«rarrk» JOHN MAWURNDJUL
JOURNEY THROUGH TIME IN
NORTHERN AUSTRALIA

Schwabe Verlag Basel

The (→**Museum der Kulturen. Basel.**) Guest of the **museum Tinguely**
a cultural commitment of roche

«rarrk» JOHN MAWURNDJUL
JOURNEY THROUGH TIME IN
NORTHERN AUSTRALIA

Museum Tinguely, Basel
September 21, 2005 to January 29, 2006
Sprengel Museum Hannover
February 19, 2005 to June 5, 2006

CONTENTS

Erika Koch/Bernhard Lüthi	Photo Essay	6
	List of lenders	21
Guido Magnaguagno, Museum Tinguely Clara B. Wilpert, Museum der Kulturen	Foreword	22
	JOHN MAWURNDJUL	24
John Mawurndjul in an interview with Apolline Kohen	"I never stop thinking about my rarrk"	25
Jon Altman	From Mumeka to Basel: John Mawurndjul's artistic odyssey	30
Luke Taylor	John Mawurndjul – "I've got a different idea"	42
Judith Ryan	Reverberation of image and essence in John Mawurndjul's bark painting	64
Jean Kohen	From rarrk to etching	70
Hans-Joachim Müller	How the rainbow serpent became art: a short manual for looking at unfamiliar pictures	76
	WORKS 1979–2005	83
Philippe Peltier	Grids, dots and territory	155
Paul S. C. Taçon	Marks on and of land: the relationship of rock and bark painting to peoples, places and the ancestral past	160
Judith Ryan	Bark painting: a singular aesthetic	176
Claus Volkenandt	Perceptible boundaries: aesthetic experience and cross-cultural understanding with a view to John Mawurndjul	181
Gary Foley	The inevitable collision between politics and Indigenous art	185
	THE KAREL KUPKA COLLECTION	190
Richard McMillan	Karel Kupka in Australia: artist, collector, writer, anthropologist	193
Christian Kaufmann	Aboriginal art from Arnhem Land – why in Basel?	222
	APPENDIX	
	List of exhibited works	227
	Artist's biography	229
	Solo exhibitions, select group exhibitions, awards and grants, collections containing works by John Mawurndjul	229
	Select works from the Kupka collection	231
	Contributors	232
	Maps	233
	Glossary	234
	Photographic credits	237
	Imprint	238

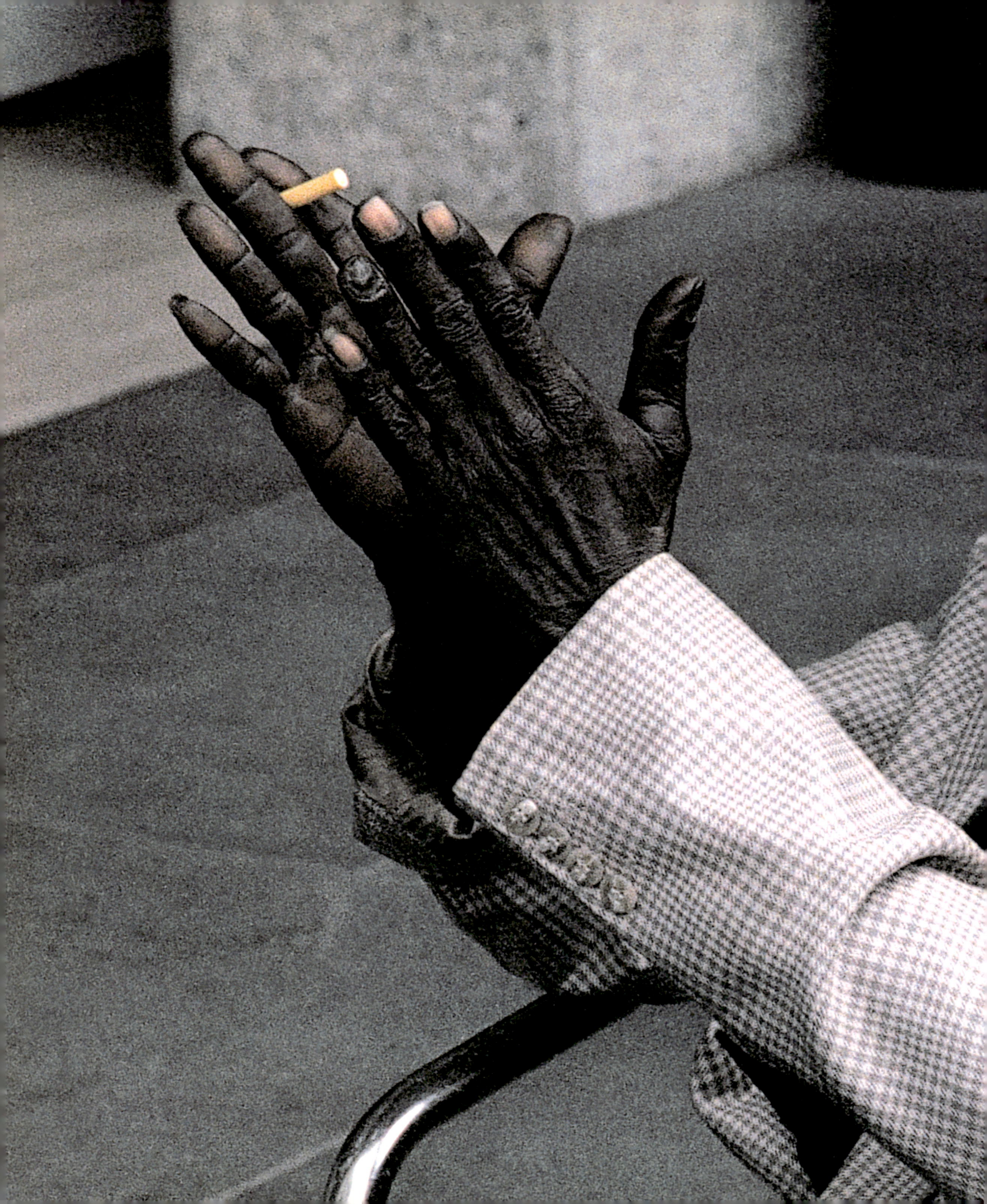

Lenders

We should like to thank all those who have lent their generous support to this exhibition:

Art Gallery of New South Wales, Sydney
Edmund Capon AM OBE, Director
Hetti Perkins, Curator Aboriginal and Torres Strait Islander Art

Art Gallery of South Australia, Adelaide
Christopher Menz, Director

Australian National Maritime Museum, Sydney
Mary-Louise Williams, MA, Director
Michael Crayford, Assistant Director
John Waight, Indigenous Curator

Groninger Museum, Groningen
Caspar Martens, Curator Collections

Maningrida Arts and Culture, The Djómi Museum, Maningrida
Apolline Kohen, Arts Director

Museum and Art Gallery of the Northern Territory, Darwin
Margie West, Curator Aboriginal and Material Culture

Museum der Kulturen Basel
Dr. Clara B. Wilpert, Director
Dr. Sylvia Ohnemus, Curator Oceania
Dr. Christian Kaufmann

Museum of Contemporary Art, Sydney
Elizabeth Ann Macgregor, Director
Judith Blackall, Head Artistic Programmes

National Gallery of Australia, Canberra
Ron Radford, Director
Brenda Croft, Senior Curator Aboriginal and Torres Strait Islander Art

National Gallery of Victoria, Melbourne
Dr. Gerard Vaughan, Director
Dr. Judith Ryan, Senior Curator

Sprengel Museum Hannover
Prof. Dr. Ulrich Krempel, Director
Dr. Dietmar Elger, Curator

The University of Sydney Union Art Collection, Sydney
Nick Vickers, Art Curator

Jon Altman

Vivien Anderson, Vivien Anderson Gallery, Melbourne

Francesca Baas Becking

Roger Benjamin and Kate Sands

Roderick and Gillian Deane

Christine Fraser

Carrillo Gantner

Bill and Anne Gregory, Annandale Galleries, Sydney

Jean Kohen

Beat Knoblauch

Colin and Elizabeth Laverty, The Laverty Collection, Sydney

Robert McG. Lilley

L.A. Moran Collection

Ian Munro

Peter Nahum, The Leicester Galleries, London

Aimé and Jacqueline Proost

Reg and Sheila Smith

and other private lenders who prefer to remain anonymous.

Foreword

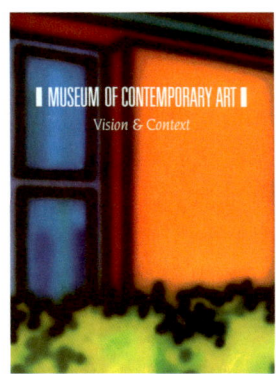

Museum of Contemporary Art. Vision and Context
Museum of Contemporary Art, Sydney, 1992,
p. 32–33

In the collection catalogue of the Museum of Contemporary Art in Sydney a double-page in colour shows a spider-like *Bascule* by Jean Tinguely on one side and facing it a bark painting by John Mawurndjul. Armed with this windfall and his extensive experience in Australia, the acclaimed Swiss artist and curator Bernhard Lüthi came to the Museum Tinguely about four years ago and suggested nothing less than putting on a retrospective exhibition for the Indigenous artist John Mawurndjul whom he had got to know during the preparations for his famous *Aratjara* exhibition in 1993/94 (Düsseldorf, London, Copenhagen). Lüthi's mind was explicitly set on a solo exhibition, an exhibition that not simply displayed the artist's works as such but placed them in the context of his artistic development over the years. The intention was to emphasise once and for all that artists 'at the back of beyond' were not, or were no longer, bound by the narrow confines of cultural tradition but had grown to become individual artistic personalities on their own merit. Moreover, Lüthi wanted to stage the exhibition in a museum of art, firstly in order to underline the work's nature as fine art and, secondly, to herald – after Jean-Hubert Martin's stunning *Magiciens de le Terre* 1989 in the Centre Pompidou, Catherine David's *Documenta* X and Okwui Enwezors *Documenta* XI – a new epoch of solo exhibitions displaying works of non-Western artists.

A pious hope, especially in a monographic museum! However, since pipe dreams have a better chance of becoming real if they are a joint dream and the museum's director himself has an enormously broad understanding of art and, for example, loves nothing better than the authenticity of Art Brut, the dream did not come to nothing after all. Things looked even more promising when the Basel Museum der Kulturen (Museum of Cultures) with its magnificent collection of Oceanic art and extensive know-how showed interest in joining the venture. During the first talks between the two museums it became clear that the Museum der Kulturen, whose own premises were to be renovated and thus the showrooms closed, was interested in obtaining a temporary but prominent showcase elsewhere.

The next step in the development of the project which was, after all, something out of the ordinary, was to persuade Roche in its function as sponsor of the Museum Tinguely to give its authorisation. One argument in favour was that a project of this kind would create an interface between some of the oldest cultural traditions of mankind and the modern and highly developed field of Life Sciences, thus opening up the kind of horizon where innovative ideas and concepts are spawned and take shape. The uncharted waters of new lands, between North and South, black and white, and art and anthropology not only provide the terrain for approaching and learning about other and unfamiliar cultural traditions but also the space to apprehend the contextual quality of globality. Thus, we are not only grateful to Roche for its financial commitment but also for the exceptional form of promotion and support gained through its worldwide engagement and experience.

Three years ago Bernhard Lüthi and the curator of the Oceania department of the Museum der Kulturen, Christian Kaufmann, set out on a reconnaissance trip to Australia. They returned with good news. Not only was the artist himself in favour of the project, but so was the local art centre Maningrida Arts and Culture and its director Apolline Kohen.

Aware of the fact that such an ambitious project demands special forms of communication we set about producing two films together with Insertfilm Solothurn and, together with Claus Volkenandt from the Department of Art History of the University of Basel, began preparations for an extensive international symposium.

For the preservation work we were able to engage Gloria Morales, an experienced bark specialist, and Tiriki Onus as our Australian co-curator with Aboriginal roots.

The whole team, now reinforced by the photographer Erika Koch, returned to Australia in the summer of 2004. It was an adventurous, nourishing and rich experience and went to show, once more, that there is no substitute for seeing things at first hand on site. The exhibition *Crossing Country* which was conceptualised and organised by Hetti Perkins as a survey exhibition on art from western Arnhem Land was complemented by a symposium. The event gave us the opportunity to meet people such as, for example, Margaret Tuckson whose late husband had been the first person to integrate Aboriginal art in an Australian museum collection (Art Gallery of New South Wales).

Experiencing the public appearances of John Mawurndjul and his companions at the opening of the exhibition, the press conference and the symposium was truly unforgettable – a star was born!

Earlier, the film crew consisting of Ivo Kummer, Pedro Haldemann, Daniel Leippert and Olivier Jean-Richard had produced a number of films under the guidance of Bernhard Lüthi and Christian Kaufmann in Maningrida, on John's outstation in Milmingkan and especially at Dilebang, one of John's clan's sacred sites. Here, in spite of one or two difficulties, the crew succeeded in shooting a number of unusual and fascinating images. Shortly afterwards Steve's car reached the magical spot Maningrida, where, from a population of some two and a half thousand, seven hundred artists make a utopia come real. Every day men and women of all ages and from different clans – armed with laptop and spear – bring their paintings and sculptures to Maningrida Arts and Culture where the works are documented, tagged and put up for sale. MAC is a success story to which a number of non-Aboriginal art advisers have made a substantial contribution, such as the present adviser Apolline Kohen, a French art curator from Paris, but also people like Ian Munro who frequently flies deep into the bush in his helicopter in search of the myriad yet undiscovered sites of rock art.

There is a dedicated community of specialists in Australia working hard to preserve and keep alive this magnificent cultural heritage. In museums across Australia we had the chance of meeting some of them, amongst them Hetti Perkins of the Art Gallery of New South Wales in Sydney, Judith Ryan of the National Gallery of Victoria in Melbourne, Brenda Croft of the National Gallery of Australia in Canberra, and in Darwin, Margie West of the Museum and Art Gallery of the Northern Territory. We also had the chance of getting to know some of the private collectors such as Colin and Elizabeth Laverty, the Belgian Aimé Proost or the late Gabrielle Pizzi whom we not only met in her gallery but also at the Art Fair in Melbourne. We also wish to thank the Australian National Maritime Museum in Sydney, where we found a number of unusual pieces, and also to thank the Indigenous curator John Waight, as well as all the museums, galleries and private collectors mentioned in the list of donors.

Special thanks also go to Ulrich Krempel, director of the Sprengel Museum Hannover who, twelve years ago, helped to organise the *Aratjara* exhibition together with Bernhard Lüthi and who has not only contributed a number of items on loan to the present exhibition but is also prepared to take over the exhibition in the Sprengel Museum from 19 February to 6 June 2006.

Many participants from the *Crossing Country* symposium in Sydney will also be present at the conference in Basel and some of them have contributed articles to the present catalogue. Among them are Gary Foley, lecturer in history, politics and education at the University of Melbourne, longstanding member of the Aboriginal Arts Council and legendary fighter for Aboriginal rights, Jon Altman of the Australian National University, Luke Taylor of the Australian Institute for Aboriginal and Torres Strait Islander Studies and Paul Taçon of the School of Arts, Griffiths University, Gold Coast. Judith Ryan of the National Gallery of Victoria, one of the most renowned scholars on bark painting in northern Australia, has written two articles on the nature of bark paintings, the different 'styles' and their iconographic properties, whilst Apolline Kohen and her father have contributed firsthand descriptions of the production of art in Maningrida.

The European perspective is represented by Philippe Peltier, deputy director of the new Musée du quai Branly (to be opened shortly) in Paris, who has written an essay on the implicit meanings of John Mawurndjul's works, Hans-Joachim Müller discusses the works in their quality as fine art, whilst Claus Volkenandt explores the intersections between art history and anthropology and fathoms the differences between the two disciplines. Richard McMillan comments on Karel Kupka's journeys and career and Christian Kaufmann, the editor of the present volume, describes the role played by Basel and its museums in discovering art on the Australian continent. The translations were provided by Nigel Stephenson and Nora Scott, Bernhard Lüthi was responsible for the graphic design and the overall layout of the catalogue and also supervised the production of the catalogue together with the Basel publishing company Schwabe AG.

The present exhibition project provides a further link in a cultural-historical process which will surely lead to further fertile meetings. After a lengthy period of absence, and in the context of the irreversible process of globalisation, the culture and art of Indigenous peoples has found its way back into the art galleries and museums, thus creating the opportunity for a new public dialogue. It is similar to the process that world literature has experienced during the last decades. The curtain falls, the cultural heritage of humankind becomes visible to be joined by world art. The unfamiliar is no longer defined as the 'Other' and at long last we are becoming, as though taken for granted, part of the whole. Even art from the 'other end of the world' with a thousand-year-old tradition is becoming familiar to us and teaching us to see and appreciate with an open mind the cultural richness of this world and its different life patterns. We hope the present project will open more than just a double-page on this journey.

Guido Magnaguagno and Clara B. Wilpert

I never stop thinking about my *rarrk*

John Mawurndjul in an interview with Apolline Kohen

A conversation between John Mawurndjul and Apolline Kohen took place at Milmilngkan outstation where Mawurndjul resided in August and September 2004, when this exhibition was in preparation. Kay Lindjuwanga (Mawurndjul's wife) helped translating Kuninjku into English when necessary. A list and images of pre-selected works were used to conduct the interview which explores the artistic career and life of Mawurndjul. Some explanations and commentaries have been added for clarity.

AK: Can you talk about the early days of your career? Who taught you and inspired you? Where were you working, for whom?

JM: I was young at the time, Balang [Jimmy Njiminjuma, now deceased], my old brother showed me, taught me how to paint. My father [Anchor Kulunba] was not a painter; he only made fish traps but he was always teaching me too. We were all camping at Mumeka [outstation about 50km from Maningrida township] at the time [1970s] when I started to paint on small barks. I made my first barks for Dan Gillespie [Maningrida Arts and Culture arts adviser 1972–1978]. They were small, a bit rough, no fine rarrk [crosshatching] on them. I was just learning. I used to paint animals such as *birlmu* – barramundi –, *ngaldadmurrng* – saratoga –, echidna but also spirit beings like *yawkyawk* – young woman spirit being with a fishtail –, *namarrkon* – lightning spirit – and *Ngalyod* – rainbow serpent.

AK: What about Yirawala and others? We often talked about them and you know some of their works.

JM: When I was a teenager I saw Yirawala and other old people [deceased artists]. I am familiar with their work and learned from them. I have put their knowledge and images into my mind. I also know their paintings on rock too, such as the ones by my uncle [Peter Marralwanga] who also taught me to paint rarrk. We have a lot of *bim* [rock art] in my country. I often visit these places. Later on in my life, when I have been travelling I saw their paintings in museums; paintings from artists like Midjawmidjaw, Yirawala and Paddy Compass. I have placed this knowledge into my head. They only used solid patterns of colours and lines of black, yellow and red. We young people [new generation] have changed to using rarrk. White, yellow, red, black, that's what we use in the crosshatching.

AK: Yes, before Yirawala and Marralwanga, there was no rarrk on early barks

JM: That's right, it was just like rock art. They took the rarrk from the Mardayin ceremony and put it on bark. They started it and we, the new generation, are doing new things. I make my rarrk different.

AK [showing two images, one of *Ngalyod*, 1980 and of *Ngalyod, the rainbow serpent devouring yawkyawk girls*, 1984] Here are two examples of Ngalyod representations that you did when you were still young. Any comments and thoughts?

JM: The first one is in the old traditional way [similar to rock art] with no red ochre in the background. I used to paint her [Ngalyod] small at the start [of my career]. Then, I had a dream which made me want to cut very large barks and so I just did it. I went and painted big barks which were a success and I kept going from there. I always thought about Ngalyod and how to paint it. In these pictures, I use dot infill like the old people but now I have changed. I have my own style, my own ideas. You don't see dot infill anymore in my work. In the bigger one [1984], I have depicted her eating [the victims]. Ngalyod is very powerful and dangerous; she killed lots of old people [ancestors].

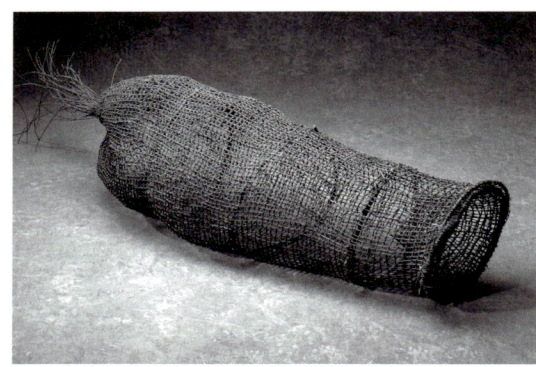

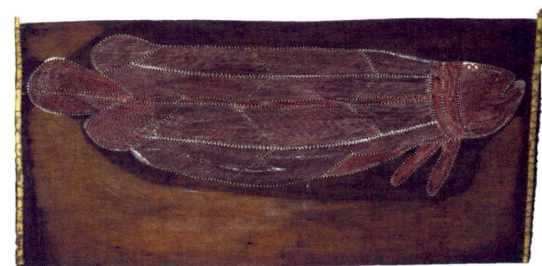

Anchor Kulunba
Fish trap
277.0 x 60.0 cm

John Mawurndjul
Ngaldadmurrng, Saratoga, 1978–79
106.6 x 53.6 cm
National Gallery of Victoria, Melbourne
(not in the exhibition)

John Mawurndjul
Ngalyod, 1980
72.0 x 56.0 cm
(see also page 89)

John Mawurndjul
Ngalyod, the rainbow serpent devouring the yawkyawk girls, 1984
123.5 x 74.0 cm
(see also page 95)

Deposit of white clay at the
waterholes of Kudjarnngal, 2004

I have depicted the bones of the women she ate. You know, at Milmilngkan where I live, that dreaming place, in the spring, a rainbow serpent lives under [the water]. That is a dangerous rainbow serpent. I paint her from my own thoughts.

AK [showing *Yawkyawk spirits: waterholes at Kudjarnngal*, 1988]. What about this one?

JM: I have painted the waterholes at Kudjarnngal [white clay mine in Kurulk estate, Mawurndjul's country]. You have been there, collecting *delek* [white clay] with me. It's an important site. Ngalyod was there too! That delek is from Ngalyod [this pigment is said to be the transformed faeces of Ngalyod], it has power. I collect delek here and use it for my painting. We also use that delek in ceremonies. In this painting, my rarrk shows that inside power of the place, the Mardayin power.

AK: I don't want to talk about the Mardayin ceremony but now you almost exclusively paint Mardayin themes. When did you decide to concentrate on Mardayin themes?

JM: I always think of new ways to paint, I always look for something different. My work is changing. I have my own style. At Kakodbebuldi [outstation on a large billabong not far from the Mann River], we go fishing there but it is also a Mardayin ceremony site and I saw there, in the water, the *dangarrk* [blue lights] glowing and flashing. I saw the Mardayin dangarrk glowing at night. I put the experience in my head and went to paint the same thing with my rarrk. I depict the lights the way I have seen it. I am just painting Mardayin now.

AK: *Balanda* [non-Aboriginal] people like your paintings, especially the Mardayin themes. They often don't understand them and keep asking me 'what is it that Mardayin, can you explain, is it secret?', what should I say?

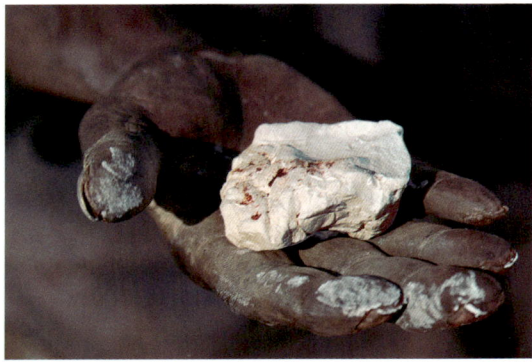

White clay, delek

JM: Tell those balanda that it's okay, there is no restriction on looking at my paintings. They can enjoy the paintings but buried inside are secret meanings they don't need to know. My paintings are travelling everywhere now, from Sydney right up to Paris or Germany. Everybody can see them, they can think, learn about my crosshatching. We, the new generation, are taking our culture to far away places where balanda live.

John Mawurndjul
Yawkyawk spirits:
waterholes at Kudjarnngal, 1988
104.5 x 51.0 cm
(see also page 101)

AK: Yes, you and other Maningrida artists exhibit works everywhere in the world and some are more successful than others. How do you see your position among Kuninjku artists?

JM: I am going first. They follow what I am doing. Sometimes, they paint in a similar fashion, with masses of crosshatching. I see their new paintings all the time in the arts centre and I can tell they're following my style. They do it differently, with their own stories and ideas but I am the one who instigated that style. I am successful and people look at my paintings. I am a teacher too and I encourage other artists to paint properly. My younger brother James [Iyuna], I have taught him how to paint. I have taught my wife Kay [Lindjuwanga] and our daughter Anna [Wurrkidj] to paint. Now, they are accomplished painters. I always teach them. I am proud of them. My wife, she can paint lots of stories, she is an independent painter now.

AK: It is a relatively new phenomenon that Kuninjku women paint. When you started painting, there were no Kuninjku women bark painters or carvers.

JM: Yes. It's something new. They started with simple things like helping with the dots and then crosshatching. Now, some women like my wife Kay or Melba [Gunjarrwanga, James Iyuna's wife] paint their own paintings from start to finish. They also make *mimih* carvings, *lorrkkon* – hollow log – or prints, just like men.

AK: While you're talking about sculptures and prints, do you remember when you first started making mimih spirits?

JM: I make carvings during the dry season when I can't get barks [barks can only be collected during the wet season when the sap is running in the trees, making the bark flexible and easier to remove]. At first, all the carvers were decorating their mimih with dot infill. I have never done that. I started much later and applied my own rarrk on mimih. I think I started to make mimih during Diane Moon's [Maningrida Arts and Culture arts adviser 1989–1994] time or maybe when it was Andrew [Hughes, Maningrida Arts and Culture arts adviser 1995–1998]. I also make lorrkkon – hollow log –, all painted with my rarrk, filled with Mardayin power.

AK: What about prints?

JM: I only started last year and I have done three so far, all Mardayin designs.[1] It's a new surface to work on but it's still my own designs, a bit different because there is no colour. The final effect is good and you can do fine rarrk too. Look, this one is *Mardayin at Milmilngkan* and I have depicted the waterholes and that spring, just like on my paintings.

AK: What are your current projects?

JM: I have lots of ideas for my next paintings. I want to use more black for the internal lines of division. Have you noticed that I have been using black lines? It's a new idea. I have to wait for the wet season as I can't get barks just now. I might start a lorrkkon soon but first, I am going to Sydney to open my new exhibition. I never stop thinking about my rarrk. Month after month, I keep putting my ideas onto my barks. I'll never stop painting.

Kay Lindjuwanga
Birlmu or namarnkorl,
Barramundi, 2004
60.0 x 167.0 cm
Museum der Kulturen, Basel
(not in exhibition)

John Mawurndjul
Mimih spirit, 1992
250.0 x 11.0 x 11.0 cm
(see also page 113)

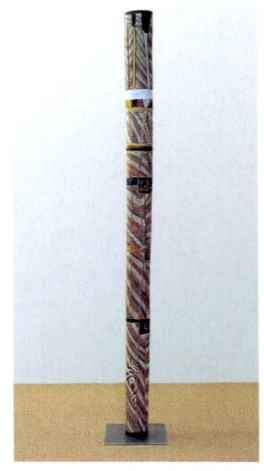

John Mawurndjul
Lorrkkon, hollow log, 1994
249.0 x 16.0 cm
(see also page 111)

John Mawurndjul
Mardayin design
at Milmilngkan, 2004
Etching
76.0 x 56.5 cm
(see also page 152)

John Mawurndjul, Balang
to the author, returns from fishing,
Mumeka, February 1980

From Mumeka to Basel: John Mawurndjul's artistic odyssey[1]

Jon Altman

Rarrk – John Mawurndjul: Journey through Time in Northern Australia is a retrospective that showcases a collection that clearly documents a leading Kuninjku artist's career development from the late 1970s to the present. This essay sets out to augment and culturally contextualise what the discerning eye can clearly see. The journey begins with Mawurndjul's birth in the bush in Arnhem Land, adolescence in Maningrida, humble origins as a novice artist at Mumeka, and then traces an arts development cycle that ends with a major retrospective exhibition at the Museum Tinguely in Basel in 2005. Mawurndjul has made this journey by the relatively early age of 53.[2] This extraordinary arts career has overcome many challenges. Some lie within the Kuninjku community and the poverty and marginalisation of Indigenous people in remote Australia. Others emerge as he and his art have moved into the national and international arenas. Mawurndjul's art is clearly dependent on his exceptional gift. But his engagement with cosmopolitan fine art also requires continuous institutional support and the assistance of cross-cultural mediators to bridge enormous geographic and cultural distances. It is impossible to capture the richness of Mawurndjul's exceptional life in a short biographical essay. Consequently, I focus here on a series of brief social historical perspectives on key phases of his career to provide some insights into its complexity. These perspectives are interspersed with biographical vignettes drawn from a long-term research collaboration and friendship with Mawurndjul that began in 1979 and continues today. Mawurndjul's exceptional success can be explained by his uncanny skill in negotiating unusual trade-offs: using deep cultural knowledge to produce modern art; and adhering to core Kuninjku values, while being a radical innovator. It is this remarkable ability to live between two worlds that this essay explicates.

Origins

Mawurndjul was born in the bush in 1952 at Kubukan on Duwa moiety country owned by Mirwi and Born clans. Mawurndjul himself is of the Duwa Kurulk patri-clan, his subsection or skin name, the common Kuninjku form of address, is Balang.[3] His mother is of the Yirridjdja Dangkorlo clan. Mawurndjul has lived almost all his life on the estates of these two clans, when he has not been residing in Maningrida, visiting Oenpelli, or other communities in Arnhem Land for ceremonial purposes, or on artistic visits to Darwin, Sydney, Melbourne or overseas.

In 1952, white colonisation had not yet penetrated the Kuninjku world in western Arnhem Land: there was a mission at Oenpelli (Kunbarllanja) some 150 kilometres west and a trading post had been established at Maningrida 70 kilometres northeast in 1949, but had been abandoned after a short time. At that time, Arnhem Land was an Aboriginal reserve established by the Crown Lands Ordinance of 1931 and entry for non-Aboriginal people required a permit under the Aboriginals Ordinance of 1918. Arnhem Land was an area of some 96,000 square kilometres of tropical savannah, the inland was occupied by Aboriginal people, the coastline dotted with the occasional mission station. There were no roads and all travel was by foot or canoe.

Mawurndjul's father was Anchor Kulunba (c. 1917–1996), a renowned 'shaman' or 'clever man' that Kuninjku refer to as *marrkitjbu*; his mother Mary Wurrdjedje was born in 1927. Genealogically Mawurndjul was the third of six children from that union, his older siblings Jimmy Njiminjuma (1947–2004) and sister Nancy Jalumba (1949–1995) and his younger brother Benny Barndawungu (1960–1999) are already deceased. Kulunba, like many men of his generation, had a number of wives, and consequently Mawurndjul has a large immediate kin network that in the Kuninjku world constitutes full classificatory kin: the Kulunba patriline was, and is, a significant political force in the Kuninjku community.

Colonial contact, adolescent years

Not long after Mawurndjul's birth, the Welfare Ordinance was passed. Under this law, the state bestowed itself powers to treat all so-called 'tribal' or 'full-blood' Aborigines residing in Arnhem Land as 'wards' of the state for their own protection. In 1957 the abandoned trading post at Maningrida was re-established as a government settlement. This occurred at a time when Aboriginal affairs policy was shifting from a focus on the protection and preservation of a supposedly dying race to the assimilation of a clearly growing Aboriginal population. Mawurndjul's early years were spent primarily living in the bush in western Arnhem Land, with occasional visits with his family to Oenpelli and Maningrida.

In 1963, a Welfare Branch patrol blazed a four-wheel drive bush track from Oenpelli to Maningrida with the track crossing Mawurndjul's clan lands. The patrol found a community of Kuninjku living at Marrkolidjban, some suffering from leprosy.[4] This disease was introduced into Australia by Chinese gold miners at Pine Creek and it was transmitted to the Kuninjku community following some peripheral contact during the Second World War.

Not long after, a medical patrol returned on the new track from Maningrida. Mawurndjul was diagnosed as having early signs of leprosy on his hands and his father was persuaded to allow him to move to a small leprosarium that had been established at Kurrindin near Maningrida.[5] Subsequently, most of the remaining Kuninjku living in the bush migrated to the growing Maningrida township, in part to be near kin being treated for leprosy. Kuninjku were among the last to embrace the regional centralisation of many different Aboriginal groups at Maningrida. It was at this time that Mawurndjul became incorporated into the colonial administrative record, given an Aboriginal Population Record number [63209] and a date of birth 000052 [00/00/1952].

Life for Mawurndjul at Maningrida during the 1960s was far from pleasant. Kuninjku people who had enjoyed a mobile hunter-gatherer existence in the bush adapted badly to the colonial regime and sedentary living at the settlement. This was partly due to their active resistance to the state policy that aimed to assimilate them, along with other Aboriginal people, into mainstream Australian society. The use of Aboriginal language and active participation in customary practices, be it ceremonial life or wildlife harvesting, or environmental management with fire, were actively discouraged and sometimes scorned. Kuninjku did not readily accept such attempted suppression. Regional politics, Aboriginal and white, also conspired against them: as the last group into Maningrida and the least sophisticated, in western terms, they were marginalised in the township.

Mawurndjul, like other Kuninjku kids, attended the local Maningrida school, but haphazardly, on an occasional basis. It was then that Mawurndjul was given his European first name, John. His formal education was quite unremarkable and his command of English has never been great. On completion of schooling he was employed on 'training allowances' as a member of a Kuninjku work gang that collected garbage in the township using a blue tractor and trailer.[6] As a member of the Kuninjku community, Mawurndjul made regular visits back to the northern parts of his clan lands to participate in ceremonies and in seasonal harvesting of wildlife to supplement the meagre living possible at Maningrida. Such trips were very arduous. While bush roads had been established, Kuninjku did not own vehicles and seasonal returning to country usually necessitated 40–50 kilometres of cross-country walking. This provided Mawurndjul with early familiarisation with ritual and the landscape and their inter-relationships, knowledge that became of great significance for his later-life arts inspiration.

Back to Mumeka as a young man

A combination of factors in the early 1970s rejuvenated the Kuninjku community. In 1972, a new national government was elected with commitments to Aboriginal land rights and self-determination, primarily in recognition of the failure of assimilation and its injustice. Kuninjku people quickly pooled their resources, purchased a tractor and land rover, and with the active assistance of an enlightened settlement superintendent, John Hunter, returned to live on their traditional lands. In 1976, land rights law was passed and Kuninjku were granted legal ownership of their ancestral lands. At that time too, a resource agency was established to facilitate remote living at tiny communities called 'outstations' with communications, provision of stores, and collection of art for sale.[7]

Outstation living was difficult, even in resource-rich Arnhem Land. Kuninjku had to readapt to living off the land by harvesting wildlife and to recalibrate their economy to generate some money to allow purchase of basic commodities (mainly flour, sugar, tea and tobacco) and technology (vehicles, guns and ammunition) to which they had become accustomed. As welfare was not available at outstations at that time, the production of art for sale flourished, but market demand was limited and prices paid were low.

Mawurndjul's life was transformed quickly: while he was poorly equipped for Maningrida township living, he was wonderfully adapted to bush living on the 1000 sq kms Kurulk and Dangkorlo lands that he regularly traversed. Despite his earlier health scare, Mawurndjul has been fortunate to be born with a strong constitution, a slight body, and great hand/eye coordination.[8] As a young man in his early twenties Mawurndjul had three things that mattered: hunting prowess for success in the harvesting economy; ceremonial expertise and experience for status in the ritual domain; and artistic and artisan skill that allowed him to earn cash. Mawurndjul's combined energy and artistic skills meant he was highly regarded in ceremonial contexts that required hard work in body decorating and in the making of ground sculptures and other ritual paraphernalia – he attained a prominent role in ceremonial contexts.[9]

Early arts career

Mawurndjul's art success was not always so. When I first met him he was an apprentice artist who was just starting to paint in his own right.[10] In fact he was renowned far more for his hunting and general bush living skills than for his artistic abilities, although that probably changed during the time I was living at Mumeka in 1979 and 1980 when his undoubted talents became increasingly apparent. Before 1978, Mawurndjul was mainly painting collaboratively with his older brother and early arts advisers do not recall any particular paintings.[11]

Mawurndjul was fortunate on a number of counts at the start of his career. First, his older brother was a fine artist who was extremely generous in the support he gave Mawurndjul. Mawurndjul also married well, to Kay Lindjuwanga whose father Peter Marralwanga was a renowned artist who also tutored Mawurndjul. Second, Mawurndjul's extensive ritual experience and his knowledge of country, including much rock art, provided many subjects for him to paint, although initially he limited his repertoire to what he was permitted and could manage, with white pigment outlines often provided by Njiminjuma and on occasions by Marralwanga as gifts. Third, the natural environment yielded the palette Mawurndjul required: white pigment from the sacred site at Kudjarnngal and yellow and red ochres from the stone country nearby at Mimadawen. The tall open forest everywhere was dense with the stringy bark trees that provide the bark for painting. And finally, regional arts infrastructure was in place in the form of Maningrida Arts and Culture (MAC) that ensured the fortnightly collection of art, by truck in the dry and by boat in the wet.[12]

It is difficult to imagine now the unbelievably difficult circumstances under which much of Mawurndjul's early art was produced. He was living in the bush, in basic shelters made of corrugated iron or from bark, and moving between camps, usually on foot. Art was frequently produced as secondary activity late at night, painting under a kerosene lamp after a long day fishing or hunting. In the late 1970s when Mawurndjul started painting this was the only source of family cash available besides child endowments (or kids' money) – economic imperatives loomed large in Mawurndjul's drive to produce art for sale.

8 This became patently obvious to me on our very first hunt together in October 1979 at Konorbo, a rich seasonal billabong on black soil where magpie geese congregate during the late dry. I marvelled at Mawurndjul's ability to glide on top of soft mud as I invariably sank.

9 Much is made in the literature of Mawurndjul's involvement in some of the last big Mardayin ceremonies performed, a theme in many of his later paintings. But he was also involved in a range of other ceremonies from an early age and I saw his artistic talents demonstrated in a number of ceremonial contexts listed at Altman, J., *op. cit.* p. 210. See also Taylor, L., *op. cit.* p. 260.

10 For a discussion of artistic age grades see Taylor, L., *op. cit.* pp. 70–101.

11 Dan Gillespie e-mail correspondence with the author, 16 February 2005; Peter Cooke e-mail correspondence with the author, 25 February 2005.

12 Established informally in 1963 as Maningrida Arts and Crafts, but then called Maningrida Arts and Culture since the early 1990s. For a more detailed history of MAC see Altman, J., 'Brokering Kuninjku Art: Artists, Institutions and the Market', in Perkins, H. (ed.), *Crossing country: the alchemy of Western Arnhem Land art*, Art Gallery of NSW, Sydney, 2004, pp. 173–187.

John Mawurndjul and his wife Kay attach a slat to a bark, Miwalaberr, September 1980

John Mawurndjul 'cooking' a bark over the fire, Kurorr, May 1980

Trimming a bark. John Mawurndjul in Mimanjar, July 1980

White outline of painting prepared by Peter Marralwanga for John Mawurndjul, Mumeka, May 1980

John Mawurndjul filling in an underdrawing with white earth pigment, Kurorr, May 1980

Jon Altman « rarrk »

In those days, Mawurndjul was very focused on living on his country, mostly at Mumeka outstation. He was often somewhat critical of those Kuninjku who drifted back to Maningrida especially during the arduous wet season. Mawurndjul's commitment to bush living was a little unusual and respected. He was idiosyncratic in other ways: he did not drive, having never learnt, and he had no interest in vehicles, unlike his many brothers and most Kuninjku males. He also had never travelled outside Arnhem Land, not even to Darwin, and showed no real interest in doing so.

It was in 1982 that things started to change when two of Mawurndjul's paintings were selected for the landmark *Aboriginal Art at the Top* exhibition and sold.[13] A career turning point for Mawurndjul might have been a visit to Canberra in 1983 when, as Luke Taylor (this volume) notes he was afforded the opportunity to see art collections in the newly opened National Gallery of Australia and to participate in an exhibition at the Canberra School of Art.[14]

Emergence as a significant artist

From 1985, Mawurndjul began to emerge as a significant artist, something that was obviously based on his artistic development and growing ritual status. But it was also linked to his management of important and burgeoning relationships with a number of art advisers, all but one of whom was white (or Balanda)[15]. These individuals, who headed MAC, increasingly operated as cross-cultural mediators and agents for Mawurndjul and helped shape his career. The fact that Mawurndjul formed close working relationships with these Balanda indicated considerable personal development because when I first knew him he was quite suspicious of whites, something that may have been linked to unpleasant adolescent experiences in Maningrida when white authority reigned supreme and institutional racism was common. Nevertheless, Mawurndjul formed close working relations with three advisers who were themselves artists, Geoff Todd (in 1984 and 1985), George Burchett (in 1985) and Diane Moon (1986 to 1994).[16]

Diane Moon travelled with Mawurndjul initially to Darwin, Canberra and Melbourne, and then overseas. Through her art scene connections she was able to negotiate with key commercial galleries for solo exhibitions. And through curatorial contacts she was able to advocate for a greater presence of Mawurndjul's art in major public art institutions.[17] In 1988, Mawurndjul had breakthroughs: he won first prize at the Barunga Festival Art Exhibition and the Rothman's Foundation Award at the National Aboriginal and Torres Strait Islander Art Award (NATSIAA). In 1991 he was awarded a prestigious professional development grant by the Australia Council and spent an entire year on salary producing a major collection purchased by Aimé Proost, a Queensland-based collector.

In 1993, Mawurndjul travelled to Düsseldorf for *Aṟatjara: Art of the First Australians* exhibition, a particularly significant event in his career, according to Moon, because he engaged with international curators, journalists and art world personalities. Equally importantly, Mawurndjul had opportunity to travel to some major European galleries. At the Rijksmuseum in Amsterdam he was impressed by the Dutch still-life paintings and interiors, but was especially taken by the Icon room where he felt a great sense of reverence. Mawurndjul also travelled to Cologne and saw a major Picasso exhibition. Moon recalls how she said to him 'One day there will be an exhibition [retrospective] like this for you' and Mawurndjul answered confidently [and with some prescience] 'I know'.[18]

John Mawurndjul's bush studio

Diane Moon, John Mawurndjul, Judith Ryan, Dolly Nampijinpa Daniels and Lesley Fogarty, Amsterdam, 1993

The road to *nambawan* (Number 1)

By the early 1990s Mawurndjul was well established as an Aboriginal artist of renown. But his artistic development was about to make a major leap into development and growth of what could be termed his Mardayin phase. By this time, Mawurndjul's seniority was beginning to give him a distinct edge over other younger Kuninjku artists; he had participated in ceremonies that younger artists hardly knew. And his establishment of Milmilngkan as an outstation locality with a house in 1992–93 provided a boost to his creativity.[19] This locality is in the southern part of Kurulk estate, near its sacred heart of Dilebang. Periodic residence at Milmilngkan stimulated Mawurndjul to increase his repertoire and to make even more powerful artistic statements about his knowledge of the sacred maps of the mythological and sentient landscape. The recruitment by MAC of Murray Garde, an exceptional linguist with rare fluency in the Kuninjku language also assisted his development. Not only was Garde able to provide excellent documentation to accompany Mawurndjul's art, but he was also able to give him his own voice through a series of published interviews and in direct translation at major events like the Sydney Biennale in 2000.[20] This facilitated fine art market understanding of, and demand for, Mawurndjul's work. Conversely, Mawurndjul gained a growing understanding that his exhibited Mardayin-style works were most appreciated.

In the last decade, Mawurndjul has had to establish creative relationships with three new senior arts advisers, Andrew Hughes, Fiona Salmon and Apolline Kohen. The collaboration between Hughes as art adviser and Garde as cultural research officer facilitated the strong promotion of Mawurndjul's art, evident for example in the joint show and accompanying catalogue at Annandale Galleries in 1997.[21] It was during Salmon's time that Mawurndjul again won the bark-painting award at NATSIAA in 1999. It was then too that Mawurndjul was given a high profile at the major exhibition *In The Heart of Arnhem Land* at Mantes-la-Jolie, France and the opportunity to travel overseas again.[22] And Salmon was instrumental in original discussions with Hetti Perkins and Mawurndjul in Sydney that resulted in the *Crossing Country: The Alchemy of Western Arnhem Land Art* exhibition in 2004 where he took such a prominent role.[23]

Apolline Kohen is now collaborating closely with Mawurndjul in his enthusiastic quest for new heights in a distinguished arts career. Recent success has included: another win at the NATSIAA in 2002; selection and success at the Clemenger Contemporary Art Prize in 2003; a solo exhibition at the Annandale Galleries in 2004[24]; and participation in a major commission for the Musée du quai Branly, Paris to be completed in 2006.

There is something unusual and driven in Mawurndjul's psychological make-up that has made him embrace the fiercely competitive fine art world and that has made him strive and take pride in excelling in the world of Balanda art. Mawurndjul is very shy in public, as is common for Kuninjku especially if talking in English. But all that changed in Melbourne when he won the Clemenger Prize and found his Kuninjku voice to state unequivocally and boldly his thanks for being awarded the prize for *nambawan* [No.1] painting.[25]

John Mawurndjul and Diane Moon in front of *Nawarramulmul*, shooting star spirit, 1988, Kunstsammlung Nordrhein-Westfalen, Düsseldorf 1993

John Mawurndjul and Lin Onus at the opening of the *Aṟatjara* exhibition, Kunstsammlung Nordrhein-Westfalen, Düsseldorf 1993

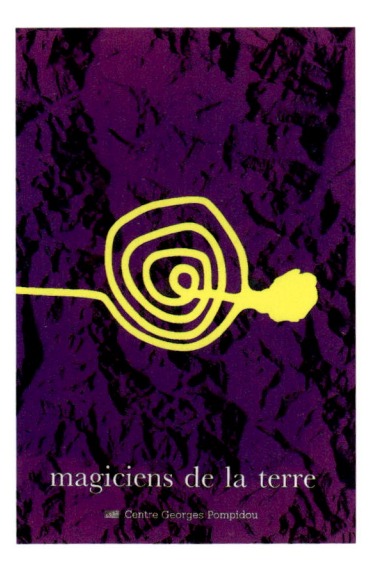

Exhibition catalogue *Magiciens de la Terre*, Centre Pompidou / Grande Halle de la Villette, Paris 1989

19 My thanks to Ian Munro for scouring his diaries to find the exact date when BAC constructed Mawurndjul's green corrugated-iron house at Milmilngkan.
20 See Mawurndjul, J. and Garde, M., 'Ngalyod in my head: The art of John Mawurndjul', in *John Mawurndjul: John Bulunbulun*, Annandale Galleries, Sydney, 1997; John Mawurndjul 'My head is full up with ideas' (translation Murray Garde), in Ducreux, A.-C., Kohen, A. and Salmon, F. (eds.), *In the Heart of Arnhem Land: myth and the making of contemporary Aboriginal art*, Musée de l'Hôtel-Dieu, Mantes-la-Jolie, 2001, pp. 51–55; and John Mawurndjul, 'I am a Chemist man, myself' (translation Murray Garde) in Perkins, H., op. cit., pp. 135–39.
21 *John Mawurndjul: John Bulunbulun*, Annandale Galleries, Sydney, 1997.
22 See Anne-Claire Ducreux, Kohen, Apolline and Salmon, Fiona, op. cit.
23 On the terrace at the Art Gallery of NSW, Sydney on 12 August 1999, with Luke Taylor, Ivan Namirrkki and me.
24 See *John Mawurndjul New Paintings*, Annandale Galleries, Sydney, 2004.
25 At the Podium, Ian Potter Centre, NGV, Melbourne, 17 September 2003. Thanks to Murray Garde, e-mail correspondence with the author, 2 February 2005, for the transcript and translation.

26 Although the amount of Mawurndjul's art in public institutions and the electronic repository of images now held by MAC might assist were he keen to revisit his own art for inspiration.

27 Thanks to Luke Taylor, email correspondence with the author 29 March 2005, for providing this viewpoint from the perspective of other artists with whom Taylor has worked closely.

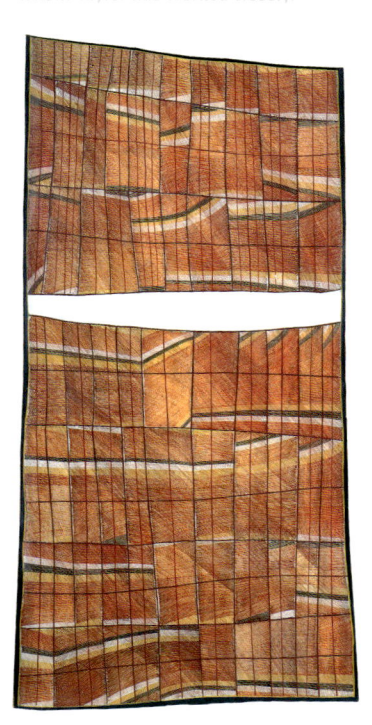

John Mawurndjul
Mardayin at Kudjarnngal, 2003
152.5 x 76.0 cm
(see also page 145)

Living between two worlds: some special challenges for Mawurndjul

The essay could end here, providing a brief narrative of key phases in Mawurndjul's journey from apprentice artist at Mumeka, Arnhem Land to doyen of an important retrospective in Basel, Switzerland. But such a narrative would grossly understate the special challenges that Mawurndjul has had to negotiate and overcome to get to where he is, despite his obvious artistic gift and unquestionable perseverance. Three instructive glimpses – termed the personal, the intra-cultural and the intercultural – are provided.

At a personal level, one might view Mawurndjul's art and think of him as a full-time artist, but in reality he is much more rounded than that, he is also a hunter, a fisher, a commercial harvester of wildlife, and a ceremonial leader immersed in numerous aspects of the Kuninjku community and wider Maningrida sociality. Mawurndjul is involved as well in many aspects of natural and cultural resource management from both customary and Western perspectives. He has worked as a leader with the Djelk community rangers and as a hunting guide with BAC Safaris: he is justifiably proud of his considerable knowledge of country, mythology, species and sustenance. He draws his artistic inspiration from sacred elements of important sites on the massive Kurulk estate, of which he is now the senior owner, and the Dangkorlo estate, his mother's country, of which he is now the senior manager. This inspiration requires him to maintain his physical links with this sentient landscape. But arts engagement draws him away, to the convenience of working in Maningrida near MAC and to numerous artistic commitments both in Maningrida and elsewhere. He must constantly manage the challenges of working most productively at his rudimentary 'studio' at Milmilngkan or at a bush camp, with the family and other pressures to reside in Maningrida. Even for a senior leader these are difficult challenges to manage, especially in the Kuninjku community where authority is difficult to exercise in everyday life.

At the intra-cultural level, there is a constant tension between securing one's personal autonomy and meeting the demands of social relatedness, a tension that is a feature of Kuninjku sociality. For Mawurndjul, autonomy is essential for his individual artistic innovation and creativity. But so too is the validating environment provided by group membership and identity: the quality and integrity of his art is dependent on Kuninjku value and belief systems. Mawurndjul has been quite masterly in his ability to carve out an individual creative space within a Kuninjku realm that tends towards conservative, egalitarian, and group-focused social values. He has negotiated this in several ways. First, in accord with Kuninjku values, Mawurndjul has shared his arts earnings with his family and immediate kin, to the point where his personal wealth is no different from theirs. Sometimes such sharing occurs in cash, sometimes with gifts or with the provision of vehicles. Like most Aboriginal artists, Mawurndjul does not own any of his art, he has no portfolio to revisit for creative inspiration, it is all in his head.[26]

Second, he has recruited others to his particular 'school of art'. He has done so directly with now established artists, like his wife Kay Lindjuwanga and daughter Anna Wurrkidj with whom he collaborates at times. And perhaps more importantly, he has done so indirectly by giving permission for other younger artists, like his brothers-in-law Ivan Namirrkki and Samuel Namunjdja, to paint the Mardayin religious style for which he is regarded as the leader and the senior ritual manager or *djungkay*.[27] In this way he has shared his talent for innovation and uncontested ceremonial rights with close kin.

At times Mawurndjul comes under pressure from kin to produce *bakki* [tobacco] or tourist art for cash, rather than the fine art for which he is renowned but he has become astute at avoiding such pressures. At other times, Mawurndjul's incentives to paint are undermined and he takes a break engaging in seasonal harvesting of wildlife or by having a holiday. There is no doubt though that Mawurndjul is a risk taker who has managed to astutely use art to push his individualism and personal autonomy to the limit, while at the same time remaining a revered member of the Kuninjku community.

Finally, to the intercultural. Mawurndjul has been fortunate in having MAC as a robust arts organisation to mediate with the market throughout his career. Yet here too there are tensions, because this organisation has been established with state support to service a large community of artists. There are pressures on MAC to provide support equitably and not just to the most successful. An artist of Mawurndjul's calibre obviously requires considerable attention – advisers have increasingly needed to operate as his agent as professional opportunities and commissions have escalated and become more complex. While Mawurndjul has not monopolised MAC he has been skilful in gaining sufficient support, not just because of his talent, but also his charm.

During Mawurndjul's career spanning nearly 30 years he has dealt with 12 senior advisers with whom he has had variable interpersonal relations. While this is not a high turnover rate for Aboriginal artists, it is in the world of fine art. Each time a new adviser is recruited, new cross-cultural relationships need to be forged with associated inefficiencies and risks. And increasingly there are pressures to travel, to spend time with curators, arts aficionados and customers. This all takes time and creates pressures. Mawurndjul is fortunate in possessing acute observational skills, evident in his hunting prowess: he is more a watcher than an active questioner. He has observed Balanda people and Balanda society carefully. This has assisted him in negotiating relationships with new advisers, appreciating other art styles in his travels, acutely observing the responses of arts aficionados and critics to his art exhibitions, living between two worlds.

And despite all these challenges, Mawurndjul has maintained a relentless commitment to the hard work of art over many years. In 1979–80, I calculated that an average bark took 40–50 hours to produce from harvested bark to finished painting.[28] Today's larger and more refined Mardayin paintings probably take twice as long, that is, 2–3 weeks of full-time work each. MAC records going back to 1978 show Mawurndjul producing bark paintings, hollow logs and sculptures at a consistently high level every year. This is no mean feat based on work effort alone. It demonstrates a remarkable, driven commitment to artistic endeavour and excellence.

Conclusion: A remarkable odyssey traversing different worlds

John Mawurndjul was born in the bush before white colonisation had extended its reach to western Arnhem Land. Within his lifetime he has seen considerable change, living through policy epochs that saw his personal standing as an Aboriginal person change from ward of the Australian state to fully recognized citizen. Today, he is a much-revered Aboriginal artist of international stature, yet within Kuninjku society he remains Mawurndjul, a member of a close-knit community. His art is beautifully executed, its *rarrk* shimmers, and yet it is also highly charged, it celebrates land rights, links to country, religious beliefs, the sentient landscape. At once, Mawurndjul has traversed different worlds, the Kuninjku world where he resides and belongs, and the cosmopolitan world of fine art where his excellence is admired and acknowledged. Mawurndjul is fast becoming a proper old man in Kuninjku society, his energy for scampering up trees to strip off barks will abate, his eyesight is wearing out from years of fine crosshatching, and he will need to find new art forms that are less physically demanding. At such a time it is most fitting to celebrate his remarkable artistic odyssey with this retrospective.

28 Altman, J., 'Artists and artisans in Gunwinggu society' in Cooke, P. and Altman, J. (eds.), op. cit., p. 14.

John Mawurndjul with his brother
James and his brother-in-law Japhed
return from hunting geese, Nandel,
July 2002

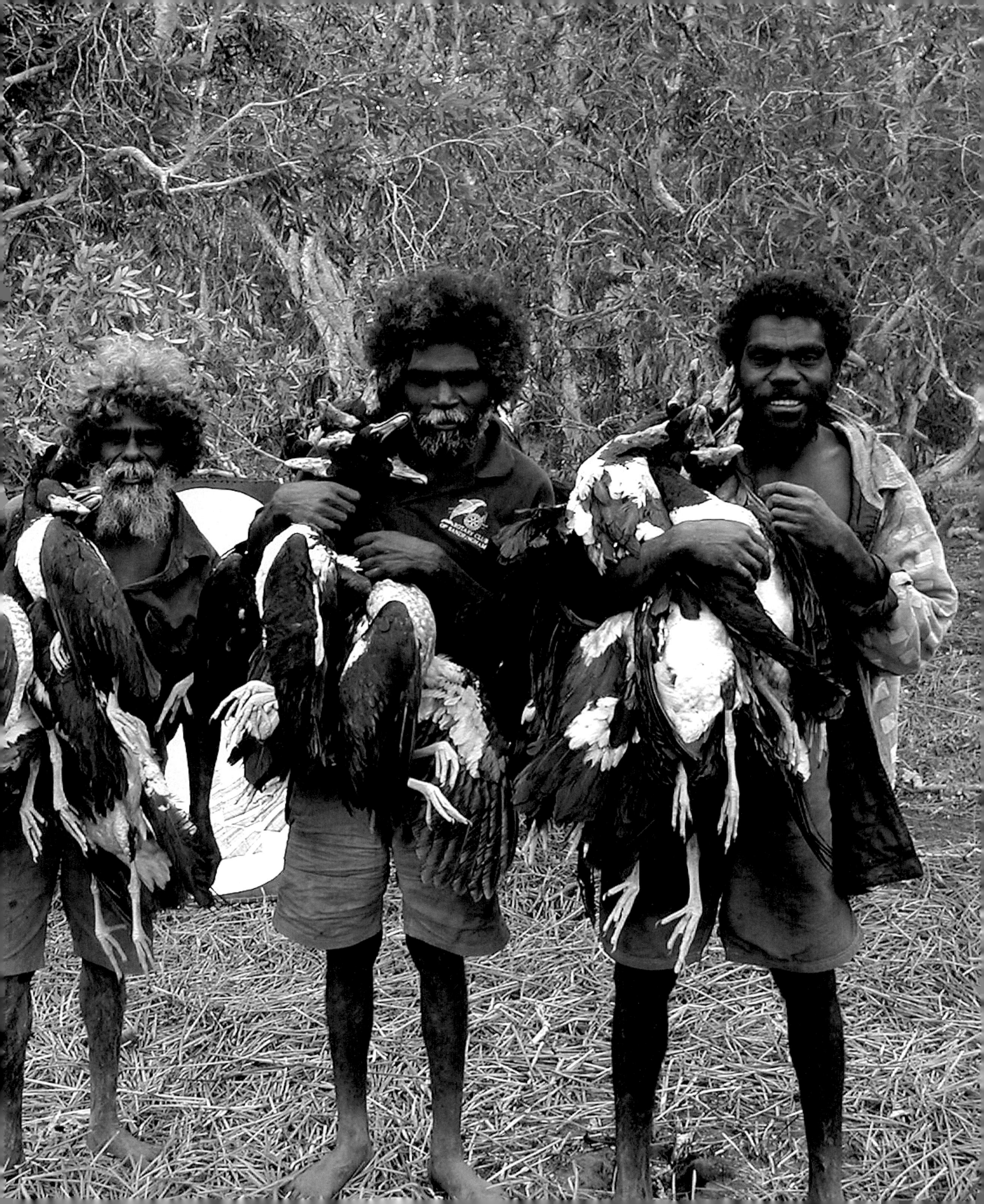

John Mawurndjul,
Milmilngkan, 2004

John Mawurndjul – "I've got a different idea"[1]

Luke Taylor

I'm doing things differently. I'm thinking about what my father told me. I know everything today from my dreams. I have ideas in my mind that can change. I paint crosshatching but over a plain colour, the light colour [white]. The old people painted with red colours. They didn't know [about using crosshatching], they only used solid patterns of colour. Red, white, black, but we, however, have changed that. The way I paint is my own idea from my own way of thinking. I changed the law myself. We are new people. We new people have changed things.[2]

John Mawurndjul is one of the most innovative Indigenous artists in Australia. He is imbued with an understanding of the history of his art and he takes a reflexive interest in his own role in bringing new ideas to enliven his works. He is a leader among other artists that come under his influence, such as his brother-in-law Samuel Namunjdja, daughter Anna Wurrkidj, and wife Kay Lindjuwanga.[3] A wider circle look to him for inspiration in terms of the general direction of development of Kuninjku art. Having travelled the world and visited some of the most important art museums, Mawurndjul understands his intercultural role and understands the term 'artist' as someone who mediates the Kuninjku artistic tradition through his own understanding and inspiration.

Mawurndjul first learnt to paint the same way that many Kuninjku learn, by participating in painting the bodies of initiates and dancers in ceremonies such as Mardayin. As a feature of the reciprocal relationship between different moieties in this region it is the ritual responsibility of *djungkay* or managers to paint the *kidjdjarn* or owners of the ceremony[4]. While every young man has the responsibility to participate in this way, not everyone is considered good at it. Mawurndjul relates that:

I saw my father doing the rarrk for the Mardayin ceremony and tried to do it myself with my back all doubled over. I ended up being better than any of them at it. They gave me a job in the Mardayin ceremony to paint some rarrk. When they all saw me doing it they said 'wow', he's got the hang of it. 'you've left us behind my son,' they said to me.[5]

Mawurndjul's father was not known as a bark painter although he taught his son his ritual responsibilities and instructed him in the production of rarrk, ceremonial body paintings that involve fine multicoloured crosshatching.[6] This was around 1968 when Mawurndjul was living in Maningrida but was not yet married. At this early age Mawurndjul had already been recognised by his peers for the ability to produce very fine rarrk patterning.

However Mawurndjul was not among the first artists who sold their work at Maningrida although his close relations Crusoe Kuningbal commenced selling *mimih* sculptures in 1968 and Mick Kubarrku sold bark paintings from 1970.[7] Rather, Mawurndjul commenced painting after his family returned to establish an outstation at Mumeka in 1973 and the production of art and crafts became an important feature of the economy of these camps located on traditional lands. At Mumeka, Mawurndjul's brother Jimmy Njiminjuma (1947–2004) was critical in the development of his artistic skills. In addition, Peter Marralwanga (1917–1987), who lived at the adjacent Marrkolidjban outstation was also influential. By this time Mawurndjul had married Marralwanga's daughter Kay Lindjuwanga (1957–) and Marralwanga exchanged knowledge about country, ceremony, and skills in bark painting as a feature of the close relationship.

In a discussion with the author in 2004, Mawurndjul spoke of three phases in his bark painting career. The first and early period of his painting from the late 1970s until the mid 1980s is characterised by predominantly small bark paintings of favourite subjects such as *namarrkon* (lightning), *mimih*, *bambil* (echidna), *yawkyawk* (young girl), *ngaldadmurrng* (saratoga fish) and Ngalyod (rainbow serpent). Occasionally he would produce larger works but not on the scale of works produced from the mid-1980s. In the second period from the mid-1980s until late 1990s Mawurndjul was painting much larger works particularly of Ngalyod and he was aware that the scale was appropriate to major world museums. At this time Mawurndjul travelled extensively within Australia and

1 This article makes use of materials I collected with the artist during fieldwork in 1982–1983 and more particularly interviews about his life and painting in 2003 and 2004. I also reference three published interviews with Mawurndjul made in 1997, 2001, and 2003. I would like to thank Apolline Kohen, Jon Altman and Jessica Weir for reading and commenting on the text for this essay.
2 Mawurndjul, J., 'I am a chemist man, myself', in Perkins, H. (ed.), *Crossing country, the alchemy of western Arnhem Land Art*, AGNSW, Sydney, 2004, p. 136.
3 For a discussion of these female artists see Kohen, A., 2004, 'Kuninjku Women and the Power of Making Art', in Perkins, H. (ed.), *op. cit.*, pp. 161–169.
4 See Taylor, L., *Seeing the inside: bark painting in Western Arnhem Land*, Clarendon Press, Oxford, 1996, pp. 59–61.
5 John Mawurndjul, 1997, in Garde, M., 'Ngalyod in my head: The Art of John Mawurndjul', *John Mawurndjul: John Bulunbulun*, Annandale Galleries, Sydney, n.p.
6 For more information on rarrk see the glossary.
7 Altman, J., 'Brokering Kuninjku Art: Artists, Institutions and the Market', in Perkins, H. (ed.), *op. cit.*, p. 176. For more on Crusoe Kuningbal see Hoff, J. and Taylor, L., 'The Mimi Spirit as Sculpture', *Art and Australia* 23 (1), 1985, pp. 73–77. For more on mimih see the glossary.

Lamilami and Bundu Bundu in the open area of the camp after a Mardayin ceremony, mouth of Liverpool River, 1952 (Photo Axel Poignant)

occasionally overseas and developed a strong knowledge of his broader audiences, relationships with curators in major institutions, and an understanding of the collections held in some of these organisations. In the current period, that commenced from the late 1990s, Mawurndjul relates that his work now concentrates on experiments with Mardayin paintings. These are relatively large works that involve elaborations of the rarrk designs painted on bodies in the Mardayin ceremony. In some way these works represent a return to the artistic practice that was the beginning of his career although he draws attention to his own role in changing these designs.

Early bark paintings

Mawurndjul started painting on bark in the same manner as many Kuninjku artists by depicting subjects that are well known to all Kuninjku. These include paintings of animals that are regularly hunted near to Mumeka as well as the lesser spirit figures such as mimih. Mimih are a kind of trickster spirit that live in the rock country and there are a multitude of stories relating to these beings that are broadly known.[8] A common way of learning to paint these subjects involves helping a more senior artist to complete a work. The older artist completes the outline of the figure as a base of white paint called *delek* (calcium magnesium carbonate) for the younger artist to infill with rarrk. Until the early 1980s, Njiminjuma was assisting Mawurndjul in this way by providing bark with the delek figure outline completed.

These early paintings reveal Mawurndjul's exceptional ability at producing fine rarrk, rarrk yahwurd (lit. little, tight rarrk). The lines in Mawurndjul's early works such as *Female lightning spirit,* 1983, and *Ngalyod the rainbow serpent devouring the yawkyawk girls*, 1984, are like fine threads in a loose-weave textile and the overall effect of the rarrk in such paintings is one of softness. Often the rarrk in such paintings is produced in a single colour red or in bands of red and orange that are very similar in tone. If this were continued across the whole work it might produce a work of soft focus that recedes into the red background of the bark. However Mawurndjul injects drama into such works by leaving body features such as the head, hands and feet unpainted. These features glow with the brilliance of the white paint delek. Delek is mined at a particular sacred place called Kudjarnngal in Mawurndjul's Kurulk clan estate. The paint is powerful in its very essence being the faeces of the rainbow serpent Ngalyod. The strength of these paintings derives from the counterpoint between the unpainted and infilled sections of the work. The white paint lends a ghostly quality to the image and is reminiscent of some of the last paintings in the caves of this region that are also completed in delek often without further elaboration.

In these decades Mawurndjul also pursued a career as a carver. He has produced painted hollow logs called *lorrkkon* as well as figurative carvings of subjects such as *komrdawh* (northern snake-necked turtle) and Buluwana, a female creator being associated with the site of Ngandarrayo in Mawurndjul's clan lands. Carving is an important activity in the dry season when bark is hard to remove from the trees.

At the close of this period of his career Mawurndjul speaks of an important visit to Canberra in 1983 which was his first travel outside Arnhem Land to attend an exhibition opening. It was the opening of the *Artists of Arnhem Land* exhibition presented by Maningrida Arts and Crafts at the Canberra School of Arts. Jon Altman looked after Mawurndjul when he visited and together they viewed the newly opened National Gallery of Australia. Altman had previously worked closely with Mawurndjul during fieldwork at Mumeka.[9] During this visit Mawurndjul remembers a first meeting with Wally Caruana, then Curator of Aboriginal art at the NGA. The gallery commenced collecting Mawurndjul's work from 1984 with the purchase of *Ngalyod the rainbow serpent devouring the yawkyawk girls*, 1984.

Works of the second period

Mawurndjul says that there was a middle period in his art that focused upon larger paintings particularly multiple interpretations of Ngalyod. Ngalyod is a major figure in Kuninjku religious life and a subject to which many artists return. Given that Ngalyod features in so many aspects of Kuninjku life there is enormous potential for individuals to investigate their own visual interpretations of this figure.

8 Taylor, L., 1996, *op. cit.*, pp. 183–189.
9 Altman, J., *Hunter-gathers today: an Aboriginal economy in North Australia*, Australian Institute of Aboriginal Studies, Canberra, 1987.

John Mawurndjul
River whale shark, 1989
233.0 x 19.5 x 23.0 cm
(see also page 112)

Lorrkkon, around 1986
224.5 x 16 cm
(see also page 98)

John Mawurndjul
Female lightning spirit, 1984
52.5 x 32.5 cm
(see also page 94)

John Mawurndjul
Ngalyod, the rainbow serpent devouring the yawkyawk girls, 1984
123.5 x 74.0 cm
(see also page 95)

Kuninjku language speakers say that Ngalyod was the first being that made the world and that every other ancestral being came out of its body. People imagine this being as the 'mother' of all other species, of all the humans, of all the ceremonies, of all the sacred objects and clan lands. Ngalyod is particularly associated with water and dwells in deep billabongs in the dry season. People say that waterlilies on the surface of the water at these places are attached to Ngalyod's back. If people damage such places, called *djang*, Ngalyod will come up out of the earth and devour them. It is both creator and protector of djang sites. Many creation myths told by Kuninjku involve Ngalyod. Typically other ancestral beings, also called collectively djang, are said to walk the earth in the creation period moulding the unformed land into features of landscape. These stories end when the ancestral being encounters Ngalyod who rises up out of the water, encircles the other being, swallows it, and takes it down into the water again. The powers of the ancestral beings remain at these places. Depictions of these moments of site creation are a very common subject in paintings. Kuninjku believe that the spirits of unborn humans also reside at these sacred places.

Kuninjku also say that Ngalyod makes the wet season. Ngalyod is said to rise up out of its watery home, arc into the sky and spit out the rain that forms a torrential downpour. The rainbow seen after the rain is another manifestation. When we imagine Ngalyod's power we must imagine the cyclonic weather that can characterise the wet season and the torrents that run across the earth and flood the low-lying country. Following the rains the earth is replenished. The otherwise dry savannah is transformed by brilliant green spear grass, animals travel to eat the grass, and birds flock to the flood plains. Kuninjku say that Ngalyod regurgitates all of the animals back into the world. Each year Kuninjku perform ceremonies such as Kunabibi to ensure that Ngalyod maintains the cycle of the seasons. Ngalyod also has this much more positive connotation as the bringer of life through the imagery of water.

Mawurndjul's painting purchased by the National Gallery of Australia *Ngalyod the rainbow serpent devouring yawkyawk girls* 1984 is an expression of these themes. The serpent loops around the painting twisting backwards across its body a number of times and the young girl figures and parts of their bodies are depicted enmeshed in Ngalyod's crushing embrace. The moiré effects of the rarrk give a sizzling energy to the snake figure much like the rainbow effects that can be seen in snakeskin.

Mawurndjul soon progressed to painting much larger works with large figures:

I painted her, small paintings of Ngalyod [rainbow serpent], at the start. I continued [painting] and, you know, my thinking. I had a dream about bark painting that made me want to go and cut the barks very large. So I went and cut a large bark. It was enormous, and I did crosshatching on it. It was a success![10]

An example of this experimentation *Ngalyod*, 1988, was included in the *Magiciens de la Terre* exhibition in Paris in 1989. In this work the form of Ngalyod fills most of the surface of the bark and waterlily leaves are incorporated in the figure form. However, the bulk of the figure allows Mawurndjul to experiment with ways of creating excitement within its interior. The sinuous rhythms of its backbone are the focus for radiating bands of colour and dotted section lines echo these forms and are suggestive of ribs. Circular elements that represent waterholes are also incorporated within Ngalyod's body and these signal the dual aspect of the image that can be read as a figure but also as landscape. Mawurndjul highlights Ngalyod's role in land creation and the figure can be interpreted as a kind of map. The work *Rainbow serpent's antilopine kangaroo*, 1991, is another beautiful example of this theme. Here Ngalyod is shown as a dual figure with the head of the antilopine kangaroo and the twists and turns of these figures writhing together fills out the body of the figure. However Mawurndjul also incorporates circular motifs to suggest the places created by the being. In essence the figures become a foil for the expression of the creative energies that radiate from the sites.

There are other large figurative works from this period such as *Short necked turtle*, 1989, and other depictions of *birlmu* (barramundi), *ngarrbek* (echidna) and Buluwana. The paintings reveal Mawurndjul's extraordinary ability to engage the viewer in the complex tension of swathes of rarrk that dance across the surface of these larger works.

10 Mawurndjul, J., in Perkins, H., op. cit., p. 135.

Ngalyod, rock painting at Dilebang, one of Mawurndjul's sacred sites, 2004

John Mawurndjul
Ngalyod, 1988
144.8 x 61.7 cm
Ill. from *Magiciens de la Terre*, p. 195.
(not in the exhibition)

Luke Taylor   « rarrk »   45

Mawurndjul was impressed with the scale of works hanging in major museums and was able to scale up his works while still maintaining the rigorous attention to fine detail in the work. Altman points out that a major exhibition *Gunwinggu Artists* organised by Diane Moon in Darwin in 1988 to coincide with an important rock art convention encouraged larger works in the manner of rock paintings.[11] In the same year he was awarded first prize at the *Barunga Festival Art Exhibition* and soon after was included in the *Magiciens de la Terre* exhibition in Paris in 1989. In 1989 he was included in the *Aboriginal Art, the Continuing Tradition* exhibition at the National Gallery of Australia and included in the *Windows of the Dreaming* book produced by the NGA to accompany the exhibition. Mawurndjul was also awarded a professional development grant by the Aboriginal Arts Unit of the Australia Council in 1991.

Mardayin paintings

Mawurndjul's experimentation with paintings of Ngalyod that can be conceived as maps reveal a broader concern for paintings of country, of the way that country can be conceived as transformations of the Ancestral essence, and of expressions of these powers that exist in landscape. Paintings such as *Yawkyawk spirits: waterhole at Kudjarnngal,* 1988, *Yawkyawk spirits: the site at Kudjarnngal,* 1988, and *Mimih at Milmilngkan,* 1989, focus attention upon the abstract representation of landscape and refer directly to the style of painting used in the Mardayin ceremony.

Toward the late 1990s Mawurndjul concentrates on these Mardayin style geometric paintings. As we have seen above Mawurndjul learnt about this ceremony as a young man and currently he has responsibility for sacred objects used in it. From his travels he was also aware that Yirawala and others had produced such paintings and created a precedent both for their production by Kuninjku and for their acceptance in Australian and overseas markets. In addition, the decline in the widespread performance of the ceremony created the conditions where bark painting became an important means of demonstrating his knowledgeable status vis-à-vis other Kuninjku and for passing on this knowledge. He makes the point that he derives inspiration from the 'inside', restricted, designs of ceremony but that his bark paintings are an elaboration and 'outside', or public, version of the themes:

Yes, I can do them [Mardayin body paintings], but I will not do them the same way on my barks. I will make them different. I will use the 'outside' version of them, or change them so they are not like the 'inside', more restricted or secret, designs. People can look at the designs, but they won't know what they mean ... but buried inside are secret meanings which others don't need to know. Other senior Aboriginal men will look at the painting and know what those deeper levels of meaning are and understand them.[12]

11 Altman, J., 2004, in Perkins, H., op cit., p. 180.

12 Mawurndjul, J., 'My Head is Full up with Ideas', in Ducreux, A.-C., Kohen, A. and Salmon, F. (eds.), *In the heart of Arnhem Land, myth and the making of contemporary Aboriginal art*, Musée de l'Hotel-Dieu, Mantes-la-Jolie, 2001, pp. 51–55.

John Mawurndjul
Rainbow serpent's antilopine kangaroo, 1991
189.0 x 94.0 cm
(see also page 109)

John Mawurndjul
Ngarrt, short-necked turtle, with its eggs, 1989
104.5 x 51.0 cm
(see also page 103)

John Mawurndjul
Yawkyawk spirits: the site at Kudjarnngal, 1988
106.0 x 64.0 cm
(see also page 100)

John Mawurndjul
Mimih at Milmilngkan, 1989
249.0 x 95.0 cm
(see also page 104)

If one compares Mawurndjul's very large geometric works with representations of the designs used in ceremony the first major distinction is the difference in scale. Early Mardayin paintings by Yirawala and others are chest-sized and the rarrk patterning is very regular. Mawurndjul's new paintings by contrast can be taller than a person. There are background grid patterns that relate the design to the ceremonial works but this element generally recedes in comparison to the focus upon the energy fields of crosshatching that swirl across the work.

Works such as *Mardayin ceremony*, 1999, that was included in the 12th Biennale of Sydney 2000 are a tour de force example of the dynamism of this theme. A fine tracery of thin dotted lines forms the background grid for the painting and indeed relates it to the grid used in the body paintings that represent this place.[13] However the energy of the painting is conveyed by the circular motifs that Mawurndjul interprets as lights glowing in the billabong at Kakodbebuldi. Rays of light and ancestral energy are evoked by the intersections and flows of rarrk around the work. These lights are described to be like sources of Mardayin power in the earth at the bottom of the billabong and the rarrk itself is conceived as an expression of this power radiating from these sources.[14] *Mardayin Ceremony*, 2000, is also a masterful representation of this theme. Here the focus is upon the rayed patterns of rarrk that move across the whole work and are only gently corralled by the grid. The fine rarrk against a light background conveys a general softness to the painting as a whole.

Mawurndjul's authority to make use of Mardayin designs and to elaborate them this way derives from his position as a senior man in a complex political landscape. At the turn of the century he had inherited the position of senior manager of the Dangkorlo clan estate and he often painted the site of Kakodbebuldi that is a key Mardayin site in this estate. By contrast there were no senior managers living nearby that could restrict him painting his own sites in Kurulk clan lands so sites such as Dilebang, Kurrurldul and Milmilngkan also feature in his repertoire.

At the height of his career, Mawurndjul is not placing such importance on the fine quality of his rarrk. In works such as *Lumaluma*, 2002 (also known incorrectly as *Buluwana*, 2002), hair-thin lines have been replaced by more robust patterning. Gone too are the minute dots that finished off the sectioning. Rather the work gains strength from various contrasts across the surface. The outer areas of the painting are not crosshatched, they are simply hatched. This creates a counterpoint with other parts of the figure which are crosshatched. Some key body parts are not infilled and are left white. Here Mawurndjul returns to skills that are seen in his early work where the delek of the outline form is left untouched in places. In this work we see a major artist making decisions that create intensity and dynamism without recourse to the minutia of patterning that was once his trademark.

In Mawurndjul's most recent works such as *Mardayin at Kudjarnngal*, 2003, which was one of a group of paintings that won Mawurndjul first prize at the Clemenger Contemporary Art Award in 2003, the paintings gain their force by a grid that is not dotted and through waves of rarrk that run across the grid. There are very subtle flows of energy in such work as bands of white and red move horizontally in wave forms. Mawurndjul told me that these days he selects the 'strong' red and yellow ochres, often trading with other artists who live further afield to obtain them. The new works gain some of their glow by the saturated quality of the paint in the thicker lines of rarrk. A counterpoint is provided by a thick band of pure delek which indeed represents the delek to be found at the site. Here again, contrast between the filled and unfilled sections of the painting creates an abrupt surprise, a tension in the heart of the work that evokes the connection between landscape and the sacred energies radiating from it. Mawurndjul is the first Indigenous artist to win this award and for him it was taken as testimony to the growing equality between Indigenous and non-Indigenous contemporary artists in Australia.[15]

13 Taylor, L., 1996, op. cit., pp. 227–234 and Taylor, L., 2004, in Perkins, H., op. cit., 126–127.
14 Mawurndjul, J., 2001, in Ducreux A.-C., Kohen, A. and Salmon, F., op. cit., p. 58.
15 The Clemenger Contemporary Art Award is a triennial exhibition and award held at the National Gallery of Victoria's Ian Potter Centre. It is an invitational award and in 2003 fifteen of Australia's finest artists were invited to exhibit. Mawurndjul was one of four Indigenous artists invited to exhibit.

John Mawurndjul
Mardayin ceremony, 1999
153.0 x 88.0 cm
(see also page 135)

John Mawurndjul
Mardayin ceremony, 2000
170.0 x 78.0 cm
(see also page 133)

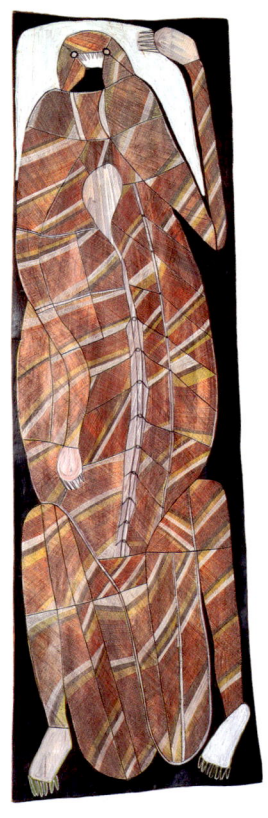

John Mawurndjul
Buluwana, female ancestor, 2001
200.0 x 59.0 cm
(see also page 141)

Energy from country

Mawurndjul is a man who impresses all who meet him with his energy and drive. He is a remarkable hunter who will work hard all day to obtain the highly prized bush foods that he will share with his relatives. In his art he tackles major works with a similar intensity. Viewers need to appreciate the concentration required to complete such large paintings with fine rarrk work; the skill needed to maintain thin and evenly spaced parallel lines as well as manage the flows of pattern across such vast surfaces. Mawurndjul talks energetically about the paints needed for such fine work, the texture of the ochres must also be fine to assist the even application. He will also talk readily about the experiments of an earlier generation of artists and about those works he has seen in art gallery and museum collections around the world. He has a strong sense of the decisions regarding colour choice and patterning made by these artists and also expresses how he has considered ways of working that are different. He is a keen interpreter of his own motivations, of themes in Kuninjku culture more generally, and readily engages in the intercultural interactions that constitute the contemporary art market. Mawurndjul's success and world recognition derive in large measure from the apprehension of this outgoing enthusiasm. It may be divined in his art and in the passion he invests in its interpretation. The enthusiasm is in turn driven by his love for his country and a desire to convince others of its richness as a source of spiritual power.

John Mawurndjul
Billabong at Milmilngkan, 2002
186.0 x 78.5 cm
(see also page 143)

John Mawurndjul
Mardayin at Kudjarnngal, 2003
152.5 x 76.0 cm
(see also page 145)

John Mawurndjul drawing rarrk lines, Milmilngkan 2004

On the following double pages:

Kay Lindjuwanga and John Mawurndjul in their studio, Milmilngkan 2004

John Mawurndjul, Milmilngkan, 2004

Milmilngkan outstation in the clearing, 2004

John Mawurndjul gathering red ochre, Milmilngkan, 2004 (left) and eucalyptus tree stripped of its bark during the last wet season, Milmilngkan, 2004

Dilebang, 2004

Billabong at Milmilngkan, 2004

Liverpool River, 2004

Luke Taylor   « rarrk »

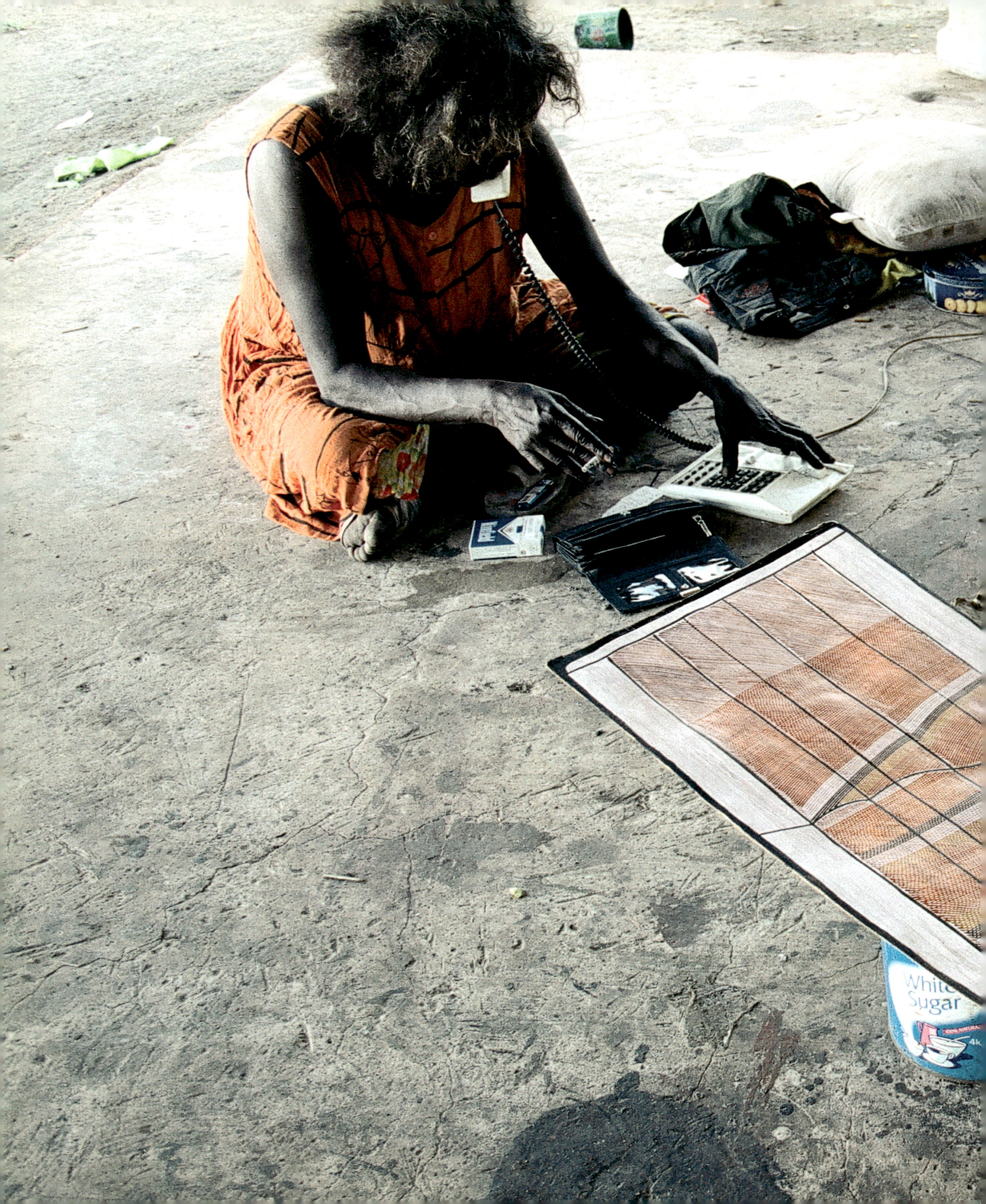
White Sugar

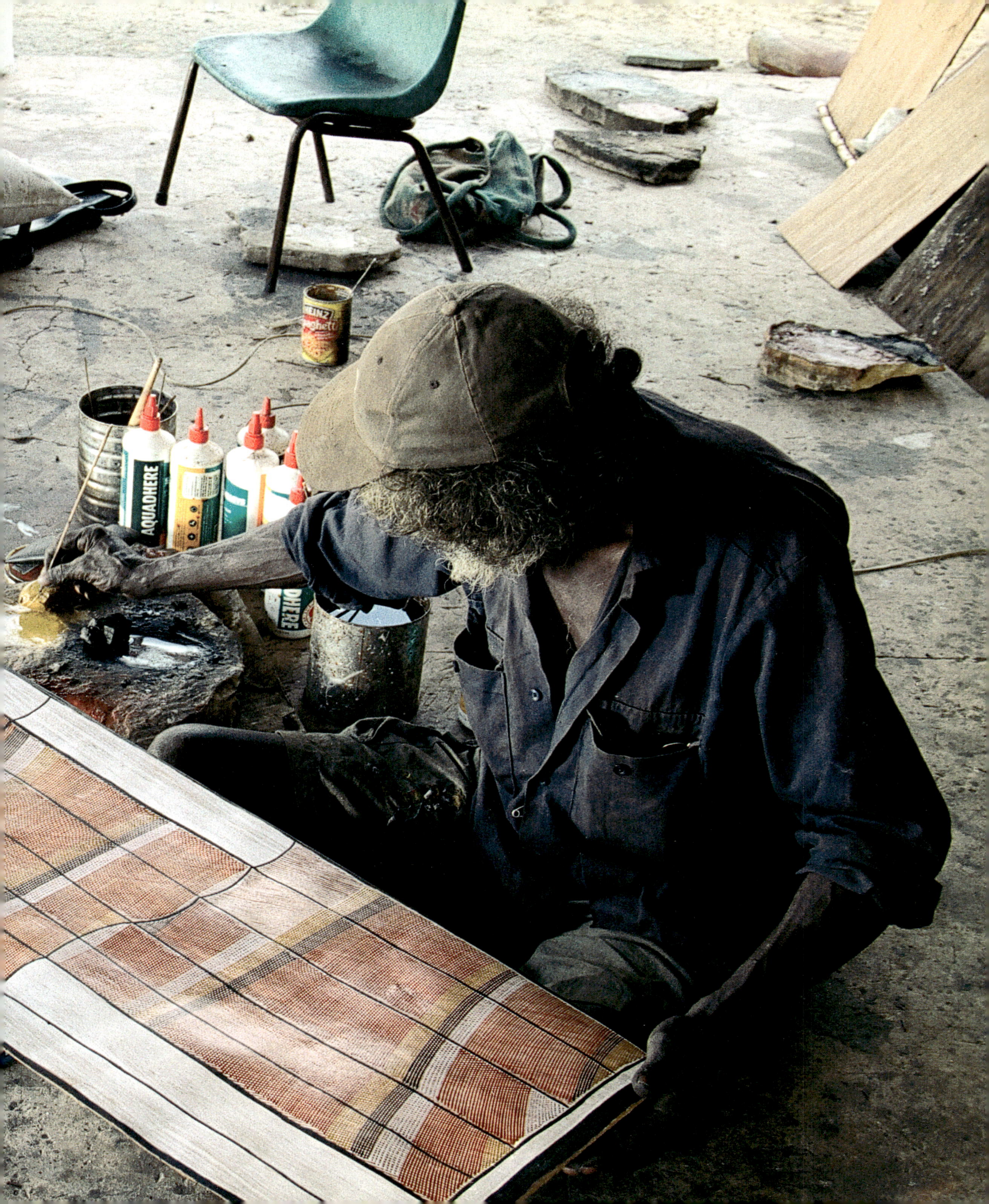
AQUADHERE

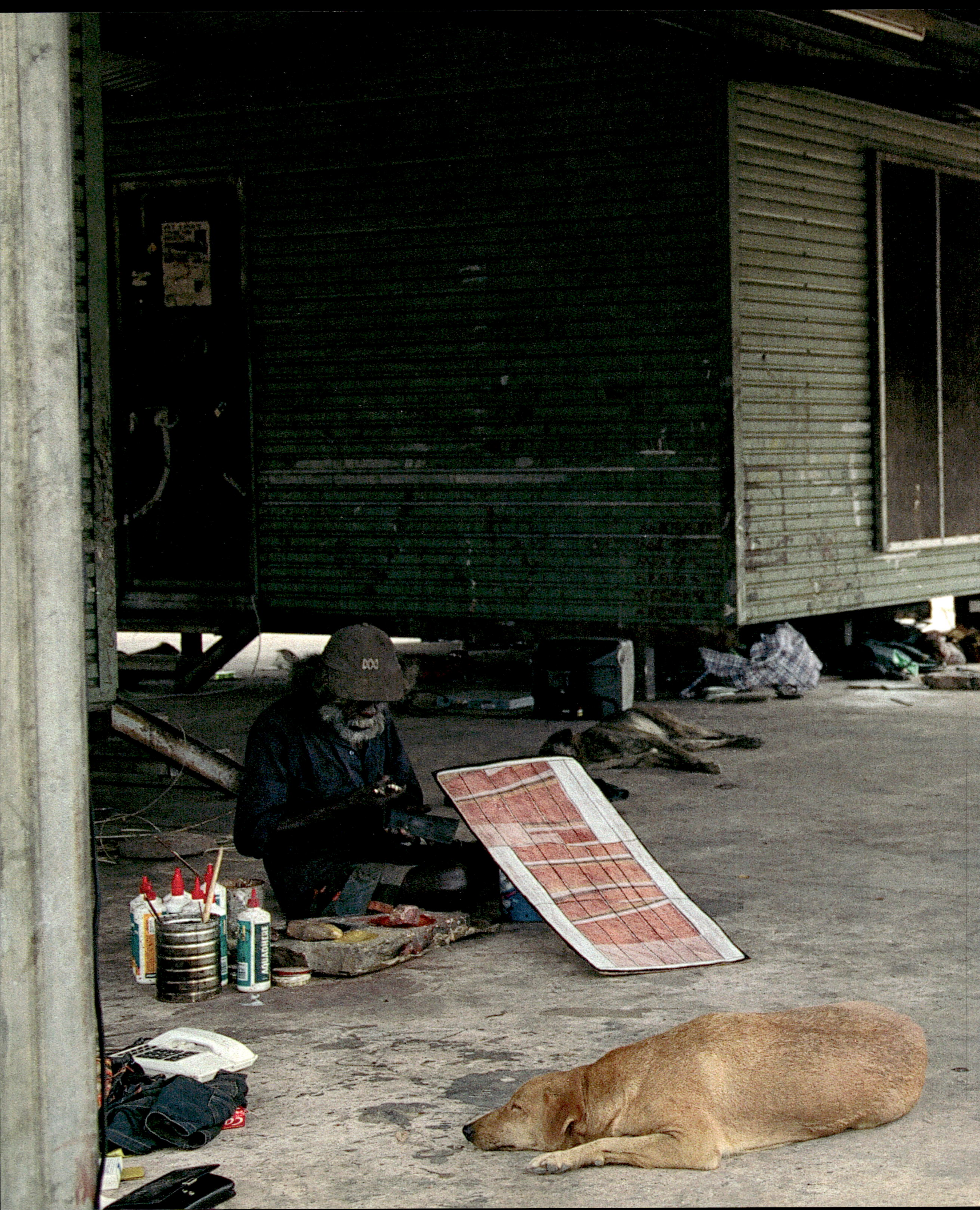

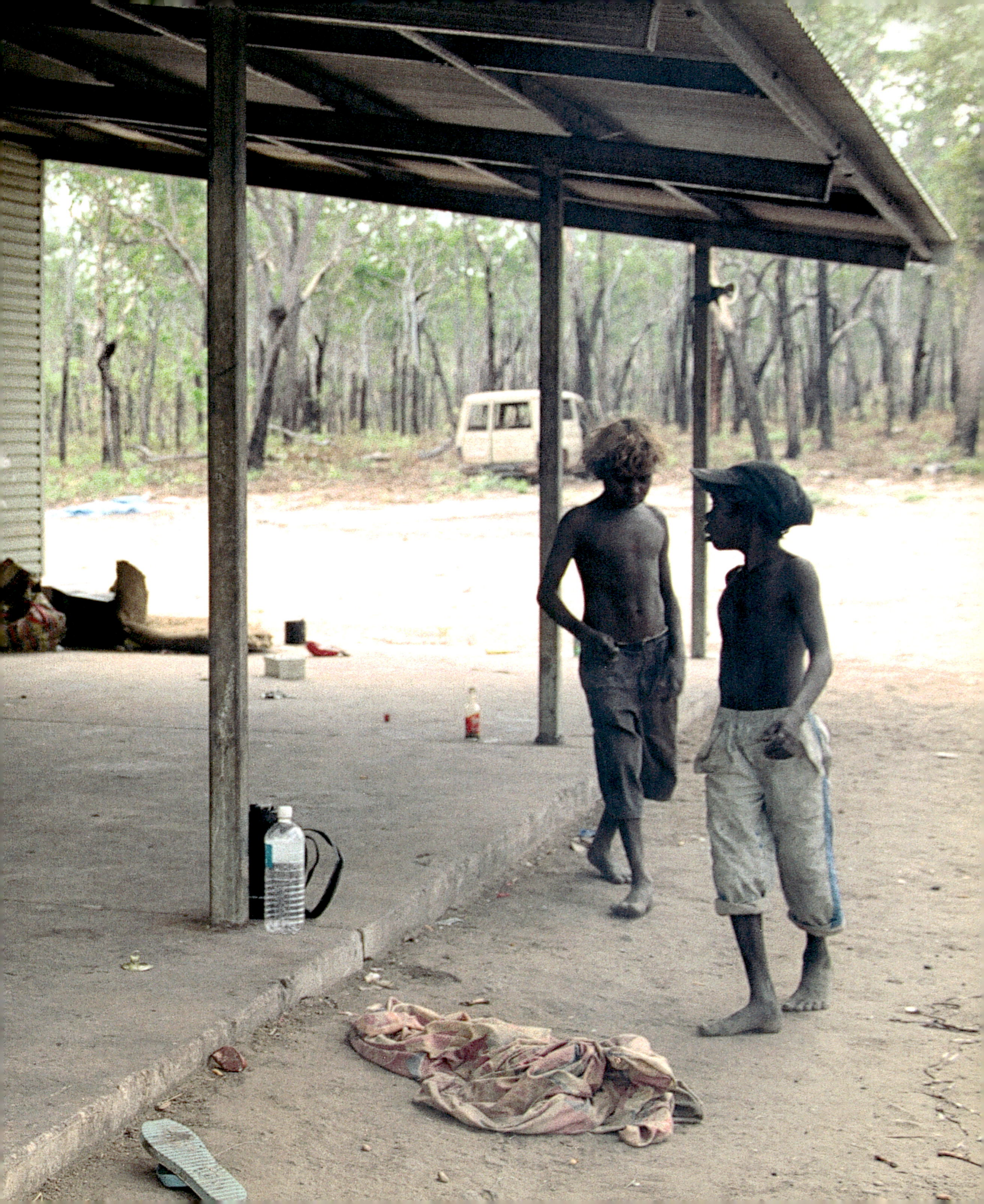

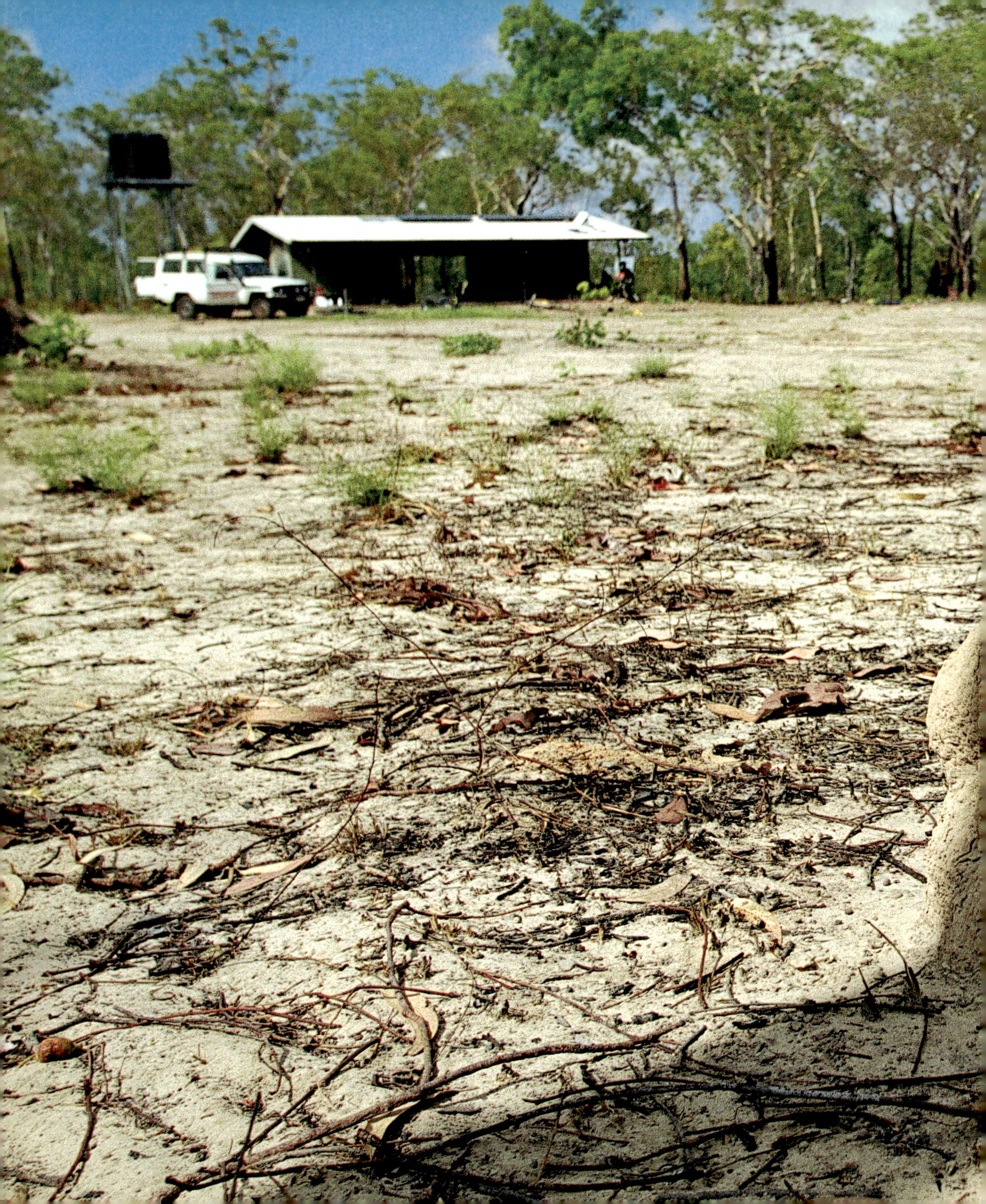

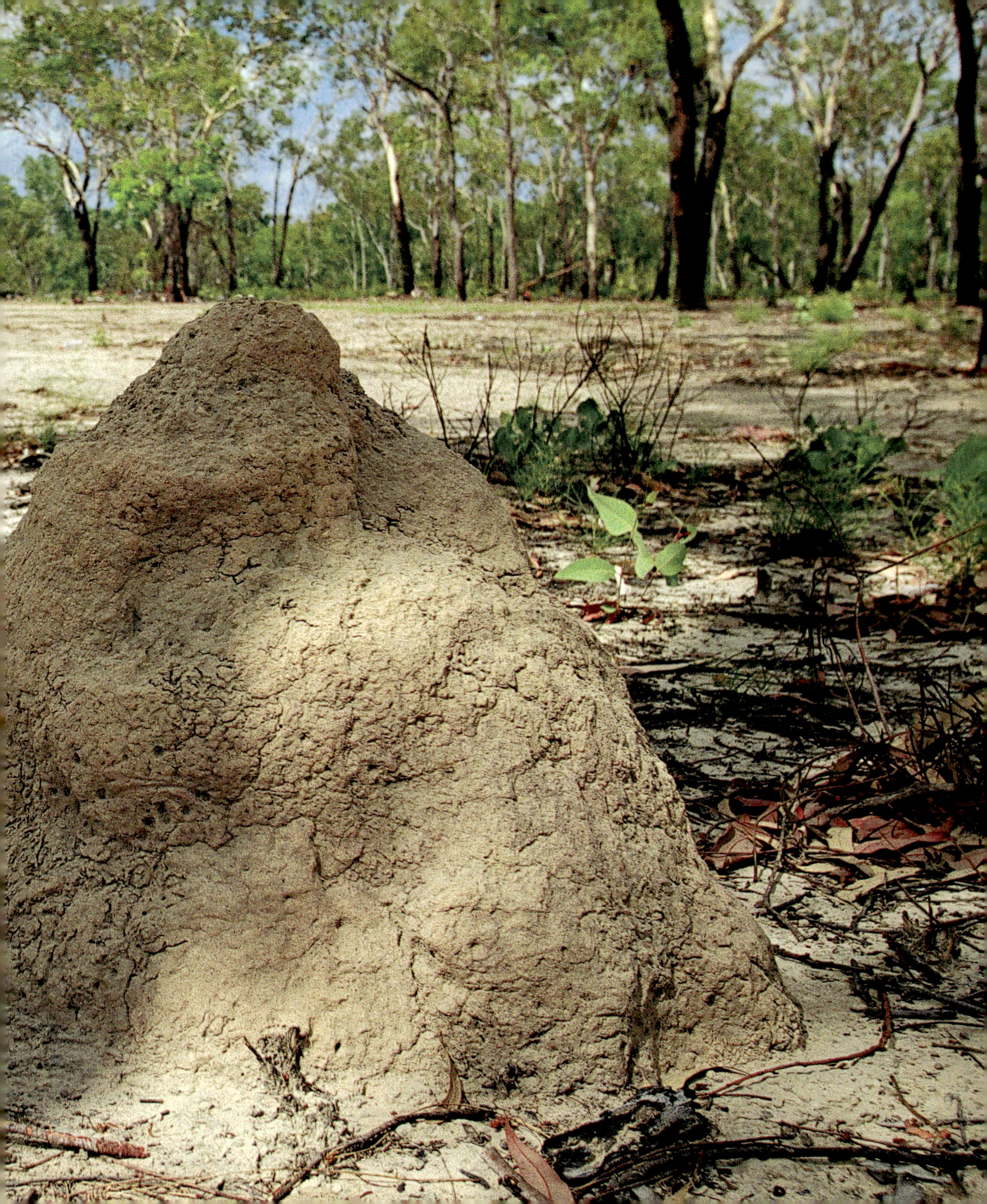

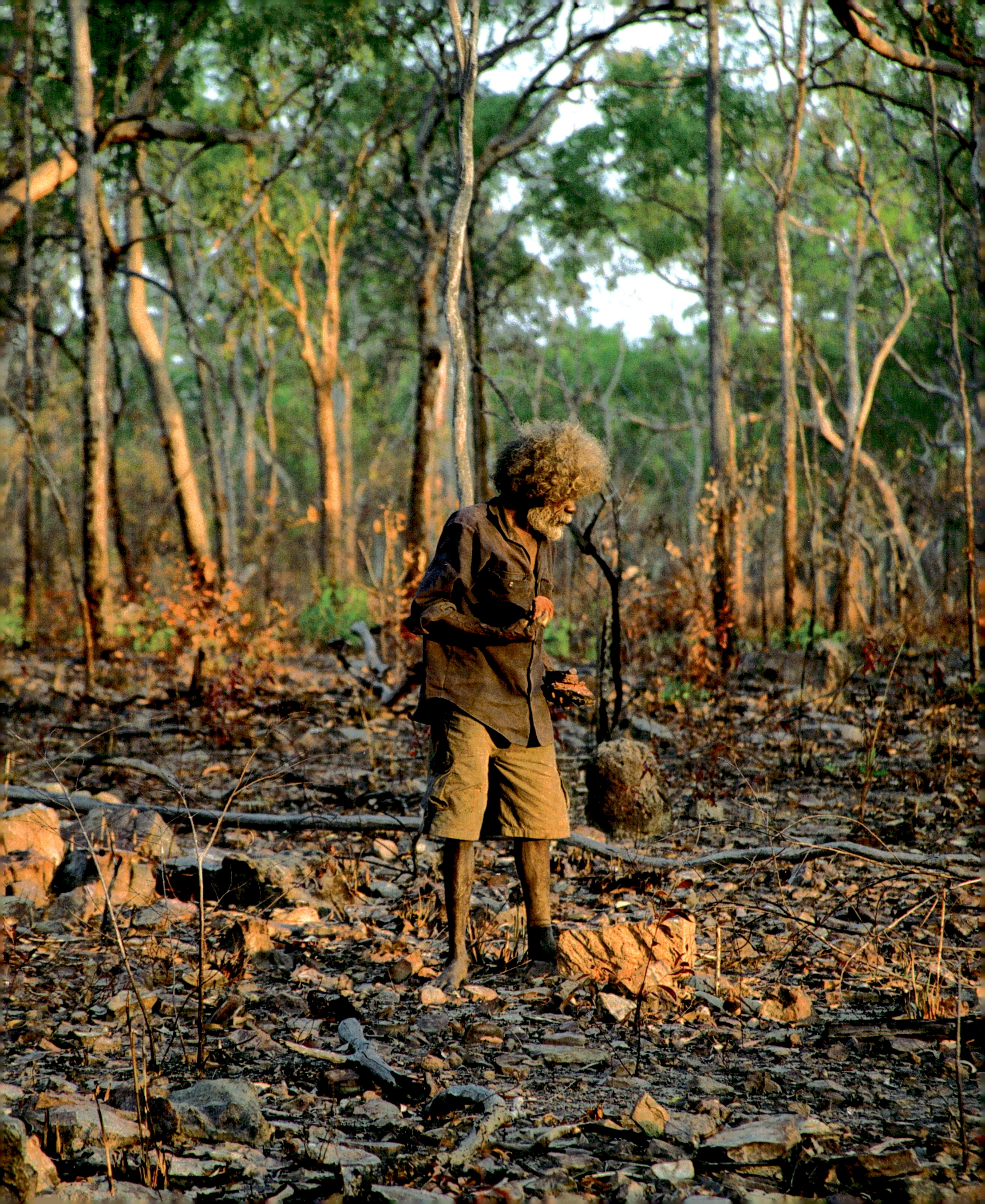

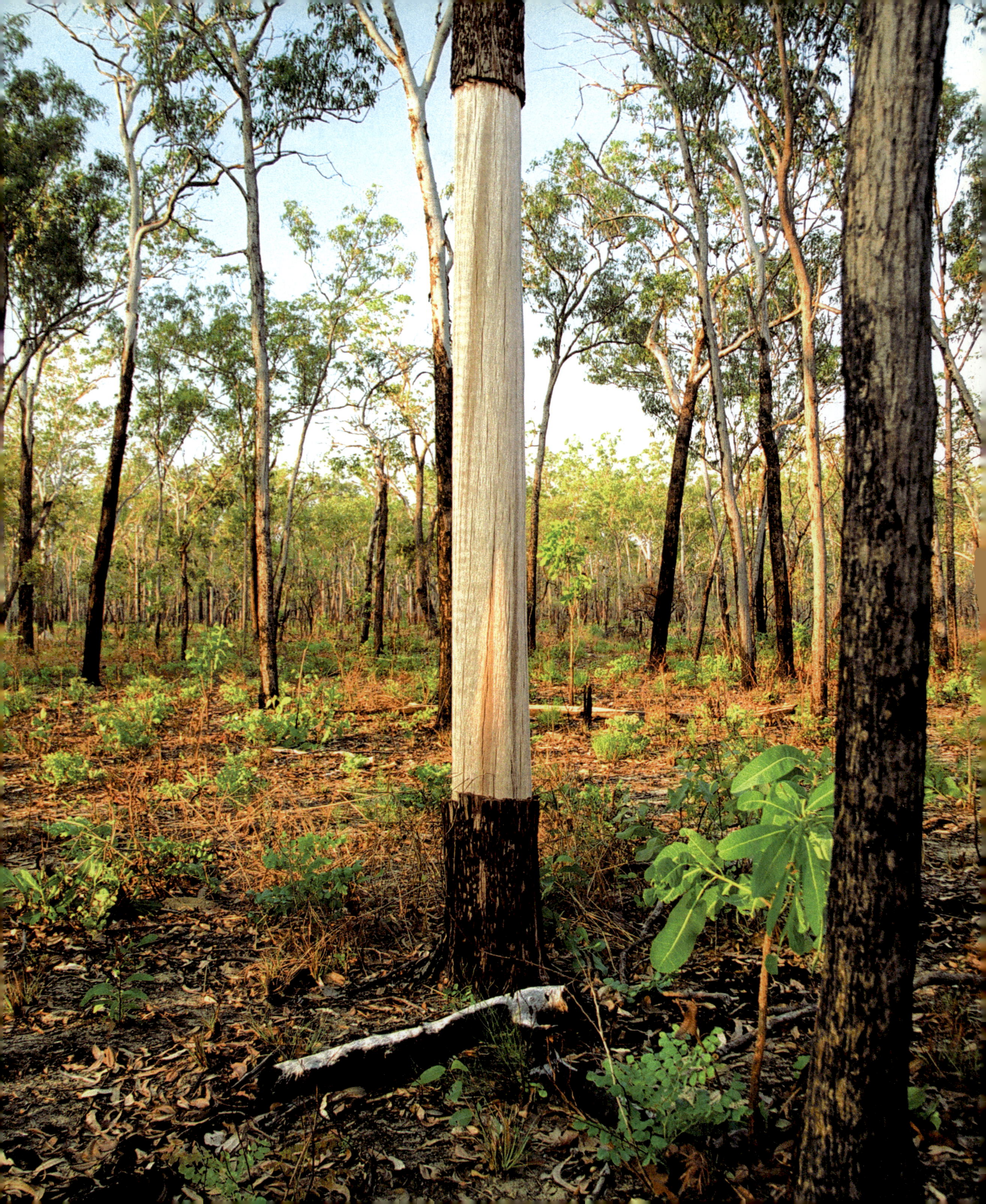

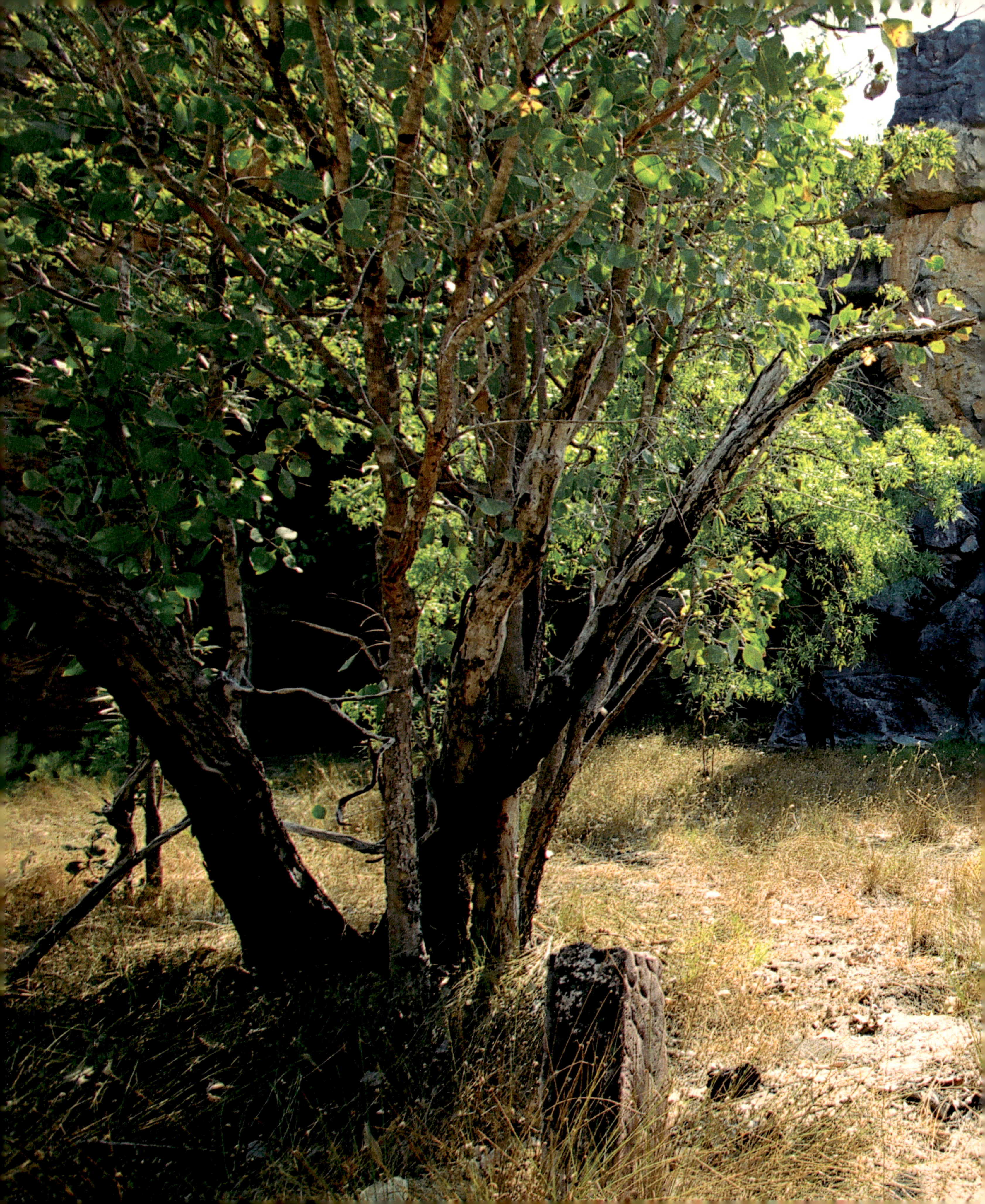

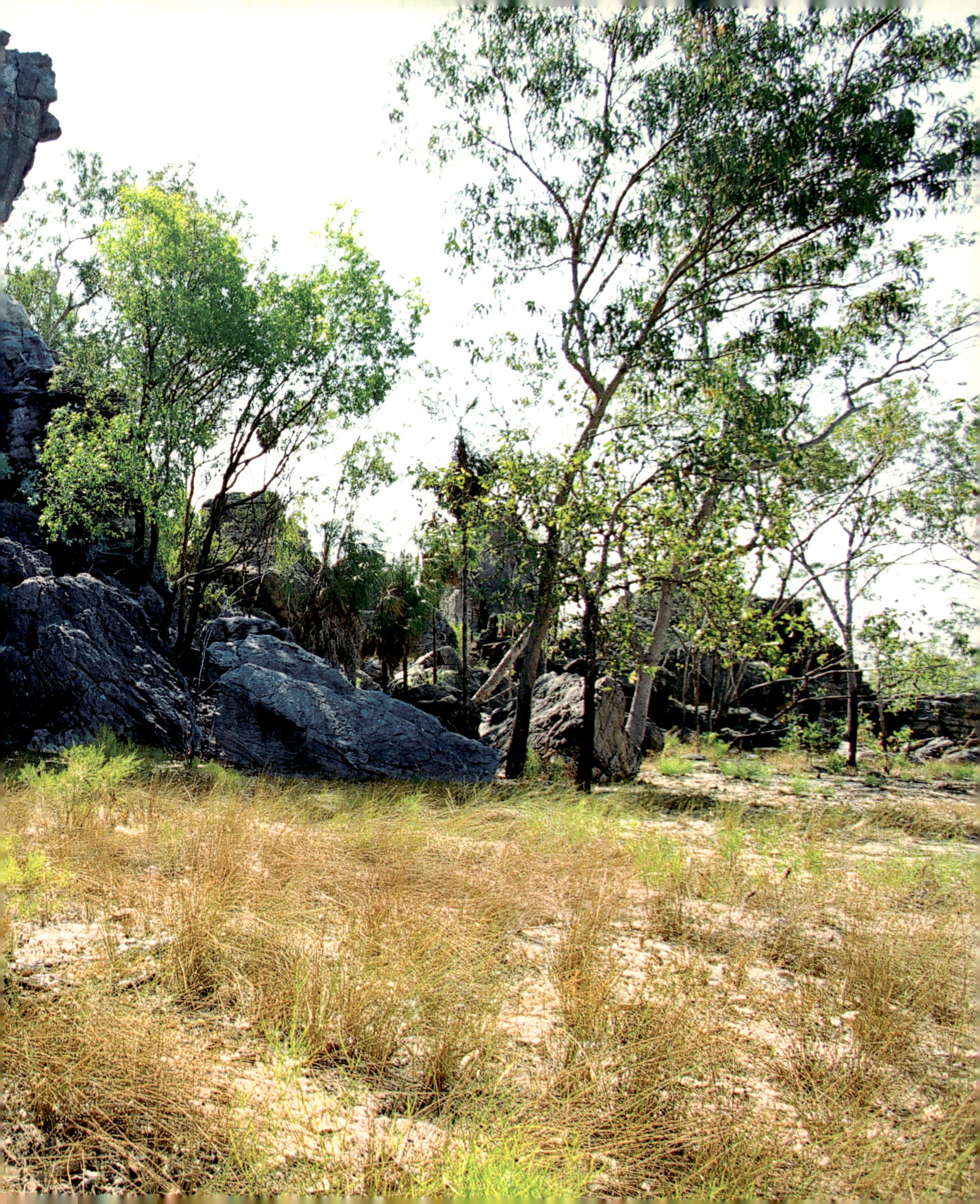

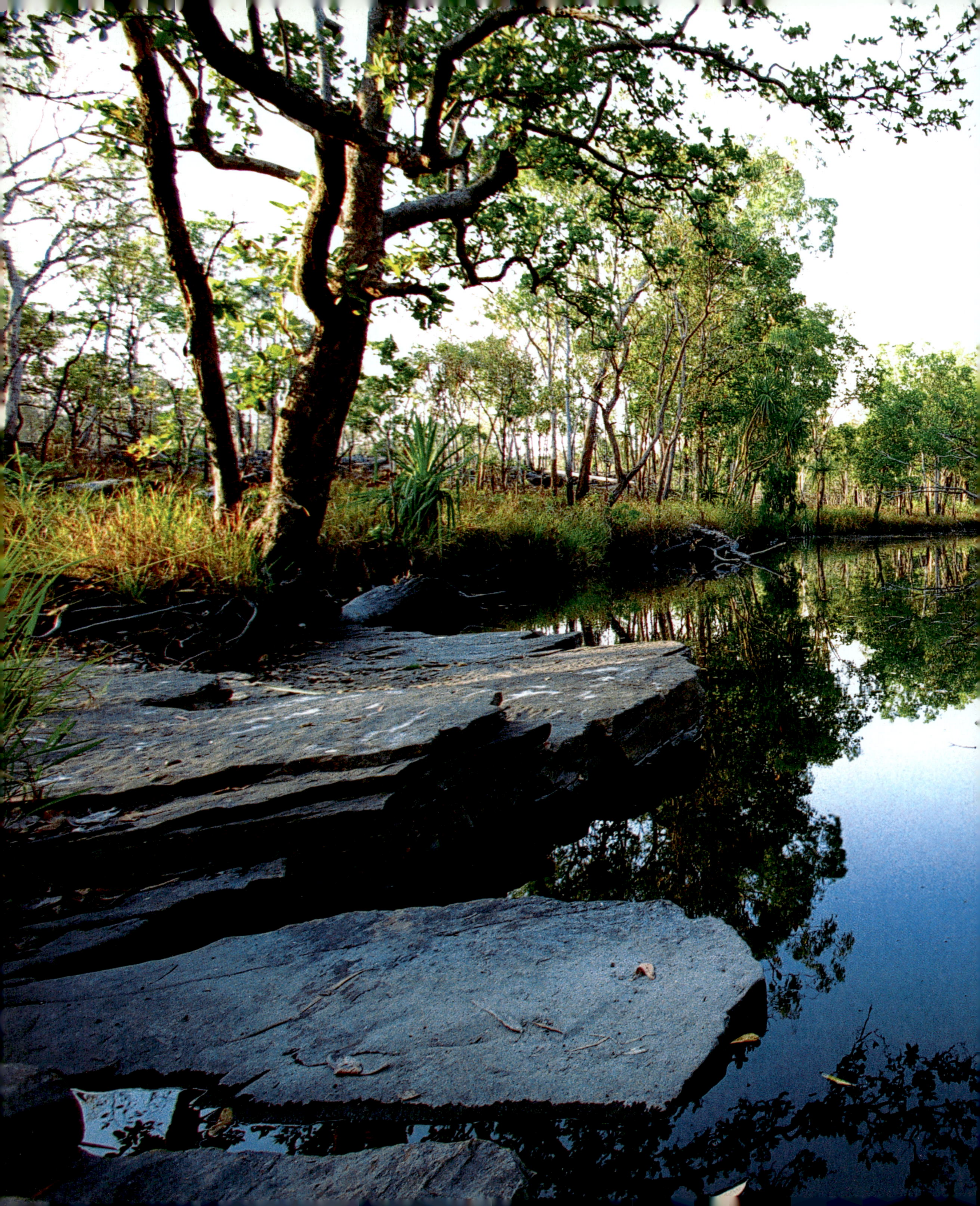

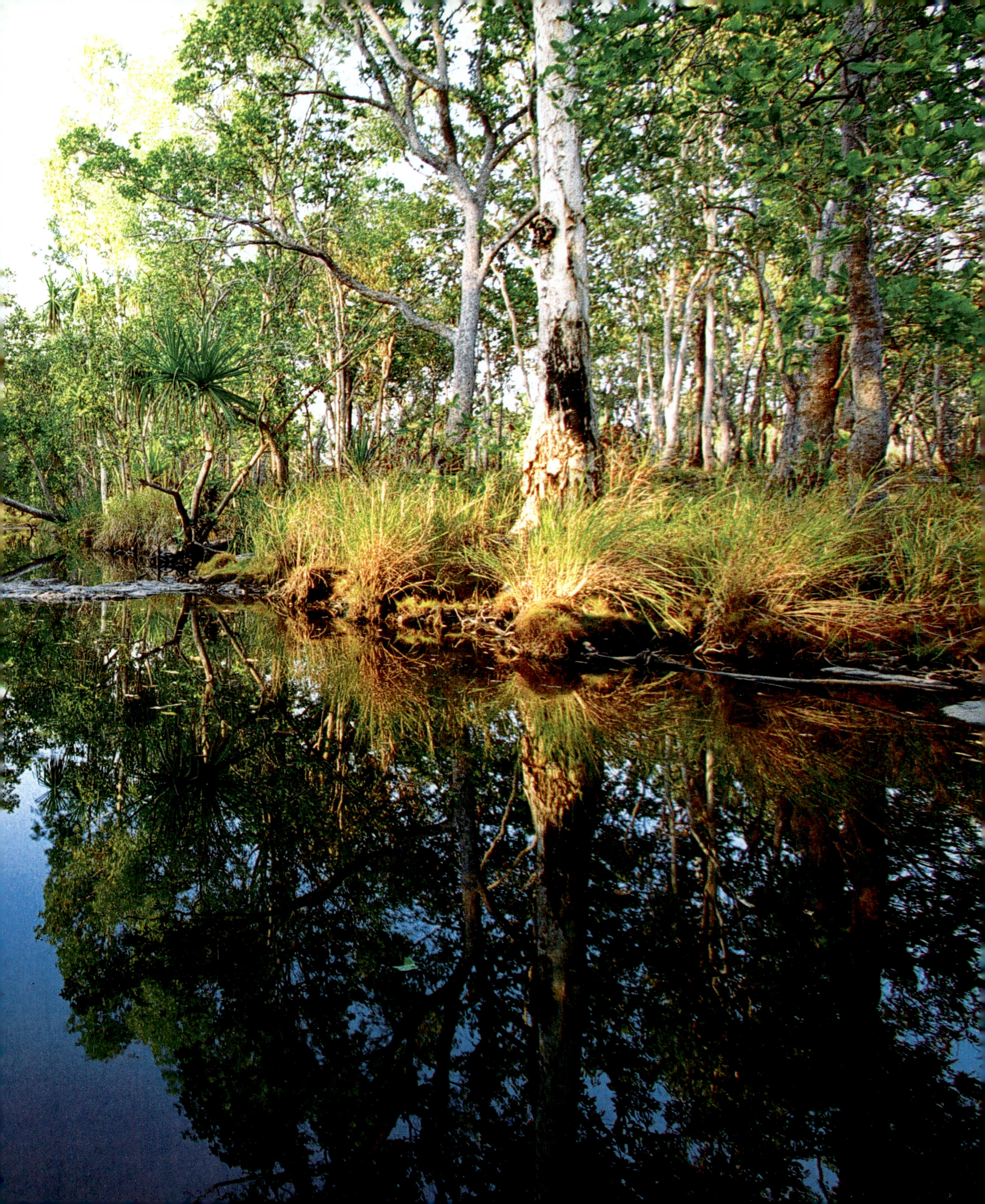

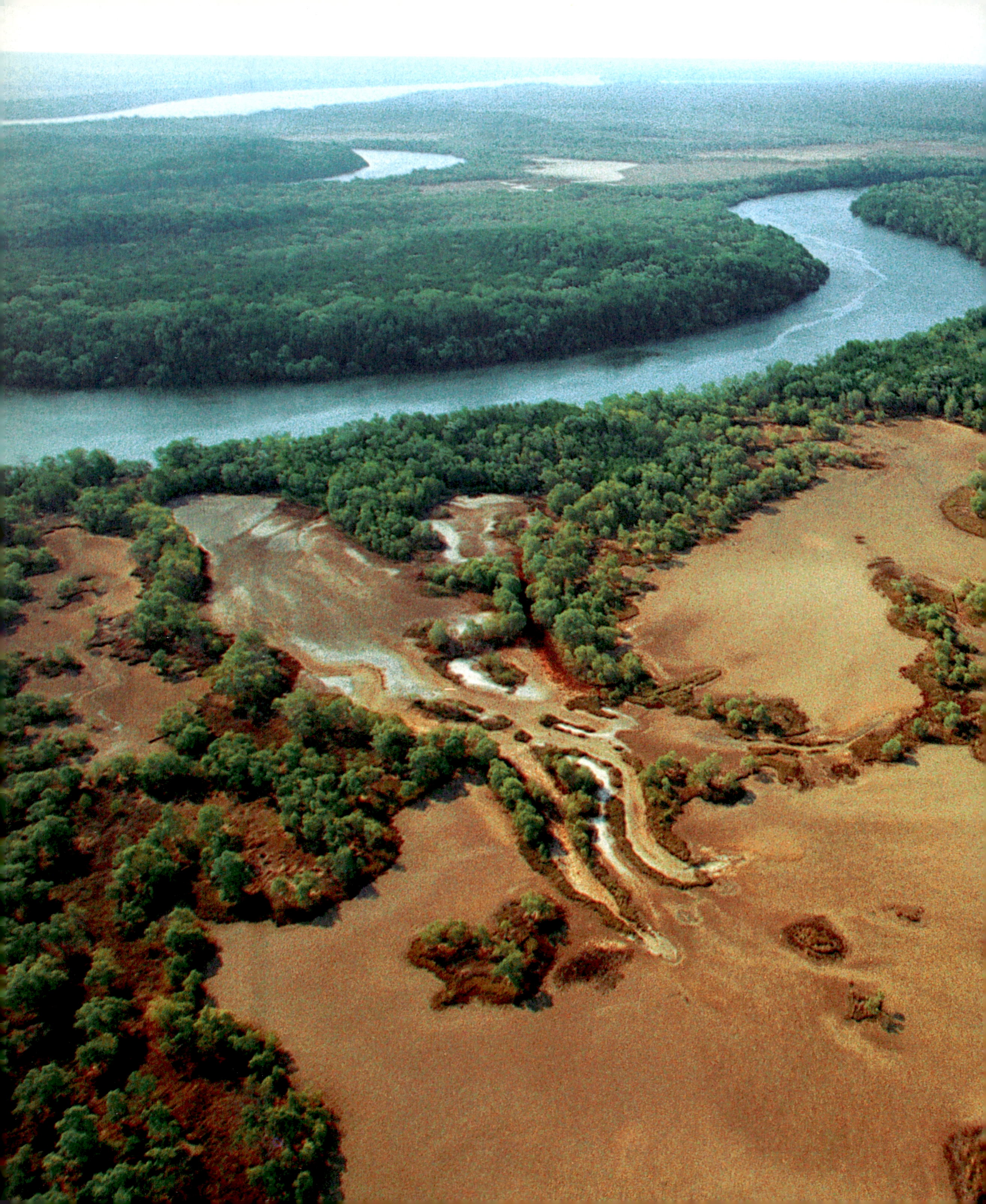

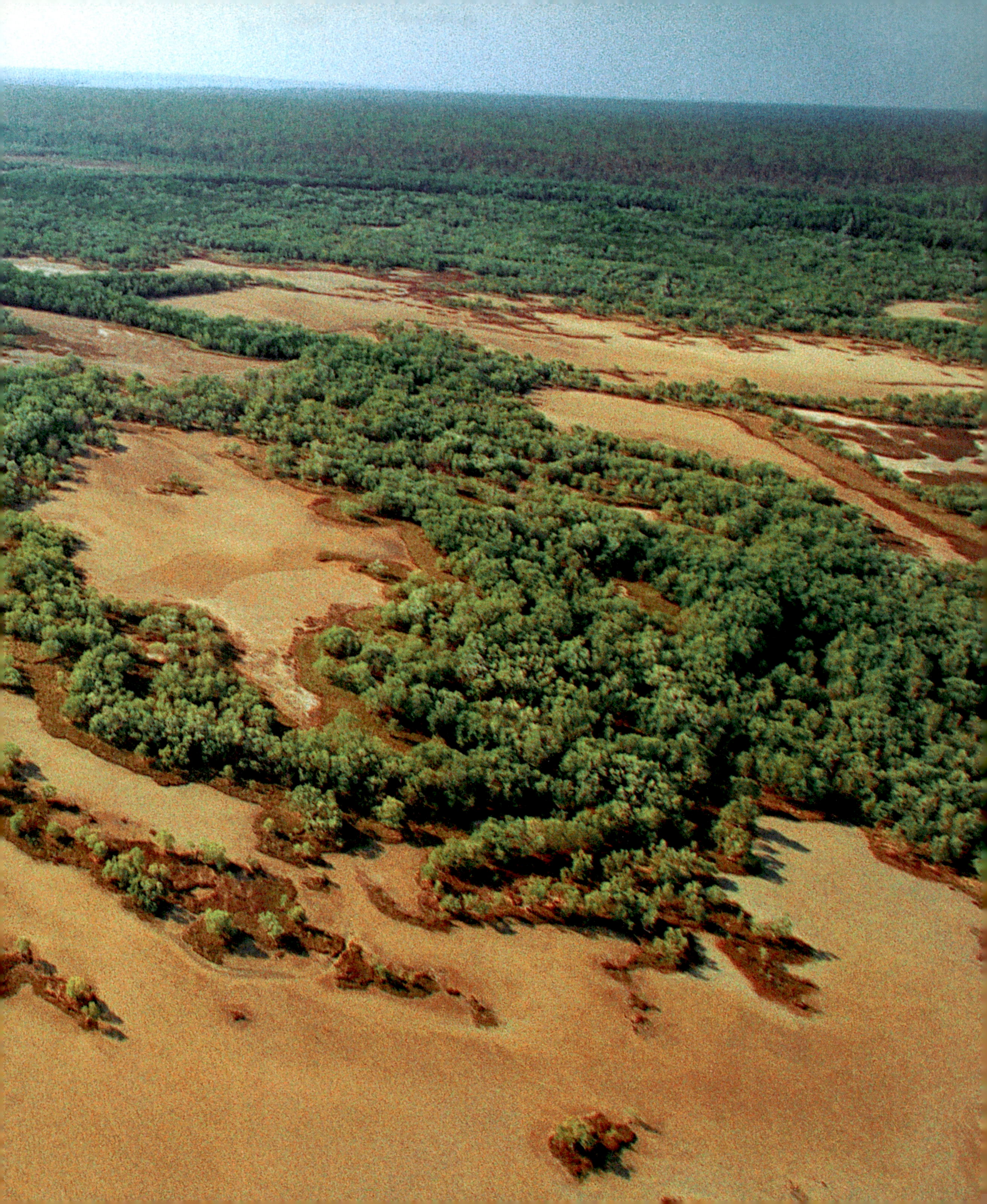

John Mawurndjul,
Milmilngkan 2004

Reverberation of image and essence in John Mawurndjul's bark painting

Judith Ryan

But me, I am a painter on bark and exclusively so. I won't change ... I only paint the things my father talked about and so I keep those things in my bark paintings, in my crosshatching. I don't go and paint on paper, paper is not for me, no. I hold on to what my father talked about and taught me and so I keep painting on bark.[1]

John Mawurndjul is an artist of substance, seriously committed to the practice of painting on bark – his medium par excellence. An innovator, restless in his pursuit of new ideas and the refinement of his technique, Mawurndjul sees himself as the leader of a new school of Kuninjku bark painting, as he proclaims:

I am the person who instigated this style and the others are copying it; they follow what I'm doing. Others have seen what I'm doing and they paint in a similar fashion with the internal lines across the whole bark and masses of crosshatching. I'm leading this movement and they are following. I'm going first.[2]

Mawurndjul has revolutionised the aesthetics of Kuninjku bark painting. When viewing his work, we no longer see stark images in crusty *delek* (white pigment) on plain grounds but large surfaces filled with masses of mellifluous *rarrk* (crosshatching) that constitute a metaphysical form of abstraction with a compelling and esoteric geometry. Thus his work is the culmination of a major shift in Kuninjku art initiated by others before him which has become more like Yolngu painting from East Arnhem Land than from Kunbarllanja to the west. The bald iconic style of bark 'drawings' derived from rock art seen in the great works commissioned by Baldwin Spencer in 1912, Charles Mountford in 1948 and Karel Kupka in the early 1960s has been transformed over generations into a complex abstract art form where images are covert and subordinate to infinitesimal variations of exquisitely drawn rarrk. Put simply, the image has become abstracted essence.

Mawurndjul places strong emphasis on individuality of artistic expression, as he explains: "Each person has their own different style and way of painting rarrk. So do I ... I have my own ideas which I employ."[3] But Mawurndjul's new way of painting masses of rarrk on large sheets of bark has not come out of a vacuum, rather it has been steadily built upon the teaching of his father Anchor Kulunba (c.1920–96) and the work of great Kuninjku masters Billy Yirawala 1903–76, Peter Marralwanga (c.1916–87) and Jimmy Njiminjuma (1945–2004): his direct artistic lineage. It has also emerged through changes in his rarrk style, which, with greater facility of technique, has become increasingly subtle and microscopically detailed over time. The development of his painting style from the late 1970s onwards also reflects broader influences beyond that of his immediate community, encompassing elements of *miny'tji buku larrnggay* (bark paintings from the east) observed in ceremony or in museums, as well as examples of Western art. Mawurndjul's encounters with paintings in ceremonial and museum contexts have created a repertoire of forms and compositions which he has 'placed in his head' as sources that fire his visual imagination, enabling him to forge a new direction and look forward, not backward. His art is a dramatic result of contact as he comments:

When Europeans arrived, the old ways of painting changed. The old ways remain there in the past but we are doing new things now. We have changed the law, the old fashioned way of painting has finished and we are new people doing new kinds of painting together for non-Aboriginal people as well. The dot infill method and x-ray was the old way. I've changed all that and I'm doing something new.[4]

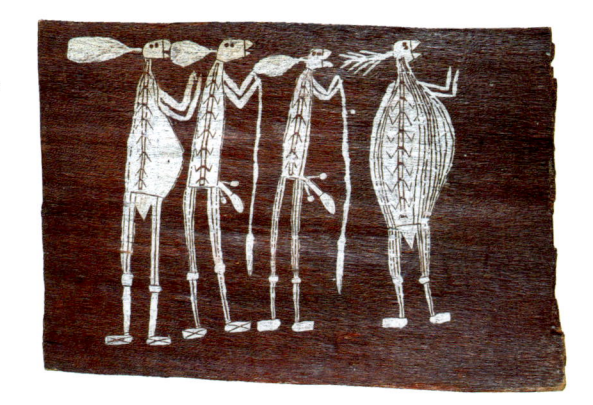

Nangunyari-Namiridali
Two mimih couples, 1960
53.0 × 73.0 cm
(see also page 215)

[1] John Mawurndjul's Speech at Clemenger Contemporary Art Award, National Gallery of Victoria 17 September 2003, translated by Dr Murray Garde, quoted courtesy of Maningrida Arts & Culture.
[2] Mawurndjul, John 'My head is full up with ideas', a conversation between John Mawurndjul, Murray Garde and Apolline Kohen, February, in Ducreux A.-C., Kohen, A. and Salmon, F. (eds.), *Au Centre de la Terre D'Arnhem, entre mythes et réalité. Art Aborigene d'Australie (In the Heart of Arnhem Land, myth and the making of contemporary Aboriginal art)*, Musee de l'Hôtel Dieu, Mantes-la-Jolie, 2001, p. 56. This conversation and subsequent statements from the artist in conversation as well as documentation of works are all quoted courtesy of Maningrida Arts & Culture.
[3] *ibid*, p. 52
[4] *ibid*, p. 59

Mawurndjul's earliest works on bark, such as *Ngaldadmurrng, Saratoga*, completed during the 1978–79 wet season at Manbulgardi, show his skill in delineating his subject, identifying the particular species of saratoga or northern spotted barramundi (*Scleropages jardinii*) through accurate depiction of its particular physical characteristics, as an outline, highlighted by the plain background. In keeping with other early barks by the artist, there is no x-ray depiction of internal organs; rather the body of the fish provides a vehicle for the artist's already refined yet subdued rarrk infill. This serves to distinguish Mawurndjul's depiction from works by Kunwinjku[5] artists inspired by rock art images in the escarpment country that invariably present the fish in x-ray, often including no rarrk sections. In fact the distinction is conscious and deliberate, as Mawurndjul comments, "I don't use the x-ray style. That's for people in the west, their style. x-ray for me is cheating on the painting if you are going to do rarrk. A painting with good rarrk on it deserves more money."[6]

The painting is unusual because it contains no yellow ochre and the artist deliberately left the foreground unpainted to represent the overhanging bank of the Mann River where saratoga shelter in the heat of the day,[7] reminiscent of "the old traditional way [similar to rock art] with no red ochre in the background".[8] According to anthropologist Dr Luke Taylor, the subject relates to a dance used in mortuary ceremonies to clear the living from associations with the deceased, in which participants stand in a circular well that represents a hollow made by the saratoga.[9] Thus, even at this stage in his career, Mawurndjul is concerned to reveal inside supernatural or ritual layers within an apparently concrete representation, a magic power or alchemy which comes from ancestors as he explains:

… my father was a great man. He was a number one magic man [clever man/shaman], my father had supernatural power. My father's power came from ancestors which he always had. I too have some of this supernatural power, which manifests itself when I paint the rainbow serpent or the antilopine kangaroo associated with the Mardayin ceremony.[10]

Mawurndjul's work at this formative point in his career is also markedly different from the paintings by Kunwinjku and Iwaidja artists working on Croker Island during the 1950s and '60s – Nangunyari, Midjawmidjaw, and Paddy Compass Namatbara. Their works were a startling discovery for Czechoslovakian artist Karel Kupka when he made his great collections of then contemporary art in the late 1950s and early 1960s. Regarding as 'absurd' the connoisseurs' preference for Indigenous works that were suitably 'aged', Kupka asserted the value of collecting current work from the source. Thus he stated "the quality of a work of art has nothing to do with its age; the only decisive criterion is its artistic value. If it imposes itself, we are naturally interested in the identity and personality of its maker, his personal vision and the reasons that spurred him to paint".[11] When searching for similarities with Mawurndjul's *Ngaldadmurrng, Saratoga*, 1978–79, Yirawala provides the key. For unlike his contemporaries on Croker Island, Yirawala incorporated rarrk from the Mardayin ceremony into his figures, rather than dotted infill alone, and also painted specific body

---

5 There are two dialects of Kunwinjku language reflecting the regional subdivision of the population into eastern and western communities. The western group or Kunwinjku live mainly around Kunbarllanjnja (Oenpelli) whereas the eastern group or Kuninjku from the Liverpool/Mann Rivers region have gravitated to outstations serviced mainly through Maningrida. The cultural division between eastern and western Kunwinjku, which is reinforced in ceremonies, is also manifest in art. In this essay, and in my 'Bark Painting: A Singular Aesthetic' essay, Kuninjku refers to the eastern group, whereas Kunwinjku refers to the western group and to early periods in Kunwinjku art before this distinction came to the fore.

6 Mawurndjul, J., 2001, *op cit.*, p. 59.

7 Letter from Dr Jon Altman, the original owner of this bark painting who donated the work to the NGV, to author March 1990, NGV archives.

8 John Mawurndjul in a conversation with Apolline Kohen at Milmilngkan in September 2004, translated by Kay Lindjuwanga, quoted courtesy of Maningrida Arts & Culture, see this volume, above p. 25.

9 Personal correspondence from Luke Taylor to the author, March 1990, NGV archives.

10 From John Mawurndjul's Speech at the Clemenger Contemporary Art Award, quoted courtesy of Maningrida Arts and Culture.

11 Kupka, K., *Dawn of art*, Angus & Robertson, Sydney, 1965, p. 63.

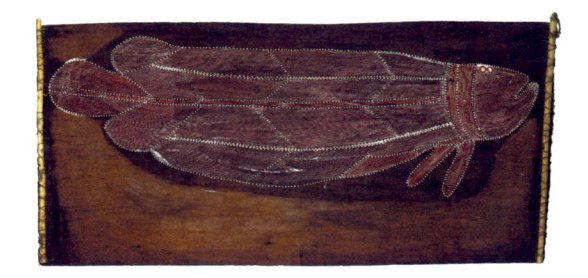

John Mawurndjul
Ngaldadmurrng, Saratoga, 1978–79
106.6 x 53.6 cm
National Gallery of Victoria, Melbourne
(not in the exhibtion)

Nangunyari-Namiridali (ascribed to)
Fish, before 1959
17.0 x 54.0 cm

Paddy Compass Namatbara
Three mimih spirits, one of them male, 1963
92.0 x 53.0 cm

Jimmy Midjawmidjaw
Namarrkon, 1960
70.0 x 60.0 cm
The earliest evidence of rarrk from western Arnhem Land in the Kupka collection in Basel

designs onto barks the scale of a man's chest. This, in turn, was taken further by Peter Marralwanga and Mawurndjul's elder brother Jimmy Njiminjuma who incorporated the subtlest tonal variations of exquisite rarrk within the envelope of figuration. Their works still occasion a vital contrast between the complexities of rarrk within the figure, its freely-drawn outline and the parts of the composition left plain.

Another early work of Mawurndjul's, *Ngalyod, rainbow serpent at Dilebang*, c.1979, following the example of mentor Njiminjuma, is notable for its complex repertoire of rarrk – parallel lines, white on white crosshatching, alternating coloured lines, lines of white dashes, over-dotted diagonals and herringbone patterns – used as infill devices within the dotted subdivisions of the body of this important ancestral creator. Ngalyod's body swells to fill almost the entire surface of the bark, a manifestation of her primordial power, and occasional malevolence, as seen by her killing of lots of people. For Mawurndjul, Ngalyod is a subject of central importance, which preoccupied him as an artist particularly early in his career when, as Mawurndjul recalls:

I used to paint her [Ngalyod] small at the start [of my career]. Then, I had a dream which made me want to cut very large barks and so I just did it. I went and painted big barks which were a success and I kept going from there. I always thought about Ngalyod and how to paint it. In these pictures, I use dot infill [subdivisions] like the old people but now I have changed. I have my own style, my own ideas. You don't see dot infill anymore in my work.[12]

As a young artist free from the glare of public attention, Mawurndjul focused on developing his repertoire of subjects and his grasp of drawing and composition. As he puts it, "I would just do it myself from my own thoughts. I think about it first and then paint. I just feel like making a change from time to time, and so I'll do a lightning spirit or a rainbow serpent…"[13] Some of his most memorable paintings from the early 1980s depict single *yawkyawk* (freshwater mermaid) or *mimih* figures, the latter in animated movement, with head bent at a sharp angle, almost snapping off due to strong winds. Mawurndjul's *Namarrkon ngal-daluk, female lightning spirit*, 1983, shows the heightened beauty and elegant refinement of Mawurndjul's rarrk, not predictable or uniform, but ever changing. Here the ethereal nuances of crosshatching float against the plain red ochre ground and are in strong contrast to the thick delek used for the head and upper body, arms and feet of the female figure. Such single-figure compositions, a hallmark of Mawurndjul's work, developed early in his career in common with work of Marralwanga and Njiminjuma and in contradistinction to multi-figural paintings of Kunwinjku artists working at Kunbarllanja.

1988 was a watershed in the evolution of Mawurndjul's iconography and the trajectory of his career: first, the year signalled his radical break with the confines of the iconic system of representation, i.e. the figurative outline, and his first paintings of metaphysical conceptualisations of specific sites in his country in terms of non-specific Mardayin designs. Secondly, the artist achieved critical recognition when he was awarded First Prize in the Barunga Festival Art Exhibition and won the Traditional Media section of the National Aboriginal Art Award. Now acknowledged as an outstanding bark painter, Mawurndjul's career was launched and a body of his work was included in a number of major exhibitions of Aboriginal art within Australia, including *The Continuing Tradition*, 1989; and *Spirit in Land*, 1990. Both of these exhibitions revealed a transition in Mawurndjul's work from figuration to abstraction: or rather his adaptation of geometric designs used in the Mardayin ceremony to represent specific sites.

John Mawurndjul
Ngalyod, rainbow serpent at Dilebang, 1979
127.2 x 88.8 cm
(see also page 87)

John Mawurndjul
Namarrkon ngal-daluk, female lightning spirit, 1983
136.9 x 40.4 cm
(see also page 93)

[12] John Mawurndjul in a conversation with Apolline Kohen at Milmilngkan, see this volume, above p. 25.
[13] Mawurndjul, J., 2001, *op. cit.*, p. 52.

The Continuing Tradition featured two pivotal transitional 1988 paintings of Kudjarnngal, associated with Ngalyod and his killing and swallowing of two young girls or yawkyawk.[14] One contains schema of concentric circles for waterholes, the other includes shapes suggestive of the main protagonists and the events that took place. The background is covered with bands of rarrk, less delicate and complex than in *Namarrkon ngal-daluk, female lightning spirit*. It is as if the artist is working through this major shift in his practice that establishes a division between formative and mature periods of his oeuvre, between figuration and abstraction, image and essence. *Spirit in Land* included two seminal 1990 works, *Mardayin ceremonial designs from Kakodbebuldi* and *Mardayin Burrk-dorreng* which both represent Kakodbebuldi, a Mardayin ceremony site in his mother's country, located on a large billabong covered in waterlilies. These monumental barks are considerably more complex than the 1988 examples, in keeping with their esoteric subject matter. Another monumental work of the same year, *Namorrorddo shooting star spirit at Mankorlod* shows rarrk designs within the figurative envelope of this frightening malevolent spirit similar to those in the paintings of Kakodbebuldi.

Significantly, Mawurndjul acknowledges that "these designs are used all over Arnhem Land."[15] His new form of Kuninjku art brings it closer to a bark painting tradition established by Yolngu artists from eastern Arnhem Land, which due to ceremonial interaction, intermarriage, the increased mobility of current artists, and the cultural diversity of Maningrida community does not exist in a vacuum. As Mawurndjul explains:

My father and uncle didn't use crosshatching: that was the old Aboriginal way. When white people appeared and became established in the area, that's when the crosshatching from the Mardayin ceremony was first used. The people from the east used it, and when the Mardayin ceremony came here, the rarrk came too. We used to just paint the old Aboriginal way (ie. no rarrk) ... and we put internal lines of division ... We only did dot infill.[16]

It should be noted, however, that the Yolngu iconographic system of rarrk signs and symbols, repeated in a sequence of interlocking clusters or patterns operates differently from Mawurndjul's rarrk because individual Yolngu clan designs within moieties are more diverse, encompassing more elements than hatching and crosshatching. The moiety dichotomy

14 *The continuing tradition: Aboriginal paintings in the Australian National Gallery*, Ellsyd Press, 1989, plates 15–16, illus. pp. 44–45.
15 Mawurndjul, J., 2001, *op. cit.*, p. 54.
16 Mawurndjul to Murray Garde, quoted in Garde, M., 'Ngalyod in my head: The art of John Mawurndjul' in *John Mawurndjul. John Bulunbulun*, Annandale Galleries, Sydney, 1997, np.

John Mawurndjul
Yawkyawk spirits: waterholes at Kudjarnngal, 1988
104.5 x 51.0 cm
(see also page 101)

John Mawurndjul
Yawkyawk spirits: the site at Kudjarnngal, 1988
106.0 x 64.0 cm
(see also page 100)

John Mawurndjul
Kakodbebuldi, 1990
179.3 x 91.8 cm
(see also page 108)

John Mawurndjul
Mardayin design, 1990
157.0 x 64.0 cm
National Gallery of Victoria, Melbourne
(not in the exhibition)

between Duwa and Yirridjdja is more clearcut in East Arnhem Land. In Yolngu art the abstract clan designs such as open or closed diamonds and parallel lines with crosshatching in-between form a precise visual language symbolic of clan identity, ancestral power, Dreaming story and place. For Kuninjku, distinctions between the rarrk of each moiety are less pronounced as Mawurndjul, a Duwa man explains: "The *duwa* [moiety] rarrk is generally finer and the *yirridjdja* [moiety] tends to be wider. These are not hard and fast rules though."[17]

Further into the 1990s, Mawurndjul's painting, loaded with a greater proportion of white, becomes more ethereal as he develops the finer and finer striations with the human-hair brush that are now his hallmark and replaces dotted subdivisions with fine single lines. The surface of each bark of variable proportions and curvature assumes a life of its own, determining the scale and structural rhythm of what Mawurndjul will paint upon it. A painting on bark is carefully constructed in layers: first a red colour is used to do the background upon which a white silhouette or *rungkalno* is painted. Next the Kuninjku artist applies an underlayer of red hatching, internal lines of division, and then red, white, black and yellow striping at different angles. A visual *frisson* or contrapuntal tension occurs through layering of tones and fine lines and the irregularities that occur within masses of crosshatching. By painting on larger and larger surfaces, the subdivisions increase in number, the range of ochre tones within the structure stretches, the crosshatching itself optically gyrates and the association with sacred body paintings becomes less literal. It is important to note that Mawurndjul's use of Mardayin designs differs from Yirawala's that are very specific to one design or totem not only because they cover the entire surface of huge barks but more importantly as he explains:

I will use the 'outside' version of them or change them so they are not like the 'inside' more restricted or secret designs. If I did them exactly like in the ceremonial chest designs, I would get into trouble or be the target of sorcery. I paint my barks in an 'outside' way for non-Aboriginal people to look at. People can look at the designs, but they won't know what they mean.[18]

Mawurndjul's conceptual abstractions increasingly demand to be seen in the context of contemporary international art, as evidenced by his success in winning the prestigious Clemenger Contemporary Art Award at the National Gallery of Victoria, Melbourne in 2003. Bill Henson, one of Australia's leading visual artists and a member of the judging panel, explained that it was the 'visual and spiritual dimension of the work' and its 'overriding presence and great beauty' that persuaded the judges to make their choice.

One of the works submitted for the Clemenger *Mardayin at Kudjarnngal* 2003 indicates the distance Mawurndjul has travelled from his 1970s barks as he explains "today the crosshatching has been elevated to a very fine level of great beauty".[19] The work is painted with a far greater degree of visual complexity and precision than previous Mardayin designs by Yirawala which are by comparison vigorously structured and free-form. The filigree linear striations are microscopically close together, shifting across a myriad of tones and colours and overlaid by rectangular subdivisions, indicated with fine lines rather than dots. Against this grid on a convex surface are placed bichrome sloping bands and zigzag markings that enliven the surface with its intense focal point provided by a brilliant shaft of white pigment indicating the presence at this site of delek white ochre deposits. Mawurndjul is still restless to develop fresh ideas within a compositional field, as he comments:

I have lots of ideas for my next paintings. I want to use more black for the internal lines of division. Have you noticed that I have been using black lines? It's a new idea. I have to wait for the wet season as I can't get barks just now ... I never stop thinking about my rarrk. Month after month, I keep putting my ideas onto my barks. I'll never stop painting.[20]

17 Mawurndjul, J., 2001, *op. cit.*, p. 55.
18 *ibid.*, p. 59.
19 From John Mawurndjul's speech at the Clemenger Contemporary Art Award, quoted courtesy of Maningrida Arts and Culture.
20 John Mawurndjul in a conversation with Apolline Kohen at Milmingkan in September 2004, see this volume above, p. 28.

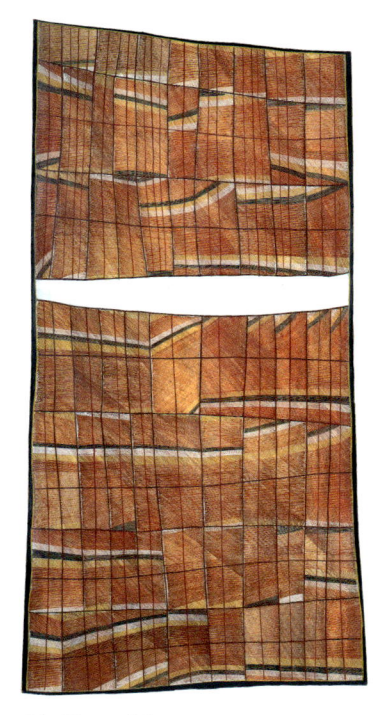

John Mawurndjul
Mardayin at Kudjarnngal, 2003
152.5 x 76.0 cm
(see also page 145)

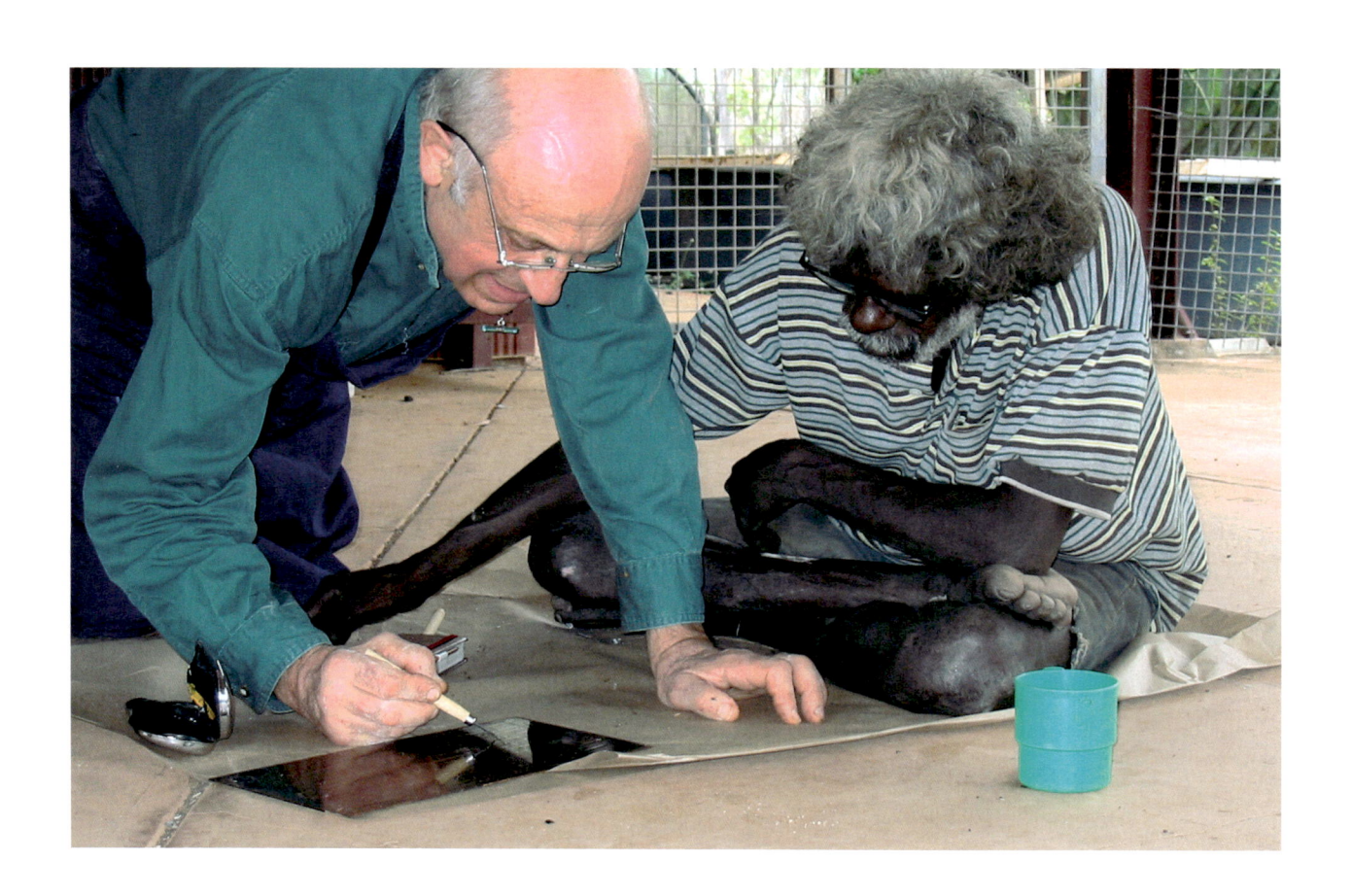

Jean Kohen and John Mawurndjul
work on an etching, Djinkarr, 2004

From rarrk to etching

Jean Kohen

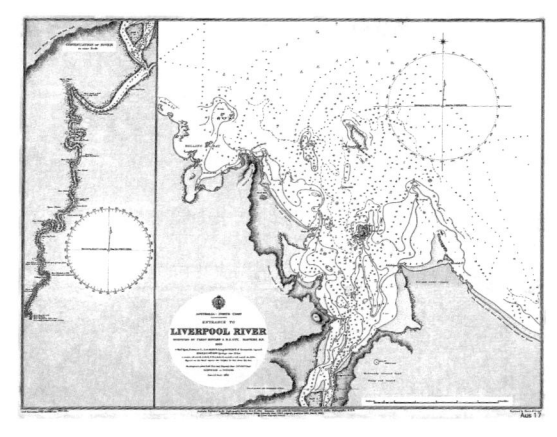

If you travel to Maningrida[1] in the dry season, you discover a warm-blue sky veiled in orange filaments stretching to the horizon. Below the plane, like a gigantic millenarian traditional representation ever renewed, is the earth with its ochres, bare of vegetation between the meagre-branched trees. The rivers have infinite meanders, while the lakes and ponds shine in the sun.

Soon a small airport rends the picture, with a smattering of houses.

It was on a British Admiralty chart made in the 1860s, in fact, that Maningrida was described for the first time.[2] Today the map of the ocean, the estuary and the river has undergone very little correction. The descriptions of the riverbanks, the land and even the trees are still reliable, even after the constructions over a hundred years later.

But you have to wait until night falls, and the moon climbs above the trees amid a flapping of wings, strange cries, unfamiliar noises. That is when you discover the bay shimmering far out to sea, the beaches overgrown with vegetation, and, beyond, the mangroves, dangerous at these hours when the crocodiles come out. The black bushes reach out their hundreds of intertwining arms, no doubt full of hidden moulds.

It is then that you turn back to the camp fires burning all around, surprised to find some of them abandoned, fanned aglow by the wind. The green wood is so full of sap that the fires burn for hours without adding fuel. Next to the houses people sit talking or telling ancient tales. It is late at night when they go to bed; everywhere dogs roam about, howl or sleep.

In daytime, the colours change nearly at every step, for the ground is always visible. The eye is surprised by the bright splotches that spring out here and there, little mounds of earth thrown up by insects.

British Admiralty Chart 1057.
Entrance to Liverpool River.
Surveyed by F. Howard and
M.S. Guy, Masters, R.N., 1866,
Published 1893, Reprint 1978

These coloured loams are used in the preparation of traditional paintings. They supply the contrasting range of shades and juxtapositions found in all the painted works.

At the request of my daughter, who takes an active part in the artistic life of the community, I agreed to transmit to certain artists my knowledge on graphic art.

In Arnhem Land, the introduction of non-traditional techniques such as printmaking began in the late 1970s. At first, the workshops were held in the towns of South Australia, and the selected artists had to leave their communities to learn the various techniques used in engraving, serigraphy and lithography. At Maningrida Art and Culture (MAC), the art centre that presents John Mawurndjul's works, printmaking workshops have been organised since 1996, in collaboration with the Darwin-based Northern Editions. Serigraphy, lithography and etched works have thus been produced by various artists. The engravings met with an immediate success, but there was a problem with the functioning of the workshops themselves, as the finished plates were sent far away for printing. The artists had to wait several months before seeing the results. For this reason, they found it difficult to realise what they had done and could not really appreciate the artistic possibilities of the engraving techniques.

I personally decided to be as up front and sincere as possible. By this, I mean that, although the engravings were made on a material that was new to these artists and with completely different tools, I wanted them to reflect the artists' personal sensibilities and, with the help of my technique and experience, to be completely *their own work*.

The outcome is dazzling in its spontaneity and truth. While it is different from their customary production, and although it keeps the same essence and spirit, we have here an astonishingly modern tonality.

The work is a bridge between two civilisations: that of the book and that of a tradition thousands of years old. These images, priceless witnesses, will have a permanent home in our libraries and museums.

[1] I would like to thank the Bawinanga Aboriginal Corporation, Maningrida Arts and Culture and especially my daughter Apolline Kohen, the artists John Mawurndjul, Kay Lindjuwanga, Kate Miwulku, Susan Marawarr, Debra Wurrkidj and Melba Gunarrwanga for having invited me to come and work at Maningrida. I would also like to thank Marc Raimondo for his help and support during the workshops.
[2] British Admiralty Chart 1057. Entrance to Liverpool River. Surveyed by Fred Howard and M.S. Guy, Masters, R.N., 1866, published 1893, reprint 1978. + Obsn. Spot, entrance I. Lat 11°58'4" S. Long 134°14'50" E of Greenwich (appr°). H.W.F & CV1. 30m. spring rise 12 feet.

In this exhibition, John Mawurndjul presents a number of prints made during these workshops.

This small, muscular man with his large laughing, intelligent eyes goes directly to the essential when it comes to assimilating technique without wasting time. From the outset, John wanted to do everything himself, at each step of the work.

Of course I was familiar with his bark paintings, totemic representations so very 'modern' in their economy and originality of line.

We need to come back to the question of the colours, varied in the paintings and, on the contrary, monochromatic in the type of engraving we have done, as we will see later.

The question of the representation of objects always arises in art, for representation means convention. Images are supposed to be viewed by a specific kind of individual; this is an inaccessible simulacrum, a mystical vision, if you will, a relation between the outer eye and the inner mind. John says: "There is no restriction of viewing anything I paint, it's free to look at. But buried inside are secret meanings which others don't need to know."[3]

Monochrome representation is not a drawback for the transmission of 'secret and sacred' thoughts. In fact, it turns out to be an advantage in the sense that the lines are purer, and, for our 'European' sensibility, it has an astonishingly modern and avant-garde quality.

In Maningrida, I came to understand a certain mode of viewing that effectively explains the images. Far from the biological truth, here the eye is not a passive receiver. It is active only because of the rays emanating from the objects together with their symbolic cargo, or, on the contrary, it is the eye that emits rays in the direction of the object thereby revealing its hidden inner substances.

This permits a relationship between the outer eye and the inner mind. To a certain extent, that is what I feel in my own work, which is never decorative but always attempts to express a sentiment or an idea.

I had only to express a few things, as did John, for us to feel close for, *basically*, there is no difference between this traditional artist and myself, schooled at the Beaux Arts in Paris and having spent my life in museums. That the traditional and the modern European ways of seeing are so similar never ceases to amaze me.

It was only after having conducted a first engraving workshop in June 2004 with four women artists that I came back in November to work more particularly with John Mawurndjul. We spent two weeks of intense work at Djinkarr, in a workshop equipped with everything we needed for making and printing the plates.

MAC provided us with all the necessary facilities in Djinkarr, at the scientific research station, located half an hour by four-wheel drive from Maningrida. During these two weeks, John Mawurndjul, his wife Kay Lindjuwanga, their children and I reaped the benefit of the peace and quiet of this spot so conducive to artistic creation. There, surrounded by trees, on a hill overlooking Liverpool River, we set up our workshop and an excellent large-format hand-operated press.

Having been a printmaker for nearly forty years and in possession of many techniques, I choose the technique as a function of the effects I want to produce. The Maningrida artists' bark paintings led me to opt for etching, which has the advantage of preserving the delicacy of the line. This choice seemed best suited to representing the rarrk – crosshatchings – much used in the painting of the region.

I taught the artists the most direct methods and the tricks of the trade so as to preserve their spontaneity and enable them to obtain the best results. We used the method of etching, which consists in varnishing a metal plate about one millimetre thick. We chose copper, which gives the most beautiful and clearest results when printed. Next the plate is scratched using various points to remove the varnish where desired. When dipped in a solution of diluted nitric acid, the chemical eats more or less deeply into the plate depending on the length of immersion. The varnish is then removed and the plate re-varnished to be worked again wherever necessary. Other tools are used as well to attack the surface directly. The aim of these operations is to obtain different depths of lines so as to create the desired tones.

Etching is the only technique that allows the artist to obtain, with a single passage, half-tones and therefore very subtle transitions. All other techniques play on the resolution of the eye: stipple or hatching, for example, on a black and white proof, give the impression of a grey.

[3] From the Apolline Kohen's conversation with John Marwurndjul, 'My head is full up with ideas', in Ducreux, A.-C., Kohen, A. and Salmon, F. (eds.), *In the heart of Arnhem Land, myth and the making of contemporary Aboriginal art*, (exhibition catalogue), Musée de l'Hôtel-Dieu, Mantes-la-Jolie, 2001, pp. 51–55.

Kay Lindjuwanga, John Mawurndjul and the family at work etching, Djinkarr, 2004

This is a simple way to tell the difference between lithography, serigraphy, woodcuts and … engraving.

But what is most important is the soft, velvety effect and the depth that emerge in such proofs. A whole world opens up to the viewer's imagination, one that is perfectly adapted, in this sense, to the traditional representations of the Australian Aboriginal peoples.

When the artist has finished with the plate, he checks his work by pulling a proof. After having chosen the shade, using a mixture of thick greasy ink, he smears it over the whole incised plate. Then he wipes off the excess with tarlatan and tissue paper.

Some ink must be left in the incised lines, and that is where technique is important for conserving the desired shading. The grooves containing more or less ink will yield darker or lighter tones. That is also where the artist comes in, for, if he is happy with the proof, he must remember that every other one must be exactly the same.

Now it is time to transfer this image to paper. We will then have what is called a print.

The paper chosen is extremely valuable, for it will have to tolerate serious constraints, as we will see. In the best of cases, the paper used is made of textile fibres in pulp collected on the mould. We used an excellent French paper made from a linen-cotton mix: the 'Moulin du gué', which is fine-grained enough to allow the artist to obtain the smallest details and yet is strong, thanks to its long intertwined fibres. The machine-made papers, although sometimes very beautiful, have parallel fibres, which can lead to warping and tearing in the printing process.

The paper is soaked in water to make it supple. The wet paper is then laid on the plate which is in turn placed on the bed of the press. Over these are placed sheets of felted cloth to absorb the pressure, for the assemblage is squeezed through two rollers, much like an old-fashioned clothes-wringer. In the process, the paper is pressed into the grooves and absorbs the ink remaining there.

The print is then allowed to dry.

I did all of this with John, our hands crossing amicably. The workshop was a gay place, for his wife Kay Lindjuwanga, also well known for her artwork, was unstinting with her jokes and teasing.

If there is a place where women are liberated, it is surely also at Maningrida. I noticed that children have very few constraints. It is true that Aboriginal children are highly attuned to nature. Let us not forget that we were in a scientific research station, and I had to set free tortoises, frogs and other small creatures … Children's education is ensured not only by their parents but by the rest of the family as well.

In this sense, I noted the constant relationship between people and life, and the natural environment. John and his wife, together with the others, were forever commenting on the different plants used for medicinal or other purposes.

The desire to transmit this knowledge is, to my mind, an admirable humanistic undertaking. It is no easy task to remember the names of the plants in the different languages, and their properties.

At Maningrida, over ten very distantly related languages are spoken, not to mention the dialectal variants – astonishing if you consider the size of the population, which is after all quite small.

The conclusion of our work, in terms of friendship which, we hope will continue and which moved me, was that John Marwurndjul regarded me as his 'father', *wamud*, and himself as my 'son', *balang*. This is a mark of trust, a precious exchange, like a bridge of crystal spanning our two civilizations.

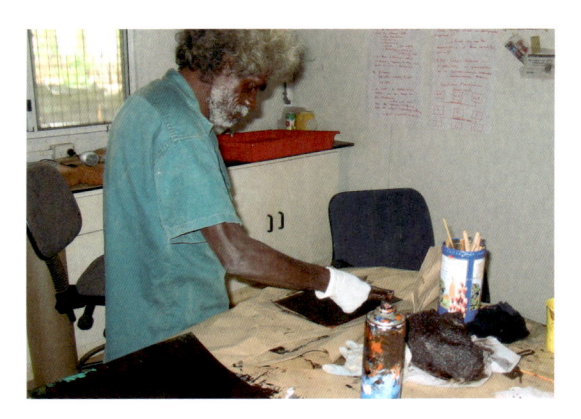

John Mawurndjul applies printer's ink to a copper plate, Djinkarr, 2004

The result of these two weeks of intensive endeavour was a surprise for everyone: a powerful series of prints that reveal, in a unique way, a hymn to the Mardayin themes so dear to John. I am incapable of explaining the hidden meaning of these themes and territorial sites that John incised on the copper, but one cannot help being moved by the strength and purity of these what are, to the non-initiated eye, abstract compositions. I was particularly impressed by certain compositions such as *Billabong at Milmilngkan*, *Mardayin at Mukkamukka* and *Mardayin design*, which, with an economy of line, go straight to the essential and lead us to discover John's artistic and symbolic universe.

When I look at John Mawurndjul's engravings and remember his words, I see their compositions of course, but also their components. That which seems abstract carries a symbolic charge. You are supposed to hear the commentaries, what is said or not said.

The mystery, in the sense of worship, may be concealed, a warning, a natural or human sign. A circle, the representation of a waterhole, of water are not a matter of style, they are means of conserving a sense of identity.

In this case, John Marwurndjul is far from the ephemeral creations he is so familiar with and which he makes, for example, in body paintings. But these are part of a life-cycle that unfolds in the space of the seasons. I personally, and this will perhaps make you smile, see a representation of the Narcissus myth, as it were, applied to a people. However this may be, these solid circular representations guide the eye. The hues are the brighter for the contrast. That is the beauty of the print.

John also made two prints in a completely different vein: a superb *komrdawh*, 'turtle', and a *kunj*, 'kangaroo', which show the force of his draughtsmanship and his sense of humour. It was after I had showed him my work that John took up figurative drawing, like a wink at some of my prints, a way of saying that he too is a talented nature artist. He also used flat tints for the first time, leaving some areas free of crosshatchings, carefully scraping the plate to obtain solid colours that contrasted with the hatchings. It was on these two plates that John spent the most time, continually laughing and joking as he made them. He clearly took huge pleasure in drawing these two bush animals. Those two weeks were only a start. John appreciates engraving and its possibilities; and in his own way he said as much to my daughter. "Good knowledge that printing, he has knowledge your father, that wamud."[4] Both of us are prepared to carry on, and I hope to return to Maningrida in July to work with John, his wife and other artists such as Kate Miwulku, who in a totally different register, has embraced the art of printmaking with a passion.

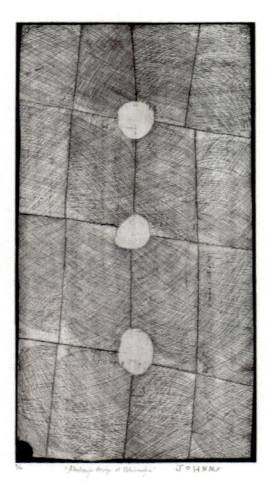

[4] Personal communication Apolline Kohen, November 2004.

John Mawurndjul
Mardayin design at Milmilngkan, 2004
Etching
76.0 x 56.5 cm
(see also page 152)

John Mawurndjul
Komrdawh, turtle, 2004
Etching
50.0 x 33.0 cm
(see also page 153)

John Mawurndjul
Mardayin Design, 2004
Etching
50.0 x 32.5 cm
(see also page 153)

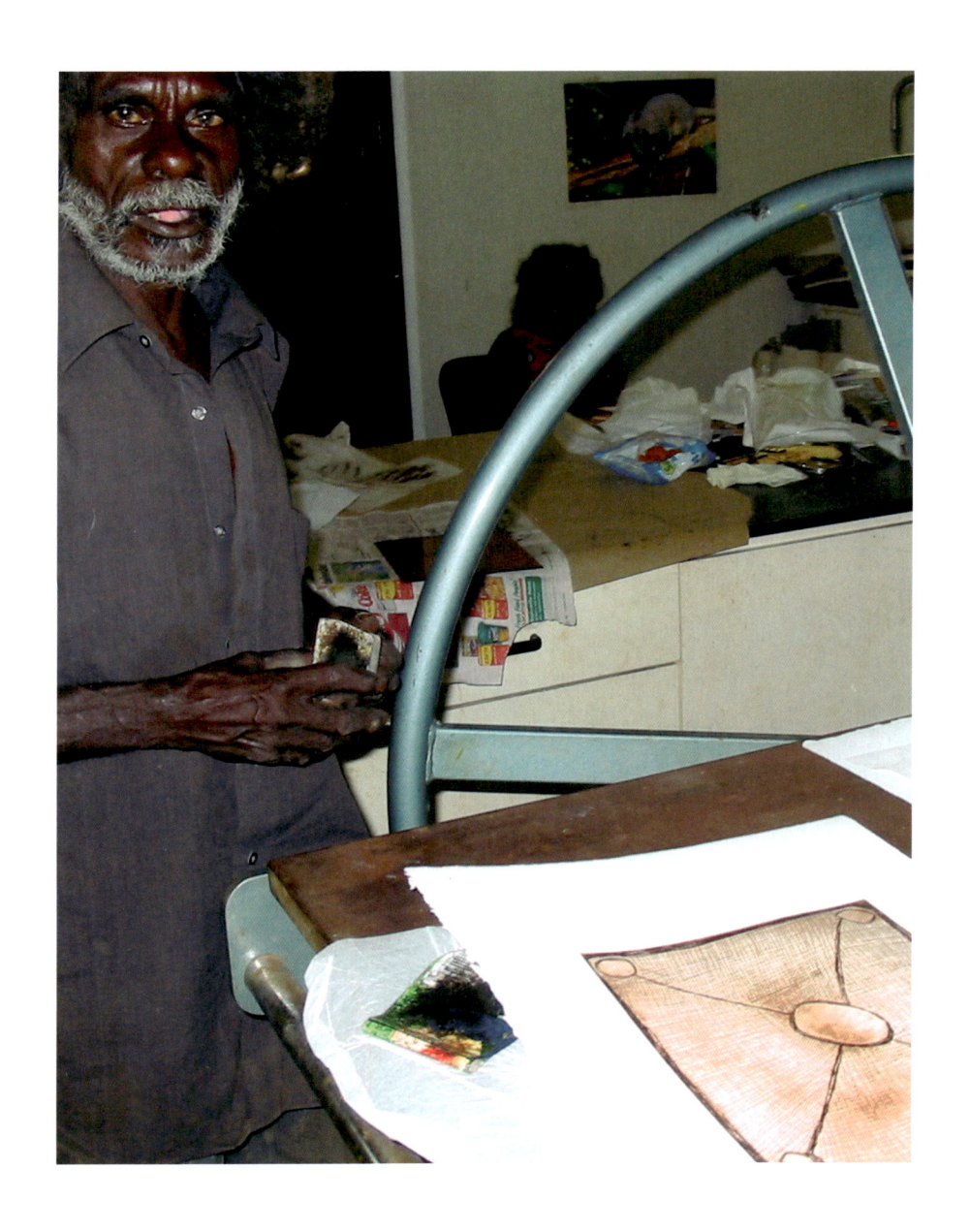

John Mawurndjul at the printing
press, Djinkarr, 2004

Jean Kohen «rarrk»

John Mawurndjul
Ngalyod, 1988
144.8 x 61.7 cm
Painting by John Mawurndjul shown in the exhibition *Magiciens de la Terre*, Centre Georges Pompidou / Grand Halle de la Villette, Paris, 1989
(not in the exhibition)

How the rainbow serpent became art

A short manual for looking at unfamiliar pictures

Hans-Joachim Müller

Mawurndjul, Mawandjul, Mowandjul, Mawurndjul. If you cannot even rely on the artist's name, what can there be to say about his art?

Aratjara – art of the First Australians was a large survey exhibition more than a decade ago that showed "traditional and contemporary works of Aborigines and Torres Straits Islanders".[1] John Mawurndjul was listed under the heading 'contemporary works'; he was one of many who had one painting on display. At that time he was amongst the youngest of the group of unfamiliar artists. Today, his work is no longer likely to be classified as 'young art', i.e. contemporary art. Although the paintings of "one of the most innovative Indigenous artists in Australia"[2] have long been discovered by the international art market and are in great demand by collectors in Europe and the United States, they do not look like 'young art'. What is missing, of what is there too much?

Everything seems unfamiliar. The colours, the colour mood, the supports, the themes, the symbolism, the literacy or illiteracy, the paintings' enigmatic provenance, their obscure function, the hieratic impression they make, their secretive transcendence, the oscillating between a far-off world, the supernatural and the netherworld. We have no firm basis for assessing them, no categories into which they could be fitted. Being socialised in the Western world of art, we probably can, for a start, do nothing else but compare the works with the patterns of tribally coined image conceptions. The mask-like faces, the empty eyes gazing from afar, the idolisation of archaic beings, the composite and transitional creatures betwixt and between animal and human, the figures' decoration reminiscent of body paintings or scar-lines, the painting's ritual equanimity, its lack of animation, its low-keyed mood, all these characteristics remind us of the singularity of images we know from different forms of non-European art, from tribal cultures. They resemble instruction sheets for unknown uses; at first sight they appear peculiarly hypnotic, more sensed than seen, more as if they had just appeared rather than having been painted. It all resembles an unspeakable secret – something that resists lucid explanation, where true meaning can only be expressed through images.

When in doubt, 'spiritual' is always a good pointer to fall back on. If there is something we cannot comprehend we immediately suspect tokens of divinatory origin. Those who try to interpret the riddle never tire of illuminating the mysterious darkness by applying the light of the sacred. Judith Ryan, senior curator at the National Gallery of Victoria in Melbourne, attempts to explain the particular spirituality of bark paintings through the material that serves as their medium: "Almost no other painting medium shares it bare, organic properties. It comes from the land – as the Aboriginal people are aware that they do as well. (…) The art form has a singular aesthetic of reticence and spiritual resonance based on the subtle modulation of ochre tones. It achieves stasis or quiescence because the artists transmit a vision of land as icon in terms of its elements: raw earth colours on living tree. The land is rendered human, yet celestial, and is revealed in symbols as if through its bones."[3]

Even if you adopt the view that land, life and art are inextricably linked, which no doubt is true, this approach almost automatically sets off the stimulus-reaction system we are so conditioned to. Images or paintings which, on the basis of their material quality, are so close to the ultimate and existential truth – ontologically earthed so to speak – stand outside the field of aesthetic competition which has become such a typical, even typological, feature of the Western world of art. This kind of 'art' is not just art on art, or art about art, it is actually tidings of being as such. From there it is only a small step to therapeutic prospects and belief in the strength of salvation. It is what we, in our progress-crazed consciousness, expect and hope from 'Dreamtime'-images or images of the 'Dreaming'. "From the artist's point of view", the anthropologist Ingrid Heermann writes, "the paintings are an invitation to deal with the world of images and the social and mythological meanings that belong to a culture that sees itself as a holistic entity, and to try and catch a glimpse, or maybe just the 'shadow' of a glimpse of what makes this outstanding work of art (…) a representation of the real as well as the metaphysical world."[4]

However, here in a Western museum, there are none of Chatwin's criss-crossing 'songlines', no dawning New Age and no arcane transformation.[5] The only reference points Mawurndjul's paintings have are the other, 'native' paintings on display. We are talking about assessing, comparing and understanding; bringing to light a metaphysical world is not our concern, metaphysical semblance is the issue. Wanting to know what the painting has to say, we are dealing with the dismantling and the deconstruction of holistic pretensions rather than with their constitution. Only fractional images render possible a form of sensory experience that goes beyond mere devotion and humility.

1 From 24 April to 4 July 1993 in the Kunstsammlung Nordrhein-Westfalen in Düsseldorf, then in the Hayward Gallery in London, in the Louisiana Museum in Humlebaek and the National Gallery of Victoria in Melbourne, see Lüthi, B. (ed.), *Aratjara. art of the First Australians*, Köln, 1993.
2 See Luke Taylor above, p. 43.
3 Ryan, J., 'Australian Aboriginal Art: Otherness or Affinity', in Lüthi, B., 1993, *op. cit.*, p. 51.
4 Heermann, I. and Menter, U., *Gemaltes Land. Kunst der Aborigines aus Arnhem Land*, Linden-Museum Stuttgart, Dietrich Reimer Verlag, Berlin, 1994, p. 7.
5 "A number of features define an art work as sacred. Sacred art always includes an act of transformation: the transformation of pure energy into a shape, the transformation of ancestral beings into animals, of animals into humans, of humans (…) into ancestral beings and the animal-like powers." In Lawlor, R., *Am Anfang war der Traum*, München, 1993, p. 313.

Experience has taught us that modernity means emphatic austerity – a kind of excitement that stems from enlightenment. The fact that everything has been disclosed is really no comfort to us. Even though all the secrets have been unearthed, something is there, an uncanny feeling that still haunts us. The fact that the frenzy of utopian ideas vanished long ago in the banality of virtual space does not necessarily set our minds at ease. No longer can faith move mountains, but still we stand there, astounded by the truth that mountains are immovable, that mountains are what they are. In the end, nobody is really happy with this self-inflicted coming-of-age and the narcissistic delusion that anything goes, that opportunities are boundless, is merely the shadow thrown by self-definition under the conditions of modernity. Nobody understands this more, and nobody is better at telling the story than art.

It was the achievement of the Early Modernists to understand that the authority of art, which in spite of all the disenchantment and de-sanctification has retained its enigmatic aura, is empowered by the authoritarian act itself of creating art, and to draw radical conclusions: art is what is declared to be art. It is art if the location where art is shown is considered to be a place of art. Art is its own context. Duchamp demonstrated this clearly in a nearly experimental manner by exhibiting mundane objects, the so-called ready-mades, in a museum and observing how they instantly, similar to a chemical reaction, underwent a process of ennoblement. The fact that the myth of art is based on nothing more than an act of designation was demonstrated by the placing of Duchamp's *Bottle Rack* in a museum.

What the test set-up does not say, however, is that when an object of a different order is raised to a noble status and becomes an object of art, it at the same time forfeits the title to a different kind of nobility. The object can only become art if and when it loses cultic properties and potency. The potent image becomes worthy as art as soon as it passes into the hands of the curators and restorers and loses its power to perform miracles. The Madonna no longer sheds tears of blood and we have nothing to fear from the spirit of the rainbow serpent that John Mawurndjul has let loose in the museum. The spirit has been stilled, like the broken gaze of the Man on the Cross, who, in the pure and aseptic timelessness of the museum, can never yield to the bestowing of a compassionate smile.

An exchange of authority is effected. One thing is lost and another is gained, humiliation and aggrandisement at one and the same time. The work, now released from its magical origin – in the history of emancipation this was called 'liberation' – is no longer the source of indescribable powers; the new context in which it re-awakens – the museum and art – has redefined its status turning it into an aesthetic object suitable for description. It is not any the poorer through this, only different.[6]

This change of spiritedness can be perceived clearly in the work of John Mawurndjul, *in actu* so to speak. "The history of the image before the age of art"[7] appears to be not quite concluded yet, at least not in Arnhem Land where, far away from Western art, a small relic of this history has been able to survive. The ritual origins of the imagery in his work are evident. Mawurndjul never visited an art academy. Instead, he assisted his father in painting bodies during ceremonies. The crosshatched designs that are applied to the bodies of initiates during the secret initiation ceremony are called *rarrk*. You cannot invent rarrk, nor can you vary it. Rarrk allows no space for modulation and fantasy. Deviations are forbidden, everything has to correspond to the original. Because, what is disclosed in ceremony is nothing less than the Law, the sacred, the dangerous. In other words: the dangerous, sacred Law. The Kunwinjku language knows one word for it: Mardayin. Although under the conditions of Mardayin it is difficult for artistic talent to develop, it did not go unnoticed that young John was in his element.[8]

Later, Mawurndjul acquired a new teacher, the bark painter Peter Marralwanga. He married Peter's daughter and started painting the rainbow serpent slightly differently from that of his father-in-law.[9] But that is another story and would be reaching ahead. Anyway, as a painter of ceremonial rarrk Mawurndjul would not have been entitled to do this and he did not do it. Unmistakably the code, the form of expression, the themes and the phrasing of this form of painting are deeply rooted in the highly secretive, ritually embedded semantics of the clan. We do not know what actually happens during a Mardayin ceremony, what types of reaction, reverie and rapture it effects, what surprises, amazements and shocks await the participants, whether people are healed in trance or whether the existing order of things is turned upside-down. Maybe Ngalyod, the rainbow serpent, rises up from deep down in the earth and once more tears off the head of a young orphan, whilst only the most sturdy and courageous do not fall to the ground petrified. We do not know and probably never shall. The fact that there are still corners of this earth from which television crews are barred, even if they are prepared to pay large sums of money, is probably the greatest Mardayin miracle of all.

But here we are in a museum where the rainbow serpent has been tamed with the help of the most advanced security equipment. But is 'tamed' the right expression here? Has art anything to do with taming? Does the rainbow serpent appear on its bark sur-

6 "Images fall under the authority of art historians only when they are collected as paintings and become subject to the rules of art. Whilst they are still part of religious wars there is no demand for art historians. Only in the age of modernism were they withdrawn from the quarrels under the premise that they were granted the status as works of art." Belting, H., *Bild und Kult. Eine Geschichte des Bildes vor dem Zeitalter der Kunst*, München, 1990, p. 13.
7 This is the subtitle of Belting's book.
8 See Taylor, L. this volume above, p. 43.
9 Peter Marralwanga *Ngalyod, Rainbow Serpent*, 1976, illustration in Isaacs, J., *Australian Aboriginal paintings*, Sydney, 1992, p.142; John Mawurndjul *Ngalyod, the Rainbow Serpent*, 1979, National Gallery of Victoria, Melbourne, illustration in Luthi, B., 1993, *op. cit.* p .53, as well as in Ryan, J., *Spirit in land. Bark paintings from Arnhem Land*, Melbourne, 1990, p. 77.

face like an illustration in an old zoological encyclopaedia – a little quaint, terrifying and gentle alike, just as we know from all the stories, as if painted out of the off?

When Mawurndjul began painting barks in the tradition of his country in the late 1970s[10] he used small barks and painted only a restricted number of themes, modifying the subjects only in detail.[11] In some way, the start to his career as an artist appears just as ritualised as the painting of rarrk on the bodies of initiates during ceremonies, but that would be a little off the mark; here he is no longer fulfilling strict obligations and following ritual instructions, now he is disciplining himself in respect to his own work. From the mid-eighties onwards he started producing larger barks, impressive paintings primed for museums and galleries. At this stage the young artist left the safe territory of his clan for the first time, visiting Australian museums and making his first encounters with Western art in both its sublime and its pretentious forms. Talk about clash of civilisations! John Mawurndjul wants to be part of it, and he is a quick learner. He soon learnt that in the world of art, a work of art can only prevail if it presents itself on a grand, self-conscious, even monomaniac scale. At this stage of his career the rainbow serpent, stepping forth from its shadowy origin, is the only figure to appear on his paintings. Would it be overstating matters to say that during this stage he focused fully on this one subject not only as a strategy for attracting attention and creating a stylistic marker for himself, but also because he wanted to test how much support the demon that has since become a fetish was prepared to grant him? And: how generously would it support him when he crossed the line from being a talented painter to being a successful artist with a claim to recognition?[12] By the end of the nineties Ngalyod had served its cause and the artist, who by now had attained international renown, remembered and returned to the hermetic system of signs from the Mardayin ceremony; not in a re-telling manner and not as if what once had been 'It' had now become 'I', not like someone who has turned his back on his church and is now ready to give an account on the time of his religious captivity. Nothing is revealed, nothing is given away or traded in. Something different, something new emerges, something that somehow ties in with the secret theurgy of an unlettered world but not in the sense that this world is now supplied with illustrations it did not have before.[13]

Bark paintings have been subject to considerable speculation. Frequently they are compared with the system of double-entry bookkeeping, implying that, when a bark is produced for the market, great care is taken that only non-secret or public designs and themes are displayed.[14] Furthermore, it is said that the traditional, ritually connoted designs are by no means suppressed, on the contrary they are treated with care, often they are modified in such a manner that they shed their sacredness and appear as mere decorative motives, ready for sale on the market.[15] Actually, this is very likely the case but it does not explain how the two incompatible levels are able to coexist: inside, there is worship in the innermost sanctuary, in the temple's cella, outside they are sold as devotional articles to gullible tourists. Can one serve the market and, at the same time, abide by the rules of the community? Can one retain one's totemic identity, safeguard one's ritual properties and simultaneously be part of the Western art industry age where ritual paraphernalia are kept in the showcases of anthropological museums. Probably one can, but how? However sharp you whet your psychological knife you will never come up with a suitable answer. And the artist remains silent; after all, what should he say?

What Mawurndjul does say is that he is doing things differently[16], that he has his own ideas, his own way of thinking. *I changed the law myself*, he says and means that he not only changed the law himself, but also for himself. He says he belongs to a new generation: *we new people have changed things*. Such a statement opens the doors to the halls of art history and echoes the act of self-empowerment that inaugurated the age of the avant-garde movement. *We new people have changed things*, says Mawurndjul. In the words of the Expressionists of the 'Brücke' movement back in 1906 this sounded as follows: "In our belief in progress and in a new generation of both creators and followers we call on youth to come together and, in the name of our future, to wrench the freedom of life and the freedom of movement from the old and well-respected forces of society."[17]

It would be misleading to regard the single stages in the growth of an artist's work as forming a straight line of development. What are perceived as steps of change does not follow any logic in the development of form, as we know too well from the history of Modernism. To suggest that Mawurndjul's paintings display a linear and growing tendency towards 'abstraction' is not the evidence we need to prove that his works are art.[18] His work becomes art because, in a much more fundamental sense: it has experienced on the journey from its ritual origins to the world of fine art the same the victories and defeats, the same moments of triumph and grief that the image went through when it passed into the age of art.

Just as Early Italian portrait painting developed out of the Byzantine icon tradition, Mawurndjul's paintings grew from their cultural background. During the last twenty to twenty-five years his work has not really developed in itself in the manner in which an artist's work usually matures or grows through alternating stages in style. Rather, he has moved away from the original, freed himself from the shackles of his cultural background. Anyone who thinks to call this 'liberation' is missing the main point, since this person does not recognize that, at one point in time, Mawurndjul decided to create art; he or she is also overlooking the authority with which the rainbow serpent has freed itself from the emblematic configurations of good or evil spirits and woven a web of its own in which it lies motionless, on hold or in the sleep mode we are familiar with from other figures in art such as Dubuffet's *Hourloupes*, Paul Klee's *Poor Angel, Forgetful Angel* and *Angel of the star* and the *Angel of hearth and home* by Max Ernst – all of them figures that Ngalyod gets along well with. Here, in a gallery, Ngalyod feels perfectly at home.

Ngalyod transformed to art cannot return to its old self. The change is irreversible. Now that it has arrived and settled down amidst Tinguely's stomping, thrusting and jostling machine-beings the serpent cannot be released back into the wild. There is no way back to the reservation of consecrated dots and lines, into the infinite Dreaming, when painting and erecting images was still an effective option. Here in the museum, even the wisest of the wise men, the oldest and best shaman of the Kurulk clan would no longer know how to perform the magic of the old rainbow serpent.

In order to understand Ngalyod in its new self, one does not need to know all about its origins, its home territory and the conditions under which it lived. All the well-meant explanations and instructions of how to approach and appreciate culturally unfamiliar images usually fall back on the kind of tolerance technique with which nowadays the enlightened citizen hopes to tackle the intricacies of multiculturalism in a politically correct manner. In the case of John Mawurndjul this certainly would be a mistake and would merely render his work harmless. It is not wrong to be acquainted with the deeds of the rainbow serpent and to know all the beautifully-scary stories that surround it, but it is not really a prerequisite.[19] The case is similar to that of the rose we see the Gothic Madonna holding in her hand. There is no harm in knowing that the Old Testament word that the flower-motif is referring to is *neser*, which is Hebrew and means offshoot or offspring and was translated as *anthos*, flower, in the Greek Septuagint Bible, but it is not essential for understanding the image. The same applies to John Mawurndjul's paintings: you do not need an anthropological glossary in order to appreciate them. To look and see, is enough. Very well then, let us take a second, closer look at the paintings.

First of all, we have to ask ourselves categorically whether we are dealing with 'paintings' here in the medial sense of the term as a configuration of signs on a surface. Though the bark is the ground for the paintings, which in the meantime have the format of pictures, it is never merely the support. The bark presses, so to speak, the painting into the room where it hangs and where image and surface weld to become a kind of shield. The paintings actually do have something heraldic about them, rather like escutcheons.[20] One can also imagine them being placed standing upright, or held up by hand or as a component of the architecture – hard and impenetrable like the wall itself, not like something that is hung on a wall. On the other hand, this does not fit with the conditions under which the paintings are produced. The artist does not work with the help of an easel but paints sitting on the ground viewing the work from above. This alone is quite a feat of abstractive ability; each new work re-lives, so to speak, the whole development history of bark painting from beginning to end, from the painting of the horizontal bodies of initiates in ceremony to the production of an upright picture suitable for a museum wall.

Because these paintings retain much of their corporeality they would still seem to lend themselves to a variety of purposes: they still have something of their old potential for the performance of symbolic acts on them, one can exhibit them or put them away, worship them or even destroy them. Iconostasis is a completely different way of dignifying pictures from exhibiting them in a museum. In terms of texture, Mawurndjul's barks are still standing with one leg in the history of the image before the age of art, with the other they have moved right into the centre of this age in which a work of art is not conceivable as anything else but a medium, a means of communication, a bearer of signs or a generator of stimuli.

To see how this artwork opens up conceptually, how it becomes part of the discursive flow of Western images and how, at the same time, it emphasizes its corporeal and not its spiritual provenance is a fascinating experience. There they hang on the wall as embodied images, they have a top and a bottom and easily adapt to the rules of Euclidean space. At the same time they could serve as table tops with sufficient room on all four sides for everyone to see *ngaldadmurrng*, the saratoga fish, swimming upside down. You would perceive that its body literally fills the entire space of what is certainly a modern surface area, with its tail fin and its lower jaw touching the stabilising slats at both ends. Geometry is absent here, so is construction. Everything appears to be in gentle movement. What looks like a straight line turns out to be a threadlike band, the innate trace of the brush (made of a stalk) being trailed along and dabbed over the surface.

19 See Lawlor, R., 1993, *op. cit.*, pp. 119f.
20 Frederick McCarthy's book contains a colour plate of a hunter from Arnhem Land holding up like a shield a painted bark showing a hunting scene. See McCarthy, F. D., *Australia's Aborigines. Their life and culture*, Melbourne, 1957, p. 160.

This also holds true of Mawurndjul's recent designs. They appear more regular and ordered than the figurative motifs but still resist the rules of the stereometric unfolding of space. Possibly, "John Mawurndjul is taking the ancient knowledge of his ancestors that is held in images and gradually transforming the themes into geometric designs." But there is more to it than that: the process is not aiming at geometry, it is not trying to establish a definite order; on the contrary, it is trying to establish an unstable linkage of parts, attempting to reassemble by hand the fragments of signs and images into which Mardayin, in memory and appearance, has disintegrated. Just as a figurative image starts with an outline drawing that encloses the sections of the body and keeps the figure in shape[21], the adjoining fields in the more recent and less encumbered 'designs' are tightly sewn together. If the picture looks more elegant, more improvised, more effortless or more intense and no longer reminds us of mythic coherence, of the power to move mountains – it is the price of expressivity that art has to, and is ready to, pay in order to be what it is.

Anyone seeking unity in these paintings falls prey to his or her own mystification. Mawurndjul's work does not bear witness to the wondrous survival of what is left of an archaic whole. Having become art it ventures forth into the residuum which the spirit of modern consciousness always tends to invade and lay claim to: *I changed the law myself*. That is why it is art! That is what art is about: it deals with dis-unity, with a lost, unimaginable, enforced and yet yearned-for unity. Even if these pictures do not suggest loss, enforcement, yearning and the unimaginable and their imposing imperturbability leaves things as they were, the central contradiction lodged in a double identity still comes to the fore: the split between the narrow confines of a pre-artistic background on the one hand and the boundlessness of the self-professed artist on the other.

At some time in the past, painting the rainbow serpent might have assisted in calling forth the spirit, the ancestor beings or the daemons, but no longer. Today the incantation of the rainbow serpent has resolved into a set of re-enactable signs and meanings that have become legend. The images have lost the power of invocation; they now serve to hallmark a personality who has transcended the boundaries of his clan. Mawurndjul has become a specialist never seen before in the 40,000 years of Aboriginal history. Some anthropologists maintain[22] these cultures never had any form of centralised authority beyond the clan and the ritual community, no outstanding personality in the role of chief. Now that John Mawurndjul together with others – *we new people* – claim entitlement as artists this figuration is doomed. The dissociating adaptations to the operating system of global art will not be reconciled to the technique of concealment through which the secrets are claimed to be kept hidden away.

The distinction between 'fine art' and 'tribal art' is part of the narrative pattern of art history in the twentieth century. The respect and veneration shown for African tribal art by representatives of Early Modernism expresses – beyond simply formal aesthetic interests – a regressive wish, a deep-felt yearning to return to the pre-modern world of imagery where nothing had yet been divided into separate spheres, collective lore on the one hand and individual creativity on the other. Here the famous sculpture, there the nameless object that the unknown artisan had created adhering to the canons of his culture. Against this background, John Mawurndjul's art is even more confounding: as works that are still embedded in traditional imagery, with no wish to dis-embed themselves, but which nonetheless represent unique artistic achievement. Given all the travesties of Western habits and the international standards by which art is judged today, Mawurndjul's paintings remain filled with the narrative and symbolic sediment of a non-Western culture. That cannot be overlooked. After all, the rainbow serpent cannot metamorphose to become world art so quickly. And that, actually, is marvellous, just as Mawurndjul's resistance to the undertow of globalised signification is commendable. Resistance and recalcitrance do not mean backwardness. This kind of defiance, the pride of owning something that is not freely accessible, of defending one's own, constitutes the foundation of the work's unquestionable status and character as art.

Since the artist moves here and there and between different worlds, the fact that Mawurndjul suddenly becomes Mawandjul, or is turned into Mowandjul, only to change to Mawurndjurl in the next moment is nothing less than a subtle punch line. Not to be able to rely on the way his name is spelt is certainly not the least that can be said about his art.

21 Australian art critics called this special form of Aboriginal Art x-ray style or x-ray art. From an analytical point of view, however, this overlooks the more synthetic nature of the paintings.
22 "Technical and artistic abilities (...) were not vested in a single few (...) they were embedded in the overarching field of social obligations (...) apart from the healer or shaman, all men and women, with growing age, attained the necessary amount and kind of knowledge according to their sex status." See Supp, E., *op. cit.*, p. 90 and p. 162.

WORKS 1979–2005

Bambil, echidna, and mimih
1979
68.0 x 46.0 cm

Ngurrdu, Emu
1980
47.0 x 38.0 cm

Namarrkon, lightning spirit
1979
96.0 x 57.7 cm

Ngalyod, rainbow serpent, at Dilebang
c. 1979
127.2 x 88.8 cm

«rarrk»

Lorrkkon, hollow log
1980
93.5 x 24.5 cm

88   « rarrk »

Ngalyod, rainbow serpent
1980
72.0 x 56.0 cm

**Namarrkon,
female lightning spirit**
1981
c. 60.0 x 20.0 cm

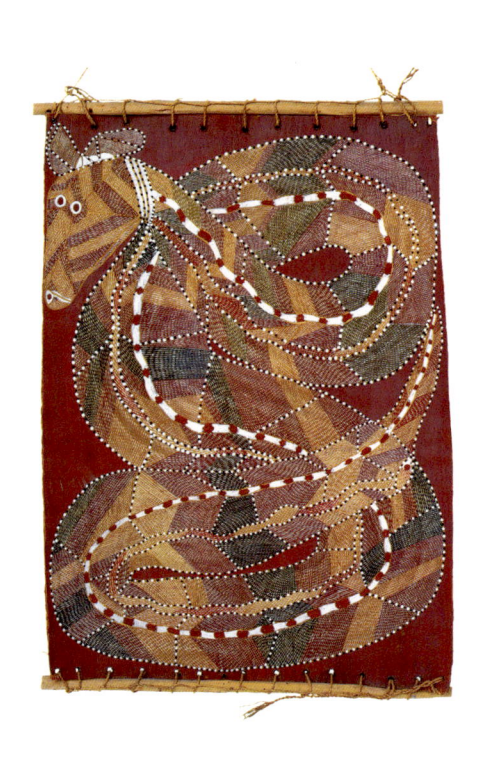

Ngalyod, rainbow serpent
1982
100.0 x 44.0 cm

**Namarden,
female lightning spirit**
1982
64.0 x 37.0 cm

**Namarrkon ngal-daluk,
female lightning spirit**
1983
136.9 x 40.4 cm

Female lightning spirit
1984
52.5 x 32.5 cm

**Ngalyod, rainbow serpent,
devouring the yawkyawk girls**
1984
123.5 x 74.0 cm

«rarrk»

**Yawkyawk, young girl –
water spirit**
1985
50.5 x 27.0 cm

«rarrk»

**Yawkyawk, young girl –
water spirit**
1985
115.0 x 60.0 cm

Lorrkkon, hollow log
c. 1986
224.5 x 16.0 cm

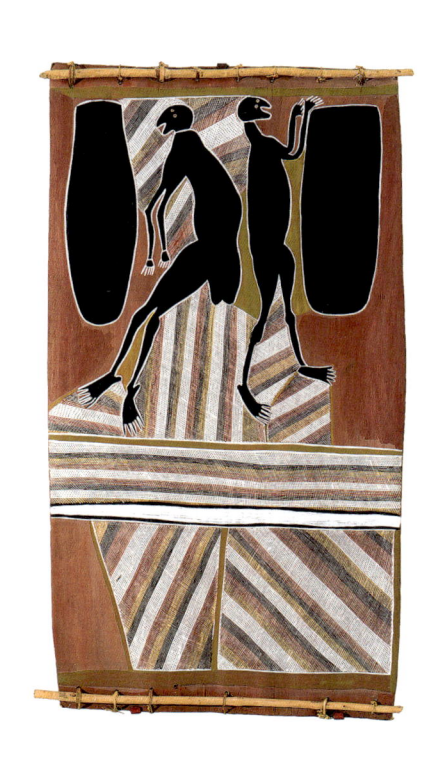

**Ancestral spirit beings
collecting honey**
1985–87
110.5 x 61.0 cm

«rarrk»

**Yawkyawk spirits:
the site at Kudjarnngal**
1988
106.0 x 64.0 cm

**Yawkyawk spirits:
waterholes at Kudjarnngal**
1988
104.5 x 51.0 cm

«rarrk»

**Nawarramulmul,
shooting star spirit**
1988
219.4 x 95.0 cm

Ngarrt, short-necked turtle, with its eggs
1989
213.0 x 96.0 cm

«rarrk»

Mimih at Milmilngkan
1989
249.0 x 95.0 cm

Namorrorddo, shooting star spirit, at Mankorlod
1990
241.0 x 116.3 cm

«rarrk»

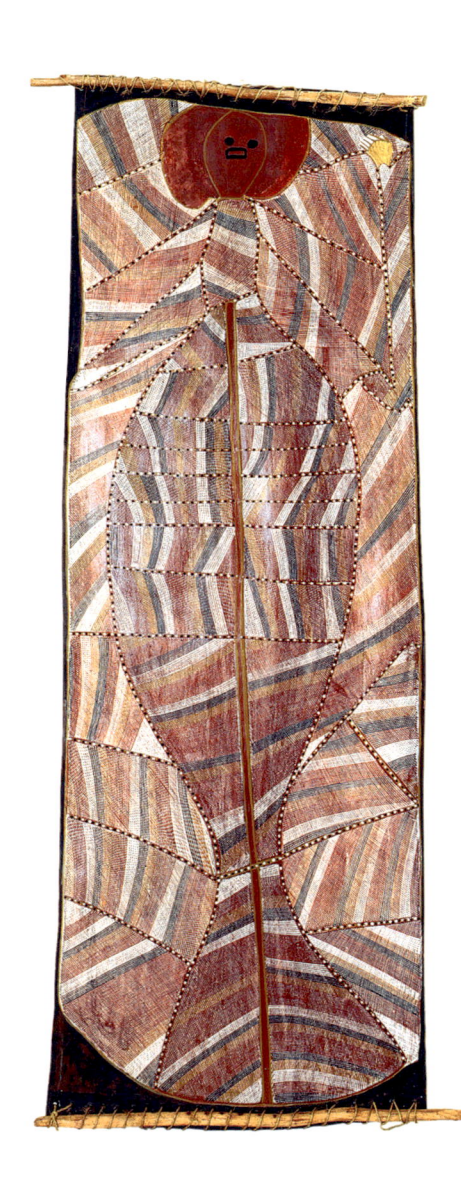

**Yawkyawk, young girl –
water spirit**
late 80s
164.0 x 69.0 cm

Buluwana, female ancestor
1989
261.0 x 77.6 cm

«rarrk»

Kakodbebuldi
1990
179.3 x 91.8 cm

**Rainbow serpent's
antilopine kangaroo**
1991
189.0 x 94.0 cm

Creator spirit
1994
c. 240.0 x 86.0 (Dm.)

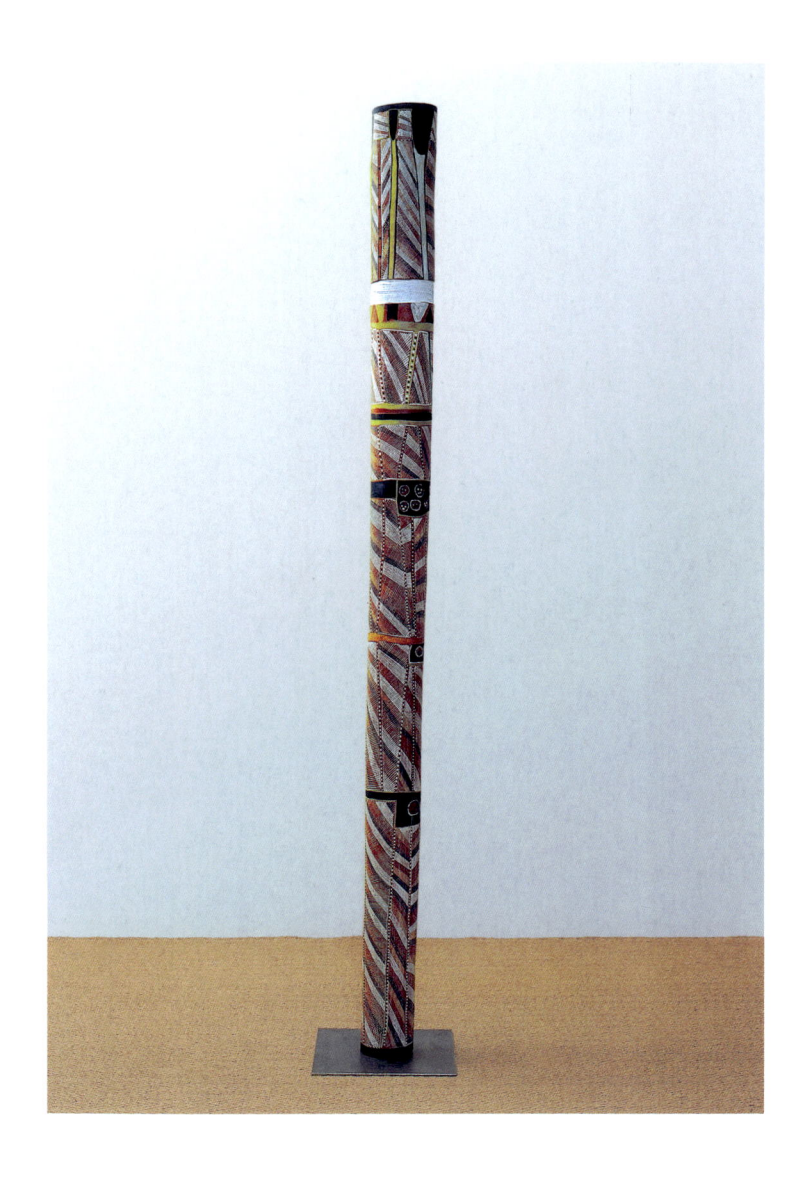

Lorrkkon, hollow log
1994
249.0 x 16.0 cm

«rarrk»

River whale shark
1989
233.0 x 19.5 x 23.0 cm

Mimih spirit
1992
250.0 x 11.0 x 11.0 cm

«rarrk»

Billabong at Milmilngkan
1993
175.0 x 49.0 cm

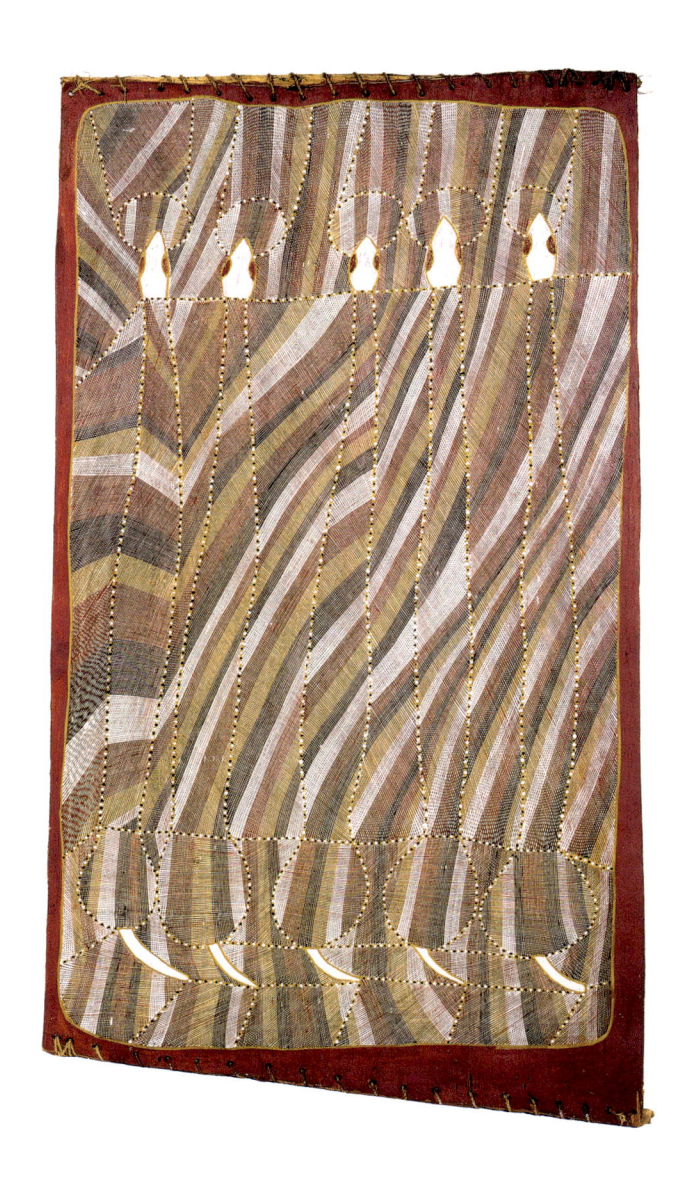

Mardayin design
1993
152.0 x 74.0 cm

Djatti, frogs
1993
175.0 x 49.0 cm

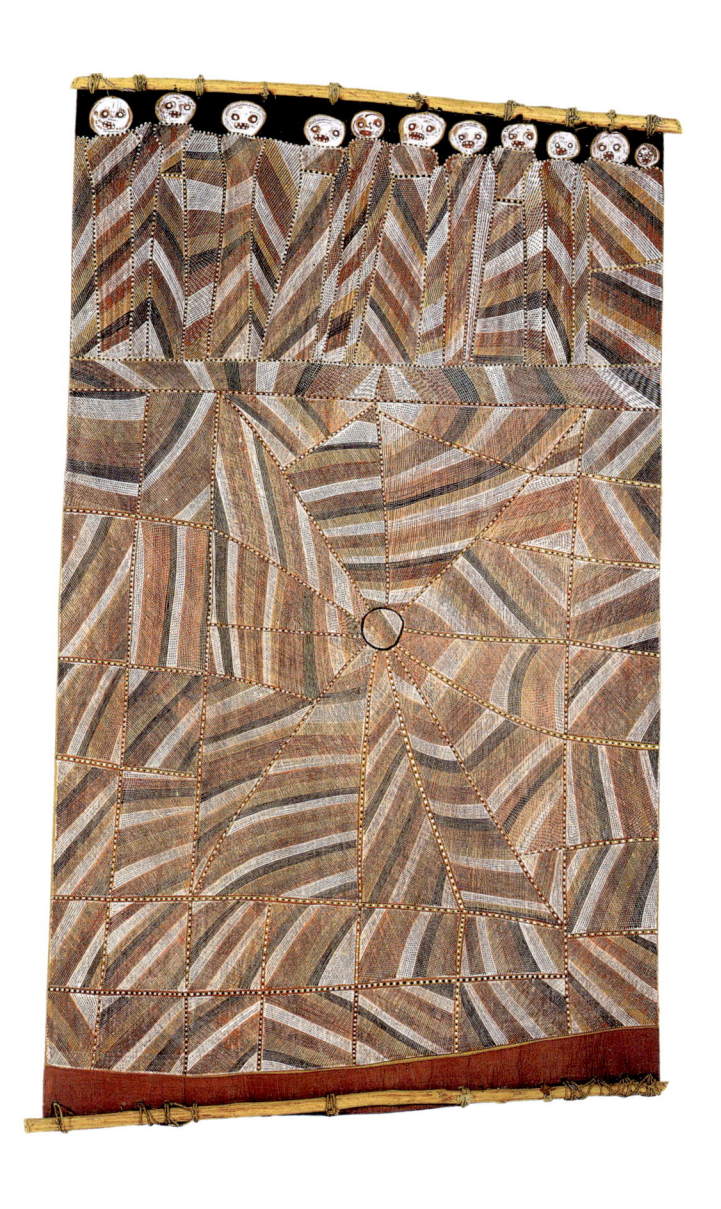

**Buluwana, female ancestor,
at Dilebang**
1993
174.0 x 74.0 cm

«rarrk»

Kunmadj, dilly bag
1996
112.5 x 59.5 cm

**Mimih spirits as dreaming beings
under a rock at Ngandarrayo**
1994
86.5 x 40.0 cm

«rarrk»

**Ngalyod and the creation
of sites at Kakodbebuldi**
1994
191.0 x 68.0 cm

**Nadulmi, the rainbow serpent's
pet antilopine kangaroo**
1995
197.0 × 74.0 cm

Wayuk, waterlily, at Dilebang
c. 1990
69.7 x 44.0 cm

122 « rarrk »

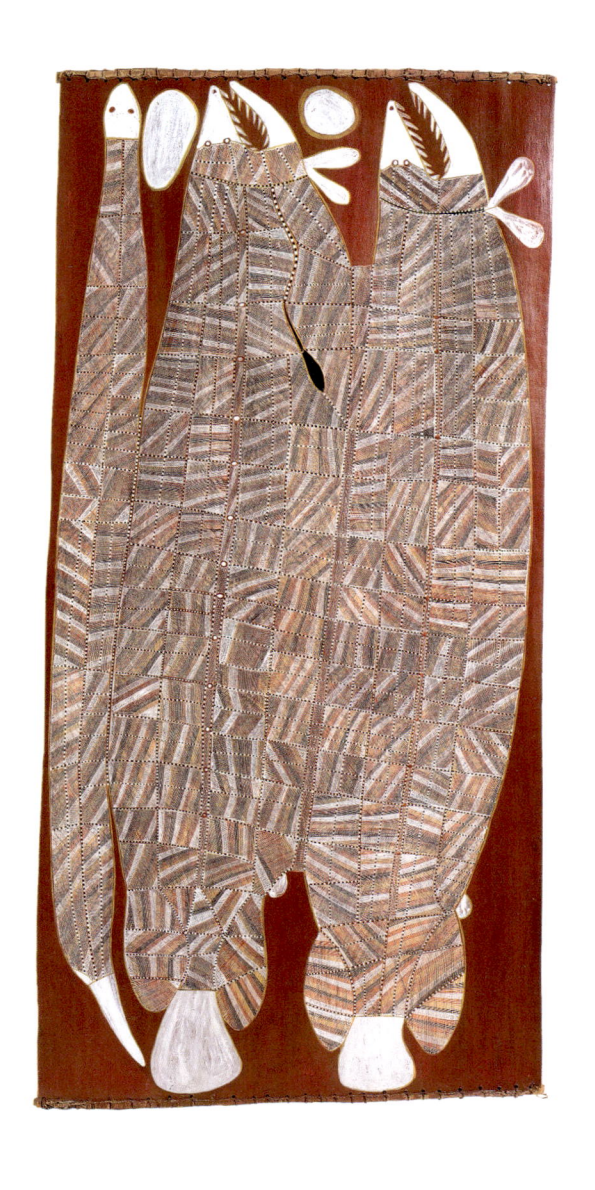

Ngaldadmurrng, saratoga
1997
189.0 x 89.0 cm

«rarrk»

Mardayin ceremony
Theme 1
1997
134.5 × 73.5 cm

Crow from Kurrurldul,
Mardayin ceremony, Theme 4
1997
154.0 x 81.0 cm

«rarrk»

Yawkyawk at Dilebang
1997
194.0 x 19.0 x 16.0 cm

**Yingarna, mother of the
rainbow serpent**
1997
183.0 × 82.5 cm

«rarrk»

Ngalyod, rainbow serpent
1999
156.0 x 81.0 cm

Ngalyod, rainbow serpent
1999
153.0 x 90.0 cm

«rarrk»

Dilly bag
1996
57.0 x 30.0 cm

130 «rarrk»

Barramundi and catfish
1997
79.5 x 63.0 cm

Mardayin at Mukkamukka
late 90s
168.0 x 95.0 cm

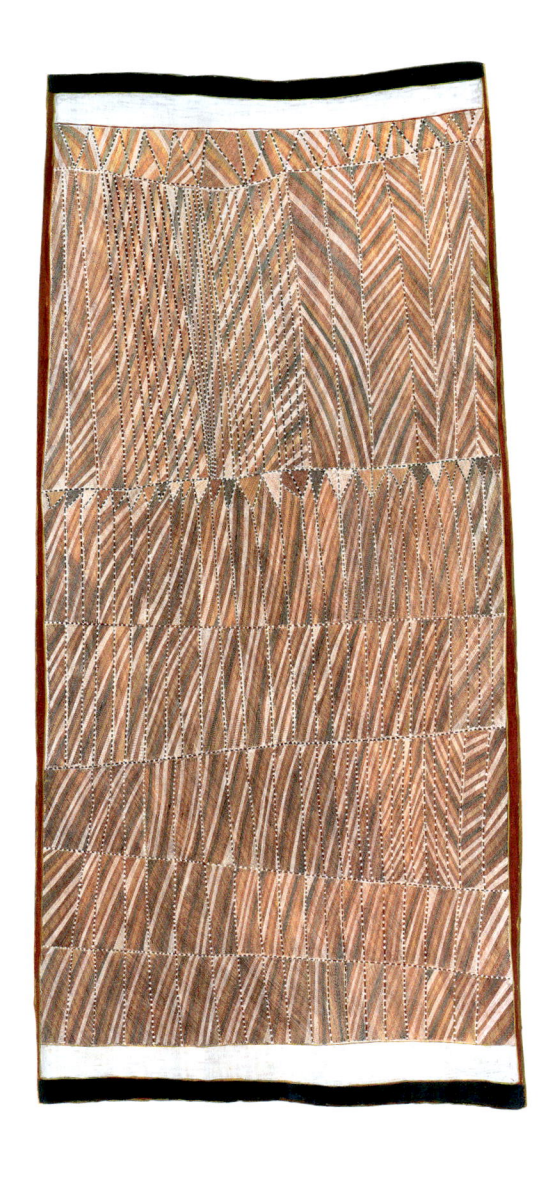

Mardayin ceremony
2000
170.0 x 78.0 cm

Mardayin at Kakodbebuldi
2000
157.0 x 66.0 cm

Mardayin ceremony
1999
153.0 x 88.0 cm

«rarrk»

Turtle
2000
153.0 x 65.0/73.0 cm

136 «rarrk»

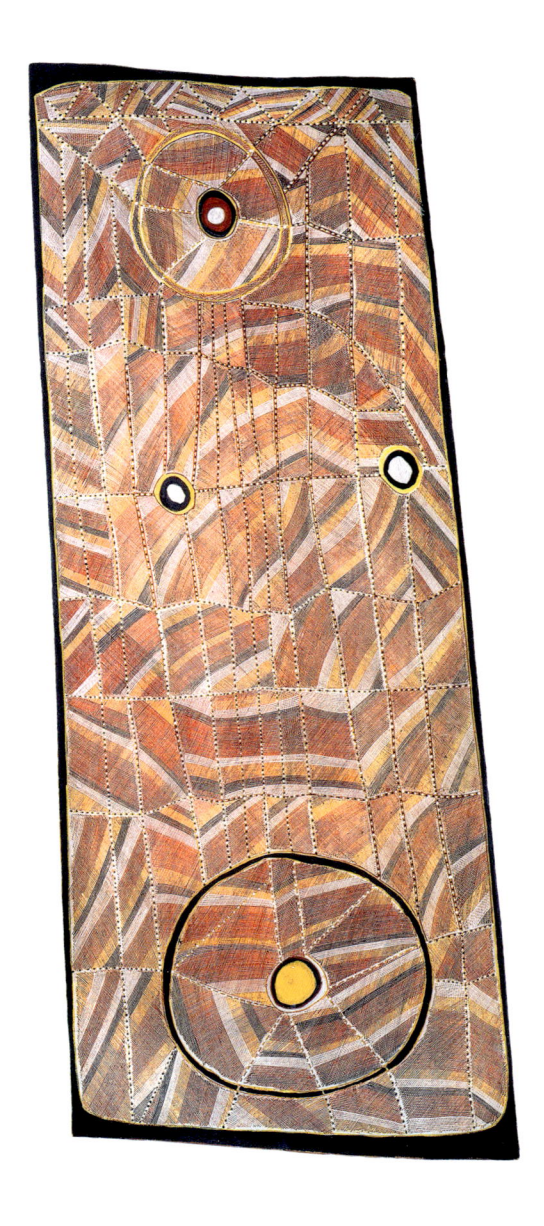

Mardayin at Mumeka
2001
168.0 x 63.0 cm

«rarrk»

Namarrkon, lightning spirit
2000
58.0 x 23.0 cm

Lorrkkon, hollow log
2001
148.5 x 14.0 cm

«rarrk»

Two fish
2002
67.0 x 58.0 cm

Buluwana, female ancestor
2001
200.0 x 59.0 cm

«rarrk»

Billabong at Milmilngkan
2002
108.5 x 36.5 cm

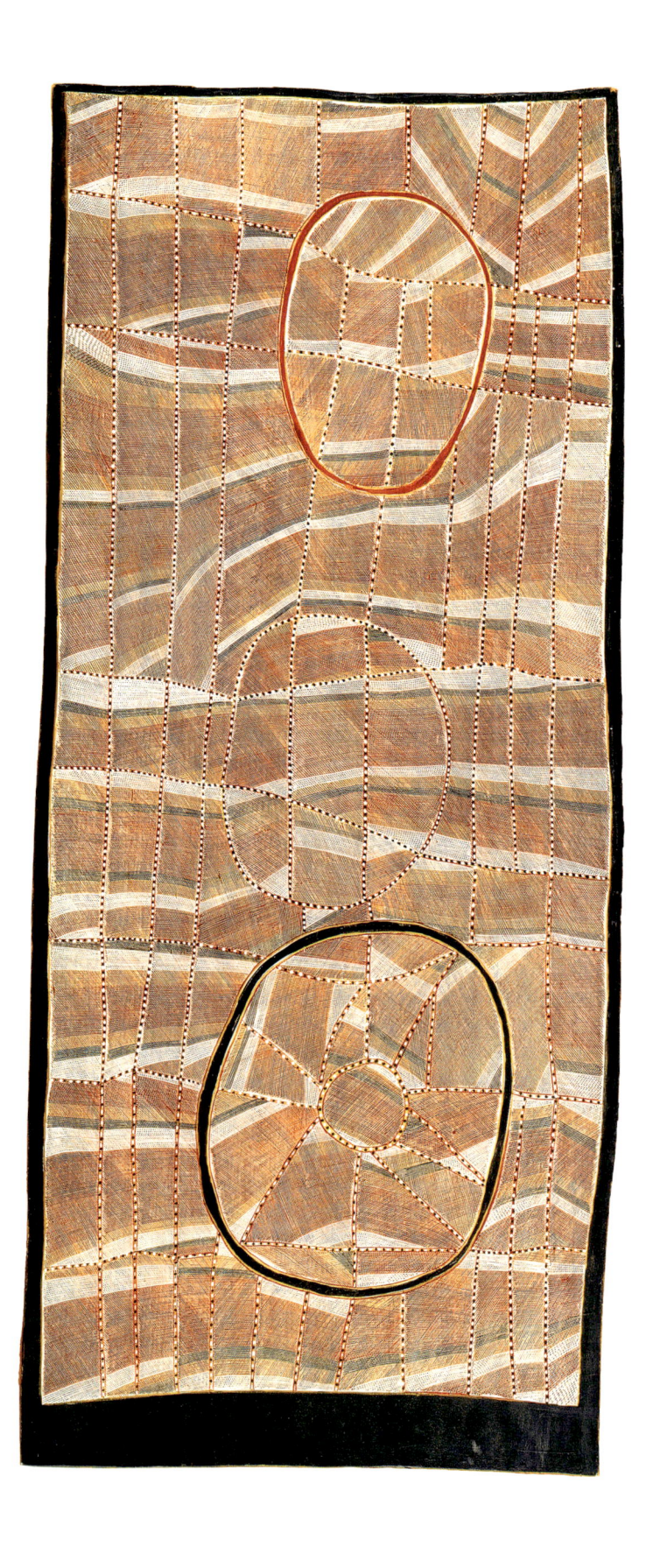

Billabong at Milmilngkan
2002
186.0 x 78.5 cm

«rarrk»

**Mardayin design
at Kakodbebuldi**
2002
172.5 x 69.0 cm

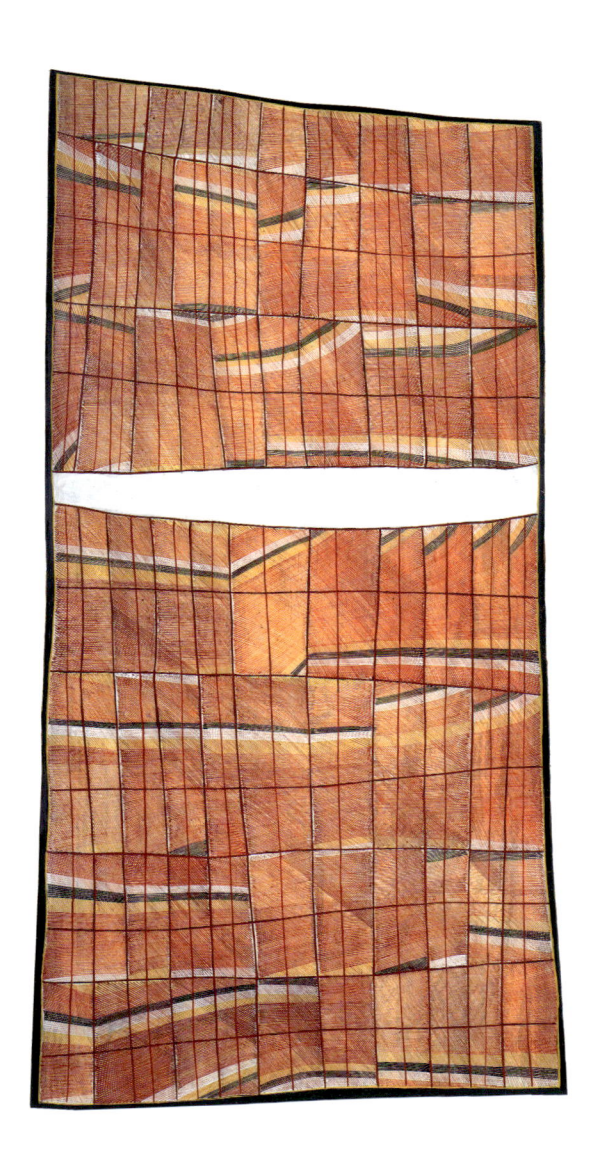

Mardayin at Kudjarnngal
2003
152.5 x 76.0 cm

«rarrk»

Mardayin at Dilebang
2003
131.6 × 63.0 cm

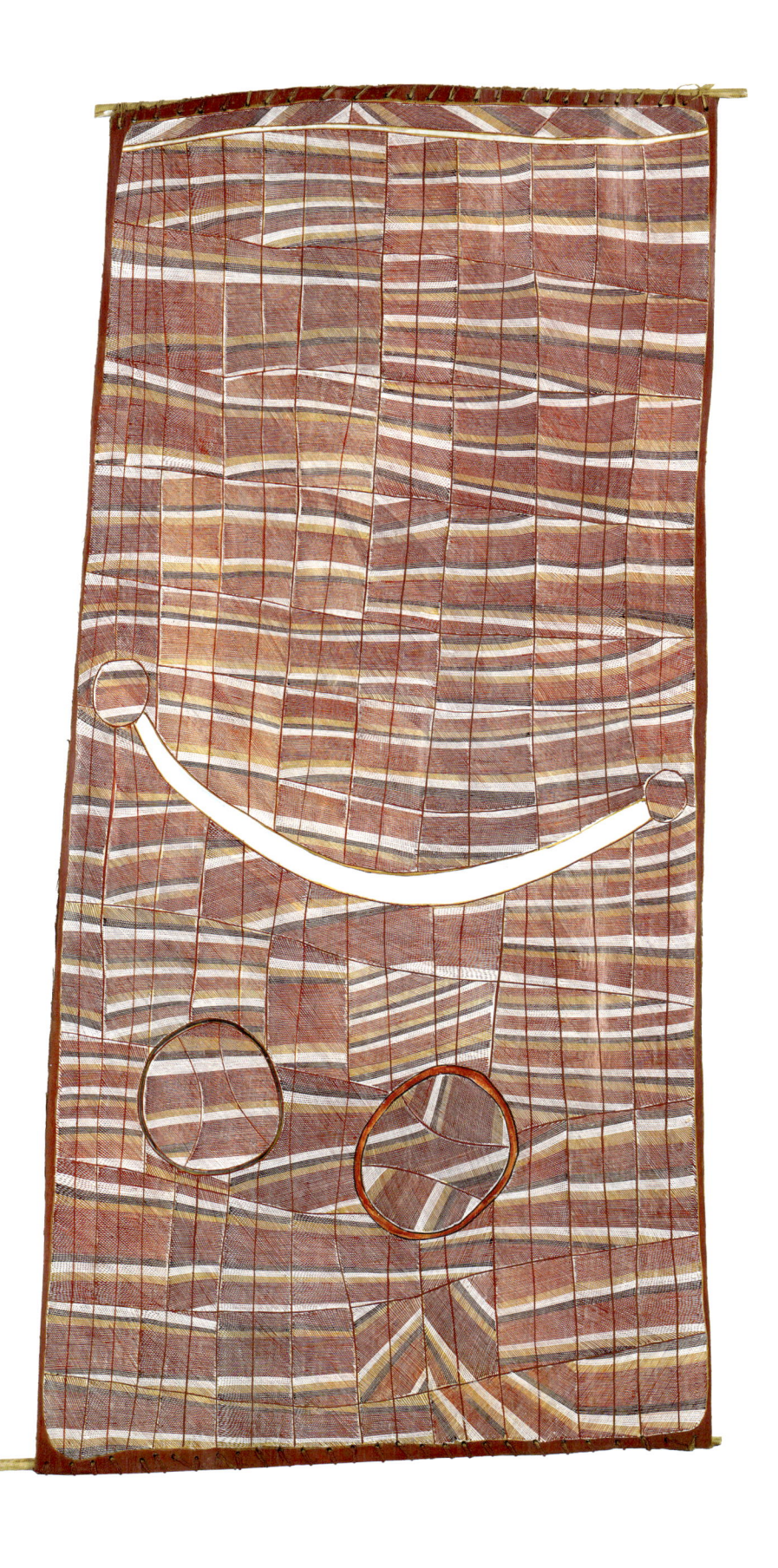

**Mardayin design
at Dilebang**
2003
212.5 × 108.5 cm

Dirdbim, moon
2003
72.0 x 41.0 cm

Billabong at Milmilngkan
2004
219.0 x 60.0 cm

«rarrk» 149

Mardayin
2004
106.5 x 36.5 cm

**Yawkyawk, young girl –
water spirit**
2005
154.0 x 72.0 cm

**Mardayin design
at Milmilngkan**
2004
Etching, 76.0 x 56.5 cm

Mardayin at Mukkamukka
2004
Etching, 37.5 x 29.9 cm

Komrdawh, turtle
2004
Etching, 50.0 x 33.0 cm

Mardayin at Dilebang
2004
Etching, 50.0 x 33.0 cm

Mardayin design
2004
Etching, 50.0 x 32.5 cm

Grids, dots and territory

Philippe Peltier

No work reveals itself on first sight. It takes time to decipher anything. And Mawurndjul's work is no exception. Looking at his paintings, you easily recognize objects (bags) or animal shapes (buffalo, snakes, fish), constructed from a dense network of lines. But underlying these shapes, your eye rapidly discovers other, often barely perceptible figures. Nevertheless, let us admit that your eye has explored the entire surface, identified all the elements; something still resists. What is it? You can't answer this question right away. Why that snake with buffalo horns? Why those squares and circles that seem to float on the surface of the painting? Who are those tall, thin figures, those others that look as if they are caught in a net? What does it all mean? What are we being told? What is this strange world that seems at the same time both familiar and alien?

A bit disconcerted by so many questions, and in order to decipher the works, you have one last resort: to call on your memory. You need to find elements of comparison, more familiar references. Yet, although this comparison, a classic method in art history, allows a heuristic approach, the terms still need to be carefully determined. You can start with details or signs, with wholes or parts. No problem with that. Alternatively, the method holds some dangers when one is obliged to draw parallels between works from one's own culture and those completely alien to it. The situation can be anachronistic and paradoxical, to say the least, if one deems that the two worlds, in this case Arnhem Land and the West, are irreducible one to the other. In the present case the paradox is reduced by a *coup de force*: the work of Mawurndjul is being exhibited in Basel, in a museum devoted to a major twentieth-century artist. The result is a shift both in the museum's boundaries (a familiar refrain since Marcel Duchamp's *Urinoir*), and in the chronological order (or what it is assumed to be: after all, aren't Aboriginal people perceived to be the oldest society in the world?). This is only an appearance, though, if one accepts the idea that Aboriginal works are first of all ambassadors, a means whereby Aborigines may lay claim to their own culture and explain it to the Western world. Once this is admitted, the question of comparison presents itself from an entirely new angle: each society has set in place a repertory of symbols that it uses to translate and organise its world view. While one cannot be reduced to the other, their comparison can enable us to identify the distances between them and to understand how each society effects its metaphorical transfers so as to give its world meaning.

Grids and Mardayin

Let us begin with a series of very strange forms. Its generic title is Mardayin.

What do we see? A first network of lines, most often drawn in ochre, broken by black or white dots. This network forms an orthogonal grid that deviates in certain places, or takes off at a tangent. Sometimes the painter has interrupted his boxes to introduce concentric circles, or more seldom, squares or triangles. These circles, squares or triangles are painted in solid colours. They float on the surface of the painting, still shapes in a world in perpetual motion. Sometimes, in a very few works, the lines of this grid curve round to form a figure, the head and body of a fish or a snake, for instance.

Each box formed by this first grid is filled in with a second network, infinitely more complex to describe. The people of Arnhem Land call these *rarrk*. Rarrk are obtained by overlaying crosshatchings of thin lines of yellow or red ochre and black and white. The tone of each layer varies according to the order in which the colours were applied: lighter if the final layer is made of white lines, darker if ochre is used. The result is a shimmering effect, very like a moiré. At first sight, these layers seem to pass under the grid. But they only seem to. If you take a closer look, you will see that the lines stop at the edge of the square made by the orthogonal grid, sometimes leaving a small strip in which the white undercoat appears. The lines of the rarrk change direction from one rectangle to the next. They undulate, stop, sheer off. They depict an unstable, moving world, where the bewildered eye wanders before discerning the shapes submerged beneath the surface, as though the painter intended once again to literally bury the figures in a system of abstract signs.

The grid and the coloured-in network are framed by a coloured rule. The empty space between the rule and the edge of the work is painted in red ochre. This margin lets the material on which the work is painted show through: it is a slab of bark. Although it has been smoothed, flattened, neatly cut, the bark retains its texture: a slight rugosity that shows through the pictural layer to create part of the effect.

Grids, dots, lines, hidden figures: these words running through our description refer us to that moment where Western artists reduce painting to its simplest constituents, where – but need we go back over the well-rehearsed history of cubist painting? – through a long labour of refining, they sacrificed everything that bespoke the figure to retain only the grid. Through this reduction to structure, the De Stijl group (Oud, Mondrian, van Doesburg and Vantongerloo, to name only the best-known figures) radically affirm the canvas surface and thereby guarantee the autonomy of art. Canvases no longer tell a story – farewell Mordecai, Melchisedech, saints, virgins or angels – they no longer map space. The work evolves in infinite variations, and painting seems to come down to a matter of pure rhythm. For the hurried viewer, the arrangement of these geometrical figures refuses to say anything other than what it is: a surface devoid of mimetic elements, an expanse that blocks out any discourse, that operates by decree.[1]

A closer look will nevertheless note that these canvases are paradoxical. Whereas modern art breaks entirely with representation, and more specifically with religious themes, these works present infinite variations on the figure of the circle, the square, but above all, the cross. The spiritual, religious dimension emerges there where it was least expected. This is a paradox. To resolve it, one has only to read the texts written by the artist-theoreticians of neoplasticism or the founders of the abstract movement. Here the artists do not talk about forms or shapes, but about the structure of things. They want to paint the organic laws that reigned at the beginning of the world. Their painting is a project, and the figures they use, the emblems of the time to come: "However, when the universal prevails, the universal will impregnate life such that art, which is so unreal compared to life, will fade away, and a *new life* will replace it, which effectively realises the universal."[2]

Does the same go for Mardayin?

Let's first see what a Mardayin is. Before evoking the painted patterns, the term designates a ceremony specific to a small group in East Arnhem Land, the Kuninjku people. This ceremony is held to ensure the transmission of sacred objects from one generation to the next. It is largely secret. Non-initiates are not allowed to watch. The Mardayin designs are painted on the young initiates during their seclusion. They show these off when they come out of their enclosure. The Mardayin paintings are therefore not secret. Mawurndjul took part in these ceremonies. His position as an elder and a knowledgeable man in his community enabled him to fulfil this weighty task: "Sometimes (rarely) the Mardayin ceremony is performed at Kakodbebuldi (a site in John's country), and when this happens I paint the Mardayin rarrk on people."[3] These designs painted on the young men are identical in every way to those on the mythic ancestors, who made everything and are the forces that inhabit or animate the world. To paint rarrk on the initiate is to give new life to the ancestor; the ultimate aim of the Mardayin ceremony is to bind the initiate to the sacred sites that are the spiritual centre of clan lands. To this effect, the execution of the grid follows precise codes. Each clan has its own signs, and the painter must accurately reproduce those that the ancestors bore at the beginning of the world and which they then bequeathed to humankind. But Mardayin are not simply reflections of the ancestors, they are their metaphorical figures. Proof of this are the interpretations given the different designs: the dots in the grid, which are the bones, and the rarrk, the 'fat' of the ancestors.[4] In one of his interviews, Mawurndjul further explains: "The blocks of the rarrk are the 'body' of the Mardayin ceremony."[5]

Abstract paintings and Mardayin are indeed eschatologies, then, if one understands this term to mean a revelation. Both kinds of painting share the same objective: to reveal the essence of things – and not the world itself. But whereas abstract painting is a utopia, which, in line with Marx's theses, heralds a new world, a world whose terms we imagine without yet being able to distinguish the modes, the second is a skin screen, the act of painting being meant to reproduce the ancestral figures on the body.

1 On the figure of the grid and the problem of its interpretation, see 'Grids', in Krauss, R., *The originality of the avant-garde and other modernist myths*, The MIT Press, Cambridge MA, 1985, pp. 9–22.
2 'De nieeuwe beelding in de schilderkunst', IV, *De Stijl*, 1, 5 March, 1918, p. 51.
3 From an interview with John Mawurndjul, in Ducreux A.-C., Kohen, A. and Salmon, F. (eds.), *Au centre de la Terre d'Arnhem, entre mythes et realité*, (exhibition catalogue), Musée de l'Hôtel Dieu, Mantes-la-Jolie, 2001, p. 54; French translation by Apolline Kohen, English transcription by Murray Garde.
4 See Taylor, L., *Seeing the inside, bark painting in western Arnhem Land*, Clarendon Press, Oxford, 1996, p. 121.
5 Ducreux, A.-C., Kohen, A. and Salmon, F., *op. cit.* p. 56; English transcription, p. 55.

Skin and screen

The act of painting once again takes on its full importance in this 'skin screen'. This has nothing to do with Western-style make-up. The body paint is not a cosmetic, not a coating to hide imperfections; it is a substance that impregnates the skin and overlays the real body with a metaphysical body. The painting is a screen whose realisation indicates the change of social status. This screen bears more than the signs that bind generations through timeless motifs. Here substance and image are inseparable. It is one skin over another, a screen on which a body is projected onto a body.

The metaphor of the painting as a surface onto which an imaginary scene is projected that continues beyond the edge of the canvas (or panel) is inextricably bound up with the history of Western painting. It was not until the German romantic painters, however, that the theoretically present screen-window came into its own as a subject. Whether this screen-window gives onto an empty sky or sometimes a ship's masts is not by chance. Everything is said about the world, but in a suppressed form, without thickness. Sometimes a girl leans on the windowsill. Her back is turned. You look at her looking, but you never see what she sees. An impossible vision that invites meditation. Your gaze, imprisoned in the artist's studio, comes back to the window frame, a grid that at once filters, structures and, by the cross it traces, symbolises the world order. A century later, grid and window become one: the screen-window, which confirms the distance between the studio and the world, becomes the figure of the world.

However, the parallel between the image of the window in Western painting and Mardayin holds only if one turns the theory around. While, among the Kuninjku, the skin screen founds the identity of the bearer (the colour is the ancestral substance, and the blobs of pigment extracted from important sites are regarded as transformed substances from the ancestors' bodies), and while the rarrk materialises the ancestor's power by standing for his internal organs, Western painting, on the other hand, absorbs the world, stage by stage, by progressively diminishing the distances, eradicating depth the better to underscore the surface. Or rather, it does not actually absorb the world, but rather conquers it by eliminating all representation from the canvas.

Territory

The art historian Meyer Shapiro was one of the first to point out that, often in neoplastic paintings, the grid stops a few centimetres from the edge. This curious device gives the impression that the grid lines might run on forever, or that the painting is a fragment of a bigger whole.[6] The work is no longer the description of a place, no longer confined to a territory; it absorbs the wall the better to deny its existence. This negation of the canvas field was one of the theoretical foundations of neoplasticism: it was supposed to enable the work to break out of the narrow confines of the image and to fuse with life.

Alternatively, all of Mawurndjul's paintings are confined within a double border: a line encloses the central design and separates it from a red ochre margin. In some works, this margin follows the edge of the objects depicted: baskets, fish or spirits. It accentuates their shape and acts as a background. In the Mardayin series, it is reduced to a fine edging that encases the subject, designates it as a site, a point in the particular territory. This organisation of the image field is identical to that of classical painting, where the frame signals a world in itself. The titles of the Mardayin series confirm that each work is dedicated to a specific point of the territory: Mardayin at Kakodbebuldi, at Milmilngkan, at Mumeka, at Mukkamukka … It is probably on this question of place that there is the greatest separation between neoplasticist paintings and Mardayin. Whereas the Western grid has a rhythm, seeks a balance between the surfaces and their extensions into the infinite, beyond the frame, each Mardayin takes as its subject a specific site, a point of the territory animated by the ancestors.

These sites are at the heart of the Mardayin ceremony, whose aim is to bind the initiate heir to the ancestral creator of this site. As everywhere in Australia, the identity of each Kuninjku is rooted in his territory.

6 See Shapiro, M., 'On some problems in the semiotics of visual art, field and vehicle in images-signes', *Semiotica*, 1 (3), 1969, pp. 223–242.

Mawurndjul's Mardayin series deals with specific sites: waterholes. As the painter explains: "Mardayin phenomena are located in water, underneath bodies of water. Water is on the top and the Mardayin is underneath … It is always in the water."[7] This sheds some light on the formal complexity of these paintings. They are supposed to transcribe the effects of one of the most complex worlds to paint. An almost impossible task given that the painter has to render at the same time reflections and transparence, surface and depth. The rarrk is a particularly effective way to render this complex universe. The overlay of fine coloured lines gives this iridescence, this shimmering impression typical of the effects of water, with the infinite variations of colour that break when the mirror is ruffled. By meticulously applying the rarrk in the first grid, the painter accentuates the impression of a world in reverse. With their uneven edges, their gentle shifts of angle from one block to the next, the rarrk lines give rise to ghostly figures that seem to lie far below the surface. The logical order is troubled. The succession of layers, the order in which the patterns are applied is the reverse of the natural world order. It is literally turned upside down.

The same inversion process is used for the circles that dot the grid and break up its geometry. These are the signs for water plants. Because of their natural ability to glow in the night and their tendency to cut or attack the skin, these plants embody, according to the painter, Mardayin power: "*Danggark* is in the middle of the water. It has roots. You know the fresh-water mangrove which makes our skin itchy if we touch it? Well, it is like that. It grows in the open. *Barrangkarl* is under the water. During the night it glows [...]. That is the body of the *barrangkarl* plant, the *danggarrk* Mardayin property of the *barrangkarl* plant. You know in the water they appear in a straight line, in creeks or running water like at Mukkamukka. It's like a grass or native sugar cane, that sharp-edged grass that cuts us when we pull it up. *Danggark* is the plant that has Mardayin power underneath it."[8]

Nevertheless, there is another possible interpretation of Mardayin. The grids and the rarrk can be read as an account of the ancestors' actions on the earth, for instance a pile of rocks or signs of an animal metamorphosis; the circular elements as the waterholes through which the ancestors emerged from the earth's crust; the dotted lines, the tunnels they used to go from one site to another.[9] Mardayin could thus be seen as history paintings that tell the birth of the landscape.

Whatever reading one chooses, the series of Mardayin is indisputably a topographical transcription of a world in motion, far from the imperturbable rigidity of the neoplasticist canvases. Mardayin are meditations on the beginning of the world and on the forces that innervate the landscape. Compared to the bark paintings of the previous generation, Mawurndjul's works are 'modern'. While the subject is the same – ancestral creative power – his paintings break with the tradition of earlier generations: "The old ways remain there in the past, but we are doing new things now. We have changed the law; the old-fashioned way of painting has finished, and we are new people doing new kinds of painting together for non-Aboriginal people as well."[10] Each painting is an interpretation of mythological happenings, the keys to which are not always provided. However that may be, the present series of paintings attests to a dynamic thinking capable of conceiving a universe in constant change. Mawurndjul repeats time and again that his "head is full up with ideas", in other words, full of other readings. As for the neoplasticist canvases, one cannot help but recognize that, while they were hymns to modernity, this modernity remains incomplete, never fixed for all time.

Billabong at Milmilngkan, 2004

---

7 Ducreux A.-C., Kohen, A. and Salmon, F., *op. cit.*, p. 56.
8 Ducreux A.-C., Kohen, A. and Salmon, F., *op. cit.*, pp. 58–59.
9 This reading was suggested by Luke Taylor, *op. cit.*, esp. chap. 10.
10 Ducreux A.-C., Kohen, A. and Salmon, F., *op. cit.*, p. 59.

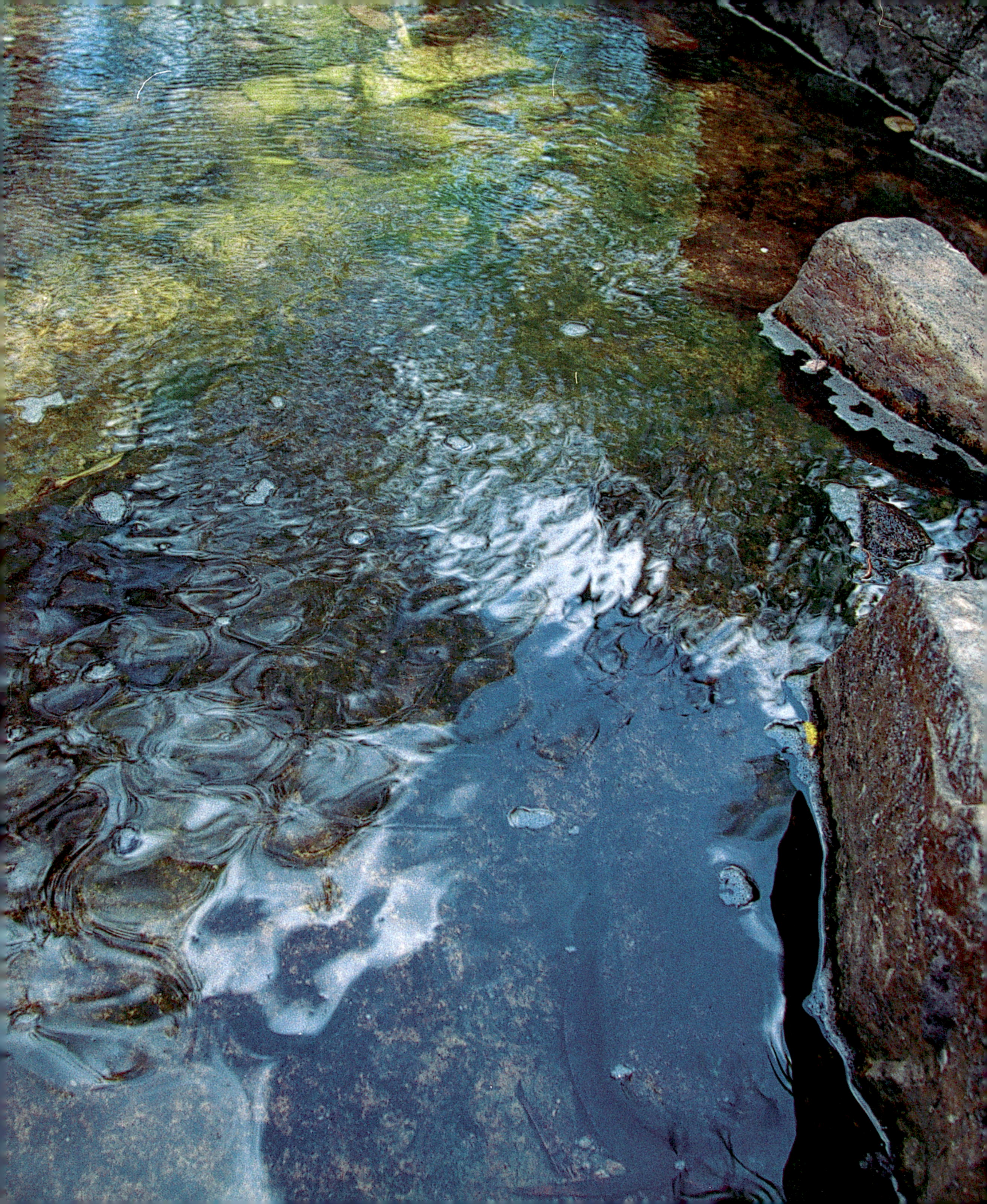

Early rock painting of Ngalyod, the
rainbow serpent, John Mawurndjul
at Dilebang, 2004

160 « rarrk » Paul Taçon

Marks on and of land: the relationship of rock and bark painting to peoples, places and the ancestral past

Paul S.C. Taçon

John Mawurndjul is an incredibly accomplished individual artist with his own unique style of representation. However, his work is also part of a much larger body of bark painting with a lengthy if not ancient history. As well, his work is grounded in landscapes, expressing webs of relationship between peoples, places, other creatures and the past. His marks on bark reflect individual identity and experience, group identity and history as well as innovation within tradition. Elements of sacredness run through all of his work but also there is emotion, spirit and story. His paintings speak of other worlds but these are places grounded in familiar landscapes.

Webs of relationships and the importance of landscapes are two key themes that dominate much of the bark painting tradition experienced by Europeans since interest in this form of north Australian Aboriginal art was sparked by Paul Foelsche in the 1870s[1]. These themes are not unique to Mawurndjul's work and also can be seen in much earlier art, such as the incredibly rich Arnhem Land rock painting tradition, spanning tens of thousands of years. In many of these examples it appears almost as if the land itself inspired, guided and perhaps compelled people to interpret and paint experience of and within it.

When one visits northern Australia, and particularly the region defined by Greater Arnhem Land and the Kimberley, one is immediately struck by the power of the land. Everywhere one looks, landscapes, many of them rocky, illustrate eras of history, times of change and the adaptation of an amazing array of creatures. Evidence of creation and creativity is all around — whether ascribed to Ancestral Beings or forces of nature one cannot escape its all-consuming power. The landscapes of northern Australia are full of colour, at times bright with life in all its glory. They also can become dark and dangerous places as the seasonal cycle of climate bakes, dries and breaks down the land before overwhelming it with thunder, lightning, wind and life-giving rain. Landscapes change over centuries, sometimes in a sudden and dramatic fashion. But they also change each year in an annual pageant of decay and renewal.

Earliest art

From the moment humans arrived in northern Australia, at least 45,000–60,000 years ago, they must have been accutely aware of these changes. Indeed, survival depended on such awareness. As they moved across the then much larger Australian continent of 'Sahul' they would have defined a new human world for the first time. They were the First People, today immortalised as the earliest ancestral beings in song,

Billabong at Nourlangie Rock, Kakadu National Park, October 1999

Rock shelter at Ngalirrkewern, September 2004

Wet season in Arnhem Land

1 Taçon, P.S.C. and Davies, S., 'Transitional traditions: 'Port Essington' bark-paintings and the European discovery of Aboriginal aesthetics', *Australian Aboriginal Studies*, 2, 2004.

ceremony and visual art. Many others arrived or were born since that long-ago time and the memories of some of their actions have also been personified or deified through all manner of art. Importantly, the First People brought knowledge of ochre with them and at Australia's oldest excavated sites, including many in Greater Arnhem Land, ochre can be found down to the lowest levels.[2]

What ochre was used for 40,000–60,000 years ago is open to debate. In Australia's south, at Lake Mungo, skeletal remains dated to this period have been found adorned with ochre.[3] In recent times ochre featured prominently in both primary and secondary burial ceremonies right across the country and continues to be one of the most important substances used in Arnhem Land for these purposes today. Of course, ochre has always been significant as a symbolic substance for the living. Its use for body art was noted across Australia wherever the first Europeans sailed and/or set foot, with many early accounts from the 1700s.[4] Ochre has been used in historic times to decorate or imbue power to objects across Arnhem Land and, presumably, was similarly used far into the past. It was especially important for some sacred objects and ceremonies, with the most potent, brightest and finest ochre used. Such was the significance of ochre that vast mining, trading, travel and exchange routes were established across the continent.[5]

And everywhere people went ochre-based designs on rock soon followed. It is estimated there are at least 100,000 separate rock art sites in Australia, consisting of paintings, engravings, stencils, prints and, from Arnhem Land to the Kimberley, figures made of beeswax pressed onto shelter walls and ceilings. In Greater Arnhem Land, including Kakadu National Park, most of the rock art is pigment-based, with engravings exceedingly rare. Although a wide range of individuals and research teams have studied Arnhem Land rock art, each year new sites are found. It is possible there are twenty thousand or more rock art sites across Arnhem Land, with thousands more nearby. Indeed, Greater Arnhem Land is one of the most abundant rock art regions of the world. It also has one of the longest time spans as well as a rich ethnography.

For contemporary Aboriginal people of Arnhem Land rock art is all about history – the history of their people, particular places, ancestral beings and other creatures. It also illustrates relationships between people and places, with hand stencils the most individual form of this. Rock art was used to teach people about hunting, sharing, ceremony and many other things. Some of it was commemorative, illustrating important events such as battles over land or women, the arrival of Macassans and Europeans, changes to the environment and the passing of individuals. There is no one meaning or explanation to the rock art we find across Arnhem Land other than that it is an expression of the human spirit, human experience, important knowledge and the special nature of some places. However, the very act of marking landscapes socialised them in ways that defined subsequent human use.[6]

2 See e.g. Jones, R. (ed.), *Archaeological research in Kakadu National Park*, Australian National Parks and Wildlife Service Special Publication 13, Canberra, 1985.
3 Thorne, A.G., 'Mungo and Kow Swamp morphological variation in Pleistocene Australians', *Mankind* 8 (2), 1971, pp. 85–89; Thorne, A., Grün, R., Mortimer, G., Spooner, N., Simpson, J., McCulloch, Taylor, M. L. and Curnoe, D., 'Australia's oldest human remains: age of the Lake Mungo 3 skeleton', *Journal of Human Evolution* 36 (6), 1999, pp. 591–612.
4 For e.g. Marten van Delft in 1705, see Robert, W.C.H., *The Dutch explorations, 1605–1756, of the North and Northwest Coast of Australia*, Philo Press, Amsterdam, 1979; for Gerrit de Haan of Batavia in 1756, see McKnight, C.C., *The farthest coast*, Melbourne University Press, Melbourne, 1969.
5 For a review of the use of ochre Australia-wide see Taçon, P.S.C., 'Ochre, clay, stone and art: the symbolic importance of minerals as life-force among Aboriginal peoples of northern and central Australia', in Boivin, N. and Owoc, M. A. (eds.), *Soil, stones and symbols: cultural perceptions of the mineral world*, UCL Press, London, 2004.
6 Taçon, P.S.C., 'Socialising landscapes: the long term implications of signs, symbols and marks on the land', *Archaeology in Oceania* 29 (3), 1994, pp. 117–29.

Red ochre

Beeswax figures on rock

Special places

Very significant places were often covered with several layers of painting. There are some sites with over a hundred metres of wall coated with vibrant, animated depictions. The earliest surviving paintings consist mainly of large animals, macropods (kangaroos, wallabies and wallaroos) and other creatures hunted for food and artefactual material. These were made in a very 'naturalistic' or realistic manner although they often appear frozen onto shelter walls. They illustrate significant creatures of the land important to survival. The oldest of these images may be as much as 15,000 years of age, possibly older. This phase was followed by a much more lively, action-packed style of art, labelled the 'dynamic figure' style by famed Arnhem Land rock art scholar George Chaloupka.[7] Dynamic figures of men, and some women, race across shelter walls and ceilings. They encapsulate movement, reaching an almost cartoon-like character at some sites. They fight, hunt, have intercourse, sit around what look to us like symbols of camp fires, carry or throw boomerangs, spears, hafted stone axes, and generally look as if engaged in frenzied activity. Some appear to be chased or menaced by composite creatures, animal-headed human-like figures that are the oldest surviving mythological beings from this part of the world (see Taçon and Chippindale 2001b for a detailed analysis and the world-wide significance and incidence of similar illustrations of the supernatural).[8] Dynamic figures are probably about 9000–12,000 years of age[9] although they may be older.[10]

Contemporary Aboriginal people across Arnhem Land refer to the people who made dynamic figures as *mimih*. For them, dynamic figure paintings are mimih paintings, showing a world that existed when the ancestors of contemporary Aboriginal people first came into being. That world has long since changed, with wild floods and dramatic climate replacing an ancient time of dryness and drought. However, the mimih world is said to still exist inside rock, behind shelter walls. The mimih survive as tall, thin spirits that can easily slip through cracks in the rock. They are generally harmless but can be mischievous. They also become enraged if contemporary hunters kill their pet animals, which resemble ordinary Arnhem Land creatures. But it was the mimih that first taught Aboriginal Ancestors which animals were best to hunt, how to butcher them and the ways they should be cooked. The mimih also taught Aboriginal ancestors some songs and, significantly, the importance of painting in rock shelters.

The period that followed 'dynamic figure' art was one of great change. The climate warmed and sea levels rose. Australia was cut off from New Guinea, land was lost to rising waters and modern coastlines were established. People were forced inland, cultural encounters took place and fertile landscapes were born. Much of this is encapsulated in the form of the rainbow serpent, one of the most powerful composite beings of all. In many ways the rainbow serpent is a symbol of change as all recorded stories, songs and ceremonies associated with it dramatically reinforce transformation of one kind or another.[11]

Mimih figure with Dilly bag

Fighting mimih. Rock painting, Ubirr, Kakadu National Park

Every year the low lying plains are flooded: mud remains in the forest

7 See Chaloupka, G., 'From palaeoart to casual paintings: the chronological sequence of Arnhem Land plateau rock art', Northern Territory Museum of Arts and Sciences Monograph Series 1, Darwin, 1984; Chaloupka, G., *Journey in Time*, Reed, Chatswood, 1993.

8 For a detailed analysis and the world-wide significance and incidence of similar illustrations of the supernatural see Taçon, P.S.C. and Chippindale, C., 'Transformation and depictions of the First People: animal-headed beings of Arnhem Land, N.T., Australia', in Helskog, K. (ed.), *Theoretical perspectives in rock art research*, Novus Forlag, Oslo, 2001b, pp. 175–210.

9 Chippindale, C. and Taçon, P.S.C., 'The many ways of dating Arnhem Land rock-art, North Australia', in Chippindale, C. and Taçon, P. (eds.), *The archaeology of rock art*, Cambridge University Press, Cambridge, 1998, pp. 90–111; Lewis, D., *The rock paintings of Arnhem Land: social, ecological, and material culture change in the post-glacial period*, BAR International Series 415, Oxford, 1988; Tacon, P.S.C. and Brockwell, S., 'Arnhem Land prehistory in landscape, stone and paint', *Antiquity* 69 (259), 1995, pp. 676–95.

10 See Chaloupka, G., 1993, *op. cit.*

11 See Taçon, P.S.C., Wilson, M. and Chippindale, C., 'Birth of the rainbow serpent in Arnhem Land rock art and oral history', *Archaeology in Oceania* 31 (3), 1996, pp. 103–24; Taylor, L., 'The rainbow serpent as visual metaphor in western Arnhem Land', *Oceania* 60, 1990, pp. 329–344.

The earliest depictions of rainbow serpents are argued to be 4000–6000 years old. They were made in what is known as the 'yam figure' style, because they are associated with depictions of yams and yam-human-like figures. The oldest resemble pipefish but also contain body parts of other creatures.[12] In more recent times they have become both larger and more varied, with elements of dozens of totemic creatures incorporated into their forms. Often they have macropod or crocodile-like heads. Some bark painting depictions of rainbow serpents and recent works on paper even include introduced water buffalo parts or have 'ceremony men' emerging from their bodies. Many recent or contemporary Arnhem Land artists paint pictures of Ngalyod, a powerful male rainbow serpent, with Mawurndjul's among the more elaborate and intricate in terms of hatch and crosshatch infill. But some of the earliest surviving rainbow serpents in rock shelters also have crosshatch infill, highlighting that recent works such as Mawurndjul's have grown out of a tradition thousands of years old.

During the period that rainbow serpents and yam figures were painted in Arnhem Land rock shelters, other forms of human-like and animal-like figures were made. Human figures became much simpler in form than the earlier dynamics but some are arranged in elaborate scenes of hunting or fighting. At two locations the earliest surviving battle scenes from anywhere in the world can be found. In each case two large groups of men are shown opposing each other, with weapons raised, spears flying through the air and front-line figures wounded or dying.[13] The first so-called 'x-ray' paintings were also made at this time and the earliest beeswax figures also date to about 4000 years ago.

Soon after there appears to have been a much more extensive use of colour, with bi-chrome and polychrome images becoming commonplace. Very detailed and colourful x-ray paintings developed with lots of internal detail. Fish became the most common subject, so much so that thousands of images of up to a dozen species were portrayed. Some rock art sites almost exclusively show fish, highlighting both their economic and spiritual significance in recent times.[14] A vast array of subject matter was depicted with x-ray features, from animal to human, from ancestral beings to introduced objects such as ships and guns. But x-ray art was not a 'style' in the strict sense. Instead, it was part of a much wider Arnhem Land style that includes silhouette/solid figures, outline figures, stick figures, stencils and so forth.[15] Within this style regional variation is apparent.[16] Historic and contemporary bark painting can be described similarly, with the same range of form and technique incorporated into regional and individual styles.

12 See Taçon, P.S.C., Wilson, M. and Chippindale C., 1996, op. cit.
13 Taçon, P.S.C. and Chippindale, C., 'Australia's ancient warriors: changing depictions of fighting in the rock art of Arnhem Land, N.T.', Cambridge Archaeological Journal 4 (2), 1994, pp. 211–48.
14 Taçon, P.S.C., 'Identifying fish species in the recent rock paintings of western Arnhem Land', Rock Art Research 5 (1), 1988, pp. 3-15; Taçon, P.S.C., 'Art and the essence of being: symbolic and economic aspects of fish among the peoples of western Arnhem Land, Australia', in Morphy, H. (ed.), Animals into art, Unwin Hyman, London, 1989, pp. 236–50.
15 Taçon, P.S.C., 'Somewhere over the rainbow: an ethnographic and archaeological analysis of recent rock paintings of western Arnhem Land, Australia', in McDonald, J. and Haskovec, I.P. (eds.), State of the art: regional rock art studies in Australia and Melanesia, Occasional AURA Publication No. 6, Archaeological Publications, Melbourne, 1992, pp. 202–15.
16 Taçon, P.S.C., 'Regionalism in the recent rock art of western Arnhem Land, Northern Territory', Archaeology in Oceania 28 (3), 1993, pp. 112–20.

Ngalyod, the rainbow serpent, Dilebang, September 2004

Picture of a yam tuber in shape of emu

A fish depicted in x-ray style

Macassan proa (sailing ship)

Bark paintings

We do not know when the first bark paintings were made as, exposed to the elements, they do not last long. It is probable, however, that Aboriginal people used temporary bark huts for shelter beginning thousands of years ago. It also is possible that they painted the walls of these huts in the same way they painted the walls of rock shelters. When the first European explorers travelled through parts of Greater Arnhem Land they found many instances of abandoned, decaying bark shelters with painted imagery on internal surfaces.[17] Some of these were collected for display in recently established museums in Australia's south and across the world in special 'International Exhibitions'. In the early 1900s Baldwin Spencer[18] obtained a large collection of bark paintings, trading and commissioning as well as collecting. The seeds of an emerging tourist art activity took hold but bark and rock painting continued to be made for more traditional reasons, including for use in storytelling and ceremony. The last major Arnhem Land rock painter, Najombolmi, passed away in the 1960s but sporadic instances of rock painting have taken place since and Najombolmi's influence has been incredibly widespread.[19] Bark painting, and since the early 1990s similar art on paper, has developed into a major tourist industry with great economic importance. However, spirituality and relatedness to particular Arnhem Land places and histories continues to dominate subject matter. This can be seen among the works of many artists but John Mawurndjul's paintings are particularly poignant in this regard.

Ngalyod and other rainbow serpents, *yawkyawk* (female) spirits, the rainbow serpent's antilopine kangaroo, mimih, lightning spirits such as *namarrkon*, sacred Mardayin designs, special landscape places, totemic animals and other ancestral beings dominate his work. All have counterparts in earlier rock paintings, with some such as animal-headed beings having at least ten thousand years of history. But these are not faithful copies. They have been invigorated through hatched and crosshatched infill, making them especially powerful and special both visually and spiritually.[20] They radiate with power, showing a long tradition is as alive as ever. Full of energy, they speak of rich lives and deep histories, and of great people of the land. The stories they tell have been passed down through countless generations but the imagery is bold and brilliant, its innovations reflecting adaptation and continuity through periods of great change. Through artists such as John Mawurndjul the spirit of ancient rock painters and storytellers lives on but Mawurndjul's own spirit and spirituality also shines strongly. It is art like his that inspires younger generations, hopefully insuring the great Arnhem Land legacies live on forever.

17 Campbell, J., 'Geographic memoir of Melville Island and Port Essington on the Cobourg Peninsula, northern Australia, with some observations on the settlements which have been established on the north coast of New Holland', p. 157, *Journal of the Royal Geographic Society of London* 4, 1834, pp. 129–81; Carrington, F., 'The rivers of the Northern Territory', p. 73, *Proceedings of the Royal Geographic Society of Australia (South Australia Branch)* 2, 1890, pp. 56–76; Wilkins, G.H., *Undiscovered Australia*, G.P. Putnam's Sons, London, 1929, p. 185 and plate opposite 177.

18 Spencer, W.B., *The native tribes of the Northern Territory of Australia*, MacMillan, London, 1914.

19 Tacon, P.S.C. and Chippindale, C., 'Najombolmi's people: from rock painting to national icon', in Anderson, A., Lilley, I. and O'Connor, S. (eds.), *Histories of old ages: essays in honour of Rhys Jones*, Pandanus Books, Australian National University, Canberra, 2001a, pp. 301–10.

20 Morphy, H., *Ancestral connections: art and an Aboriginal system of knowledge*, The University of Chicago Press, Chicago, 1991; Taylor, L., *Seeing the inside: bark painting in western Arnhem Land*, Oxford University Press, Oxford, 1996.

Rock painting by Nayolmbolmi, Djimongurr and Djorlom, 1963–64, Anbangbang rock shelter, Nourlangie Rock, Kakadu National Park, October 1999

Detail from illustration on the left

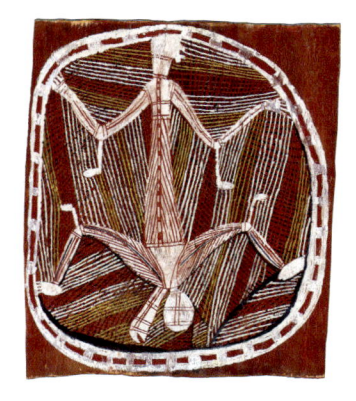

Jimmy Midjawmidjaw
Namarrkon, 1960
70.0 x 60.0 cm
(see also page 192)

John Mawurndjul
Namarden, female lightning spirit, 1982
64.0 x 37.0 cm
(see also page 92)

Paul Taçon « rarrk »

Over-hanging rock at Ngalirrkewern,
September 2004

Ngalirrkewern, September 2004
Detail from illustration on the left

Paul Taçon   «rarrk»   167

Crocodile, with rainbow serpent
underneath, at Ngalirrkewern,
September 2004

Ngalirrkewern, September 2004
Detail from illustration on the left

On the following double pages:

Stencils of hand and axes, rock painting at Dilebang, September 2004

Rock shelter, hollows in rock for grinding in the foreground, Ngalirrkewern, September 2004

Overlaid rock paintings, the two fish on the left (in x-ray style) were painted after 1928 (Photo by H. Basedow, information A. Kohen), Kunumidjara, September 2004

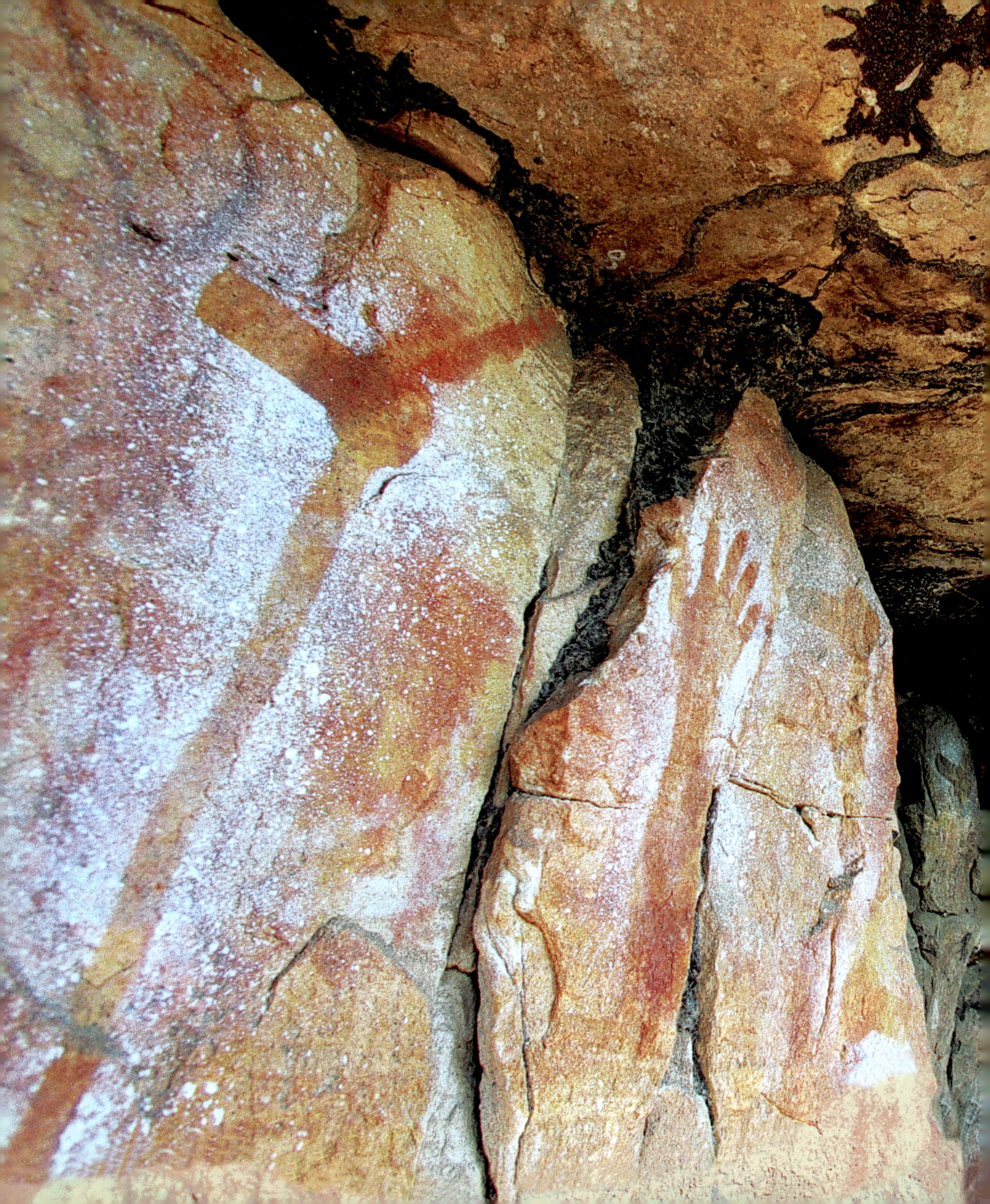

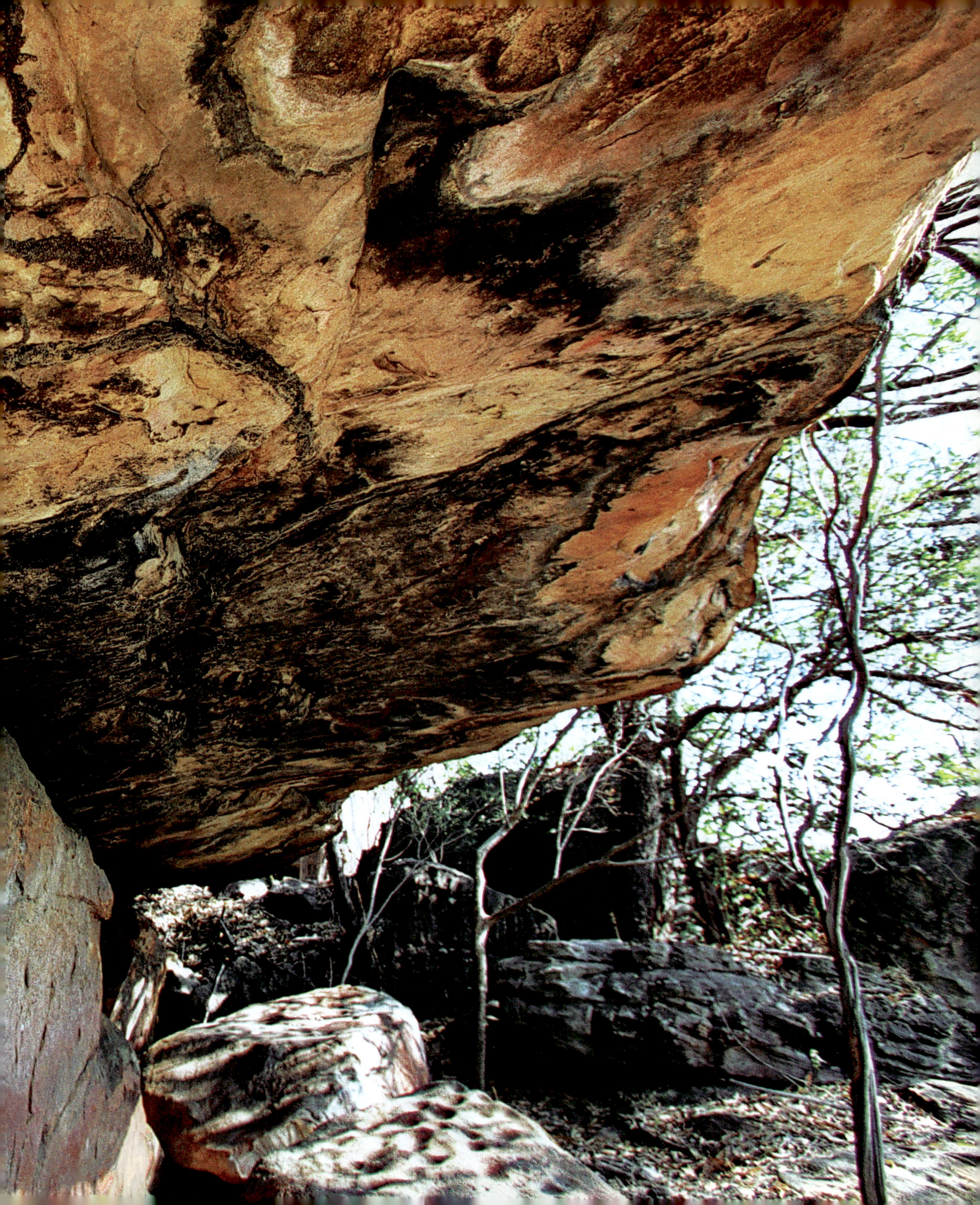

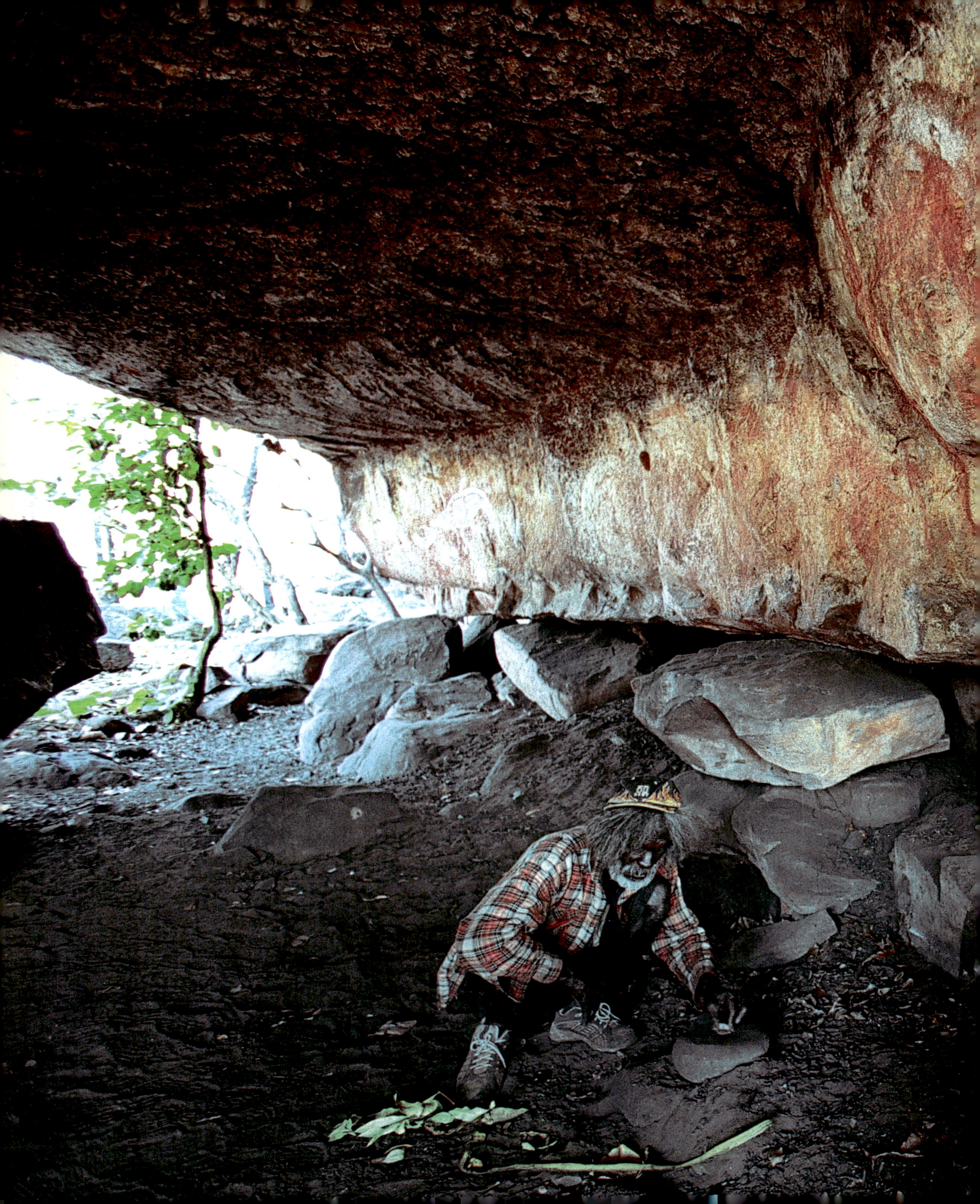

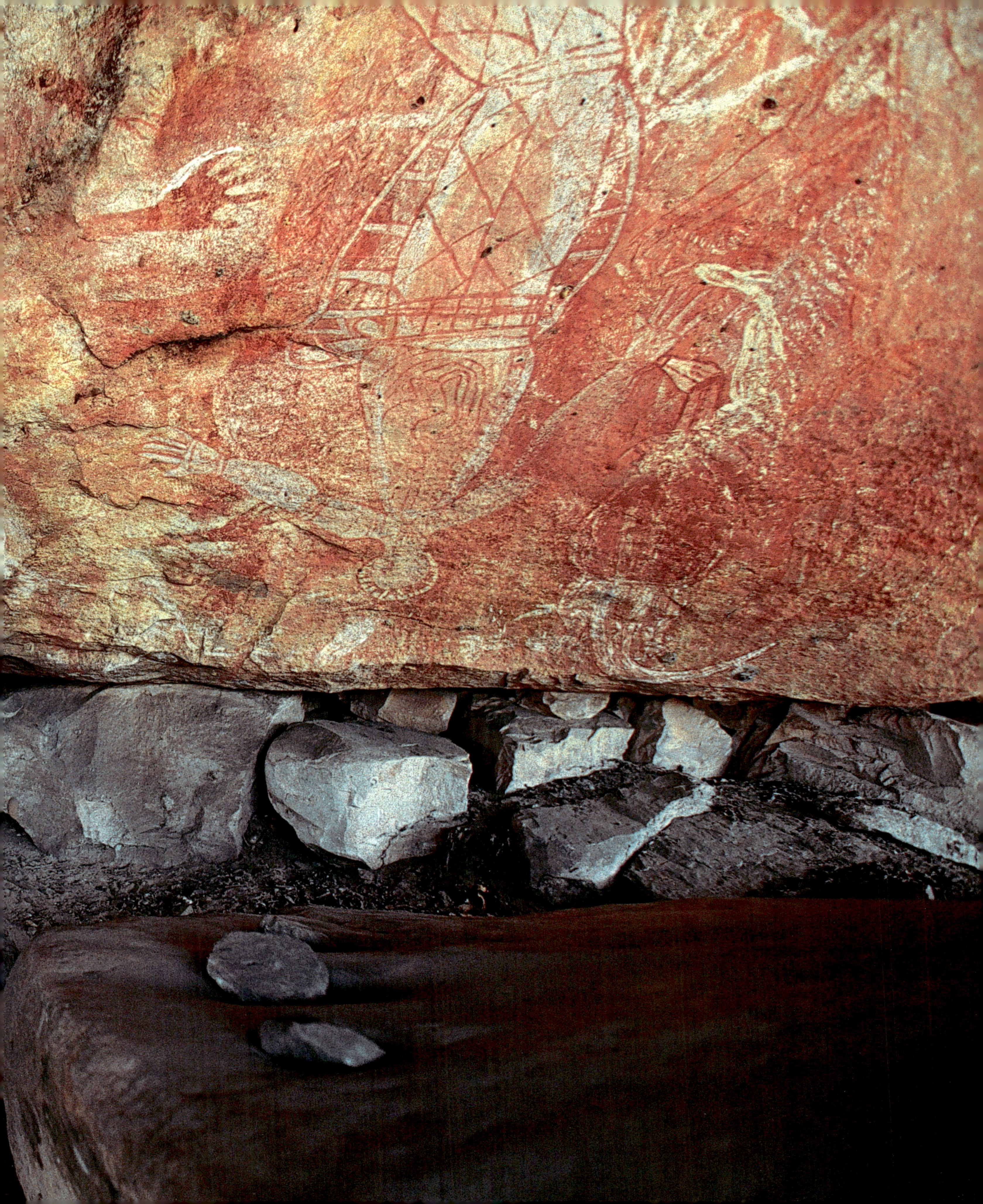

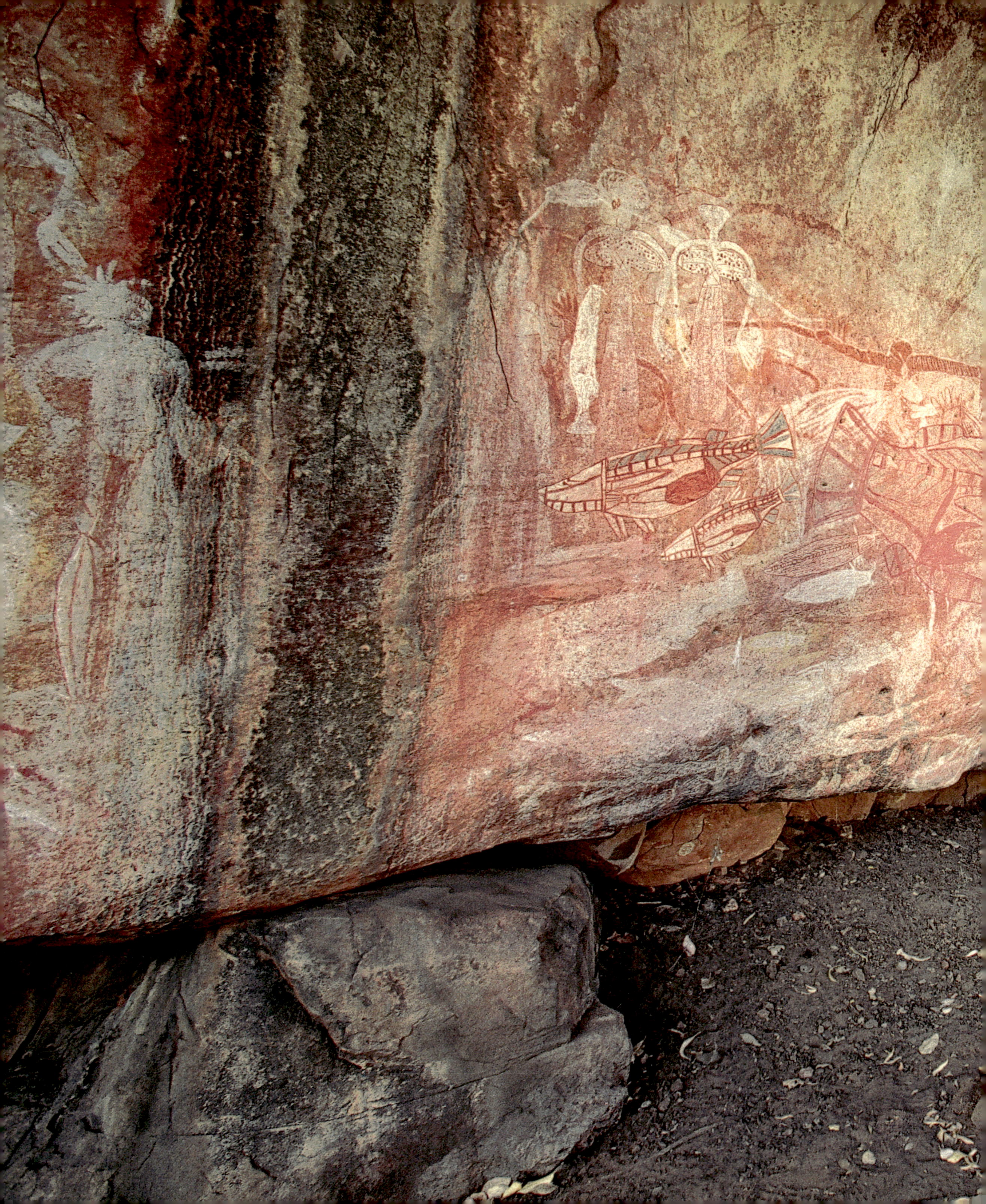

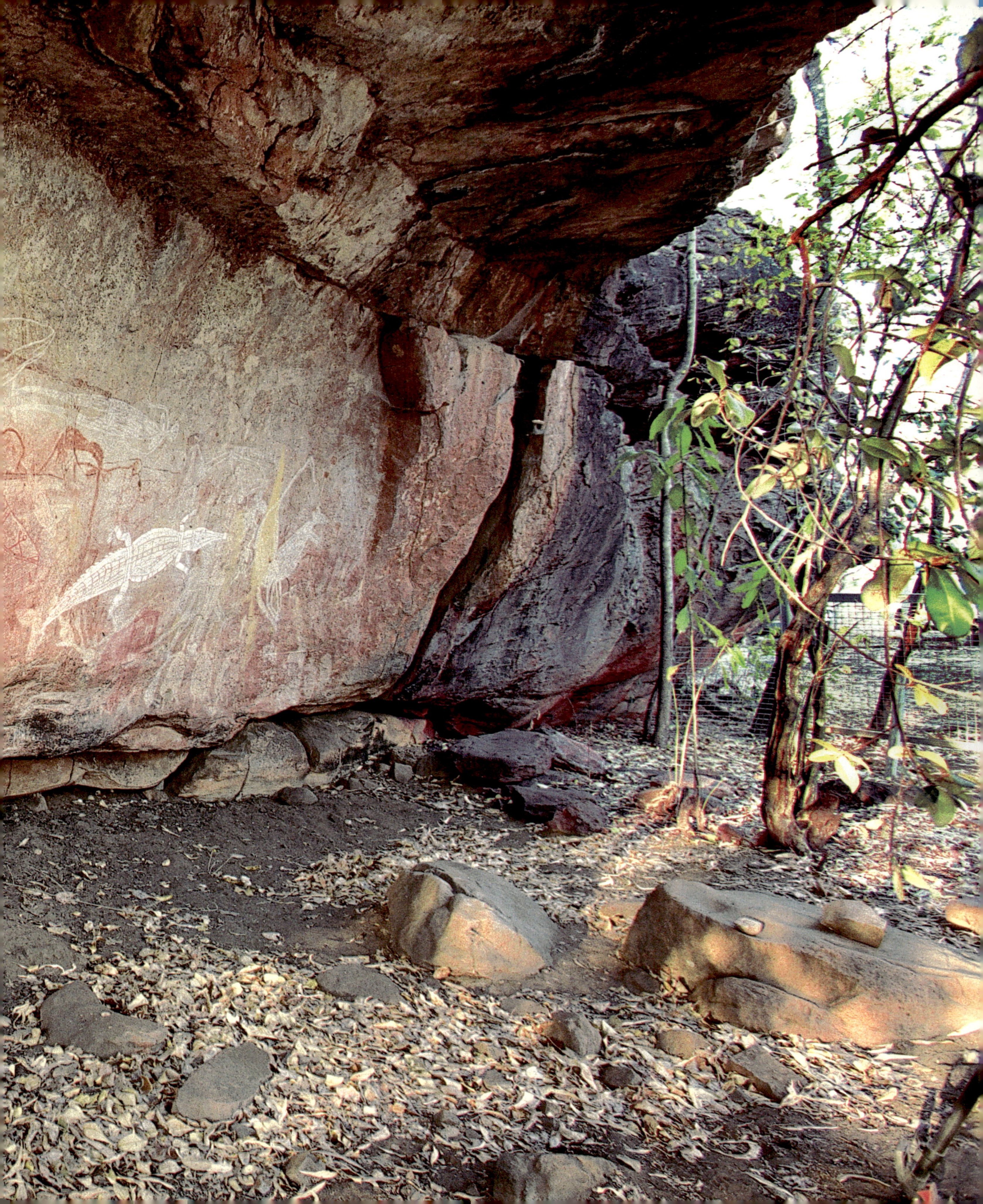

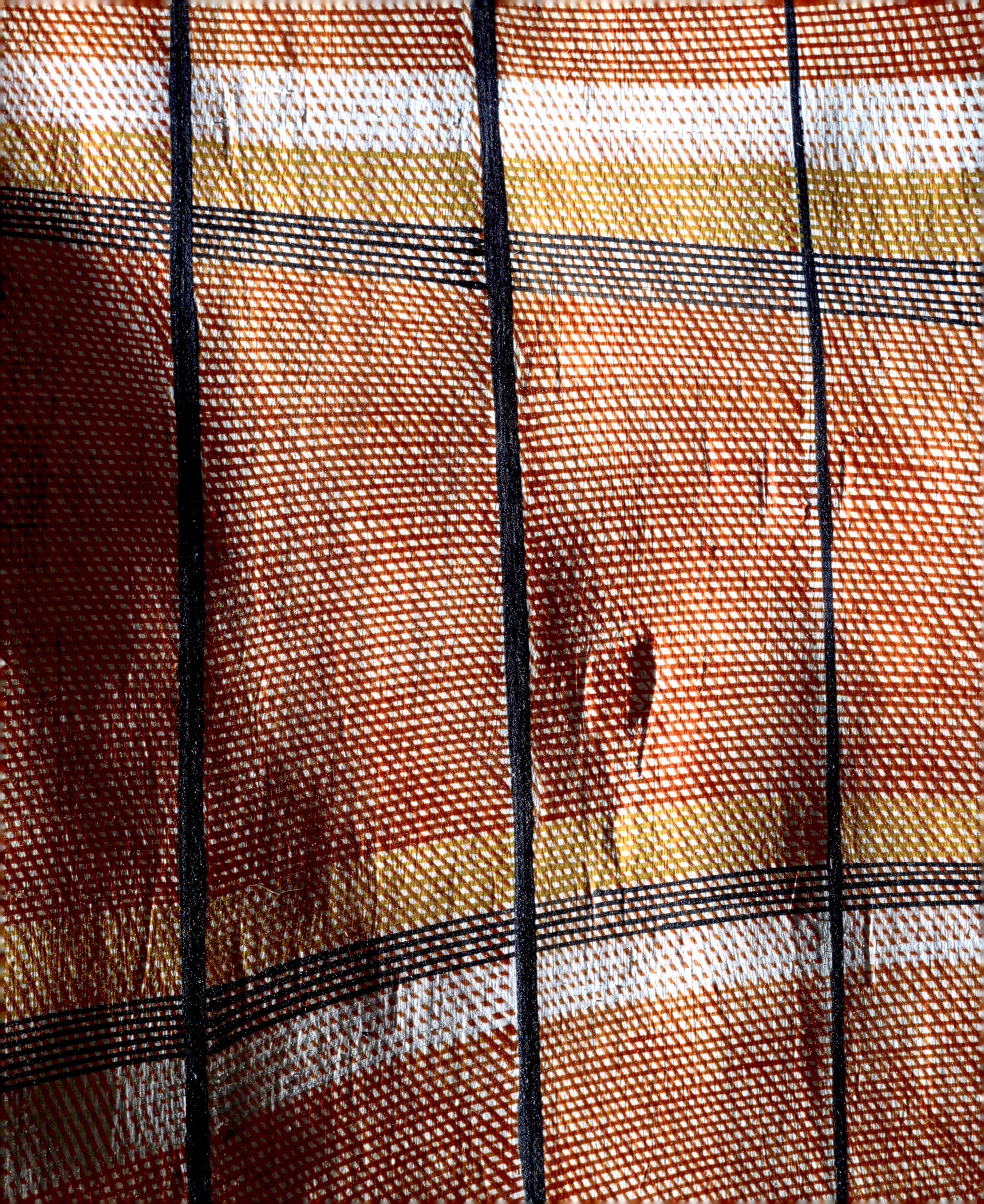

Bark painting: a singular aesthetic

Judith Ryan

Painting to me is like lambs born in spring, rain, wind, sun. Like chopping down trees in the wilderness and living with the slaughtered stumps, of not seeing the beauty I look for, and also seeing the beauty of another world ...[1]

Bark painting has been developed by generations of Aboriginal artists from Arnhem Land and other parts of northern Australia into an art form of singular spirituality and aesthetic power. This development is not the fossil tradition of an unchanging society, as is borne out by a study of the stylistic evolution of painting on bark since Spencer commissioned the first works on bark from the Gagadju in 1912. It is further exemplified by an analysis of John Mawurndjul's constantly evolving oeuvre which has not occurred in a vacuum and exemplifies the words of Ricoeur: "A tradition is not a sealed package we pass from hand to hand without ever opening, but rather a treasure from which we draw by the handful and which by this very act is replenished."[2]

Each piece of bark cut from the *Eucalyptus tetradonta* (stringy-bark) tree is organic, textured and retains its indissoluble link with the artist's country. On this uneven relief surface, artists paint while sitting on the ground, applying crushed earth pigments with anything from a twig to a *marwat* (Yolngu word for brush of several strands of human hair). Today, commercial brushes may also be employed, and wood glue is used as a fixative for the ochres instead of the orchid juice or other plant resins favoured previously. On one level the medium is the message: its organic materials are a metaphor of the way Yolngu and Kuninjku people – the greatest bark painters from eastern and western Arnhem Land – see the world. A piece of bark begins as a 'poor fellow' stripped from a living tree – just as many Aboriginal people, from areas other than Arnhem Land, have been dispossessed of their land but retain an intrinsic connection. The whole process of painting on bark and the materials of its creation express the artists' reverence for their country, and for ancestral beings and the things that grow and move in the created universe. The artists are the land they paint. This sacred affinity is ever present when we behold a bark painting as revealed by the words of Rirratjingu artist Wandjuk Marika: "Painting is very important: it is the design or symbol, power of the land ... The land is not empty: the land is full of knowledge, full of story, full of energy, full of power."[3]

John Mawurndjul
Mardayin, 2004
106.5 x 36.5 cm
(Detail)

The aesthetic uniqueness of an Aboriginal bark painting lies in its irregularities of surface, shape and design, its matte paint layer and variations of texture. We are dealing with an art work that is raw and not cooked.[4] Its design layer consists of vital, sensitive drawing and living lines that strongly reflect the hand of individual scholar painters, analogous to those of Chinese literati who work with ink in contemplation of the essence of nature absorbed over a lifetime. These qualities flow from the assurance of artists working directly with one line on to a stringy-bark surface with the finest of human-hair brushes. Like jazz musicians who improvise, rather than constantly consult the score, there is no need for practice, preparatory sketches, rulers or set squares, digital technology, air brushes or tracing paper. There is no pressure to contrive the subject, the conceptual meaning: that is the artist's birthright, identity, purpose and blood – the indelible cultural law that emanates from each bark painting, as John Mawurndjul states:

I paint the Dreaming stories and places which were instituted by the first ancestors, the sacred sites.... These are the stories my father explained to me and I put them into my head...I kept thinking and learning about these stories until they were firmly fixed in my mind and they entered my heart. I filled my head to the brim with all of this knowledge and now it is full.[5]

A bark painting calls to mind the words of Colin McCahon, "I hoped to throw people into an involvement with the raw land, and also with raw painting. No mounts, no frames, a bit curly at the edges."[6] It can never be an absolutely flat, framed rectangle contrived for the Western lounge room of the 'Home Beautiful', sitting in a 'tidy town' but is composed of elements of the artist's country. A bark painting – crooked, three-dimensional, vertical, tree-like, ephemeral – has a singular aesthetic which is a product of its materials. The ochre with its gritty particles has a matte and dull, as opposed to a shiny or smooth texture, giving the work an irregularity of surface texture which contributes to a

1 McCahon, C. in *Colin McCahon/a survey exhibition*, Auckland City Art Gallery, Auckland, p. 30.
2 Ricoeur, C., *The conflict of interpretations*, North-Western University Press, Evanston, 1974, p. 27.
3 Marika, Wandjuk, 'Painting is important', in Beier, U. (ed.), *Long water: Aboriginal and literature*, Aboriginal Artists Agency, Sydney, 1986.
4 '*The raw and the cooked*' is the title of volume 1 of Claude Lévi-Strauss' *Introduction to the science of mythology*.
5 John Mawurndjul, quoted from his statement after winning the prestigious Clemenger Contemporary Art Award, 2003, translated by Murray Garde.
6 McCahon, C., *op.cit.*, p. 30, fn 15.

quality of sensibility identified by British art historian Roger Fry.[7] The sheet of fibrous stringy-bark also constitutes raw painting, being shaped like an organism, a living thing, rather than a rectangular grid. The bark is sculptural, not flat or parallel with the wall; its edges are crooked, not uniform. It still wants to be a tree, a living thing rather than a geometrical figure, and behaves accordingly. The ochres evade permanence, the bark splits and bends: the edges do not confine or circumscribe the image on the organic support, which like life itself is ephemeral.

Based on his 1970s and '80s fieldwork amongst the Yolngu of north-eastern Arnhem Land and the Manggalili clan in particular, Howard Morphy identified the quality or qualisign of *bir'yun* – brilliance, shining – a visual effect that for the Yolngu signifies a manifestation of *wangarr marr*, ancestral power, as an aesthetic characteristic of Yolngu bark paintings.[8] He also quoted De Kooning's statement that "content is a glimpse of something, an encounter like a flash".[9] According to Morphy's definition of bir'yun, it is the crosshatched sections of a bark painting called rarrk that produce the shining resonant effects that connote a flash of ancestral or spiritual power. It should be noted, however, that crosshatching was relatively sparse in the earliest Yolngu bark paintings of 1935 onwards and consisted more of freely hatched infilling of sections of the composition, with parts of the background left plain. In some cases figurative elements were painted in solid blocks of white pigment against plain red ochre grounds, with little or no rarrk in marked contrast to the ordered and meticulous patterning of the entire surface characteristic of Yolngu bark paintings of the east coast from 1960 onwards. The artists' facility with the medium developed considerably over time resulting in more and elaborated and refined rarrk that created visual gyrations or *frisson* within *miny'tji* on a monumental scale. The substantial yellow ochre borders above and beneath the rarrk sections gradually diminished in size, until virtually disappearing whilst the proportion of white in the composition increased, serving to accentuate the painting's shimmering visual effects overall.

Similarly dramatic stylistic changes have occurred in Kunwinjku[10] bark paintings of western Arnhem Land from 1912 onwards as Mawurndjul comments, "Before Yirawala and Marralwanga, there was no rarrk … it was just like rock art. They took the rarrk from the Mardayin ceremony and put it on bark. They started it and we, the new generation, are doing new things. I make my rarrk different."[11] The abstract geometry of Mawurndjul's mature style seems to encompass and draw upon some of the defining characteristics of *miny'tji buku larrnggay* (bark paintings from the east).

Now, Kuninjku[12] and Yolngu paintings alike consist almost entirely of rarrk designs that symbolise identity, ancestral power and place and mesmerise the viewer. No section of the composition is left plain or unadorned. It should be noted that Kunwinjku artists working at Kunbarllanja and associated outstations still paint in an iconic often multi-figural style derived from rock art but most commonly choose to work on Arches paper rather than bark. A transition to paper and canvas has also occurred at Ramingining and Galiwin'ku to the east, leaving Buku Larrnggay Mulka at Yirrkala and Maningrida Arts and Culture the main centres for bark painting today.

Apart from the Yolngu concept of bir'yun, whereby the dense linear striations of rarrk create a shimmer of refinement, the actual organic materials have a contrary visual impact which is confined to this medium. The physical properties also have a metaphorical dimension as suggested by the words of Dhalwangu artist, Gawirrin' from Gangan in north-eastern Arnhem Land, who stated that "I am the people of water, earth and mud."[13] He further explained that his place is "mud, rock, sand, earth, clay" and that the painting, like earth and rocks, is not for fun but from the heart of the people. It tells us something, for the old people in the past and for people to understand today."[14] He also asserted that the miny'tji (paintings) displayed at the National Gallery of Victoria in 1995 made the room in which they were hanging *ngarra*, a sacred place, and that the ochres are also deeply sacred, a source of sickness, a danger if touched.[15]

Many of the aesthetic properties specific to bark paintings result from the ochres which are from rock, earth, clay, sand, mud – the artist's homeland. This also makes them ngarra, sacred, through their use in and association with ceremony, making them dangerous to be touched. The ochre on bark is a metaphor of the artist's country – the most precious things are mud, earth, sand, rock, clay and water. For Gawirrin', the ochres used in his *Barrama*, 1994 (Fig. below) spell Gangan and the presence of the ancestral being Barrama. Similarly, Kuninjku artists use specific pigments to connote places of spiritual power in their country where ancestors or *djang* went into or became the land. John Mawurndjul's *Mardayin at Kudjarnngal*, 2003, for example, refers to the site of Kudjarnngal where Kuninjku people collect *delek* – white pigment, believed to be the metamorphosed excreta of Ngalyod the rainbow serpent whose sacred power is therefore eternally present at the site. Her spirit essence is manifest in the brilliant shaft of white ochre towards the centre of the bark (Fig. below).

This is other than bir'yun (brightness, shininess): it is the colour of mud, of ochres. Reticent tone meets subdued tone – tonal colours of earth. Its sound is quiet – from rock, mud, earth, and serious, serious of heart, it tells us something: it is ngarra. The aesthetic is a product of the materials – mud, earth, rock, bark and what they mean to the Yolngu. As Raymattja comments, "The symbolism behind the designs can be seen by someone who knows, to be in all the little details and shapes and colours of the work of art. The deepest knowledge is abstract: it cannot be put into words."[16]

The bark painter builds up a painting in layers, following the procedure established in painting the body for circumcision. First a red ochre, yellow ochre or black ground is applied equivalent to the action of priming a canvas. Upon that ground, with a free hand, the artist paints in the outline or under-drawing, vigorously, setting down the main compositional elements, dividing the work into blocks. This gives the bark its compositional structure and is almost invariably undertaken by the artist concerned. Sometimes the rarrk sections are assigned to the wife, son, daughter or other assistants. Today a Kuninjku or Yolngu painting that is not filled in with rarrk is considered unfinished because it lacks the full design with all its tonal colours. Yet without the under-drawing, which supplies the bones of the composition, it would lack cohesion, structure. The under-drawing indicates the artist's hand or drawing style which also informs the subsidiary details. The fascination for rarrk – bark rarrk – the cross-hatched details which catch the light in splinters and the magic of the *marwat* (human hair) brush has sometimes led the viewer away from the drawn elements which determine the music and rhythm of the design.

[16] Raymattja, 'Talk to language learners at the museum', 26 March 1990, *Museum Catalogue*, Buku Larrnggay Arts, Yirrkala, 1990.

Gawirrin Gumana
Barrama, 1994
203.5 x 71.0 cm
National Gallery of Victoria,
Melbourne
(not in the exhibition)

John Mawurndjul
Mardayin at Kudjarnngal, 2003
152.5 x 76.0 cm
(see also page 145)

The spontaneous drawn elements take centre stage in the Kunwinjku and Iwaidja paintings collected by Karel Kupka from Croker Island in the early 1960s. Here images float against plain grounds as they do on the rock escarpment and artists employ negative space to heighten the power of the icons. Artists such as Midjawmidjaw, Nangunyari or Paddy Compass Namatbara worked by drawing in one or two colours only on a red ochre surface, creating spontaneous and brazen sketches, blocked in vigorously (see Figs. below). Their pure and dynamic drawings often executed rapidly in one layer are works imbued with the indelible magic of the artist's hand. Such sketching in one layer is now the starting point or cartoon for a composition that is painted in many stages and in exacting detail until the whole surface of the bark is elaborated.

The greatest bark painting contains a sensibility of design and surface texture, an inner life, a vital rhythm in the drawing that eludes mathematical definition. The art form has a singular aesthetic of spiritual resonance. Its power is not the result of technical facility or neatness, but the reverse. It is uncontrived and fluid, rather than calculated, cooked or overworked. Unlike much Western art, it is not concerned with mimetic truth, the mirroring of nature, or using the brush as a camera but with elements of life revealed through earth pigments and living lines directly brushed. The land is rendered human and is painted from the inside, with the mind's eye, and is revealed in symbols as if through its bones. The image on the rough and irregular, crooked piece of bark in its vertical, tree-like shape may vary from the minimal to the densely marked, the iconic to the abstract, the plain to the flash, but the organic properties of the bark medium create the dominant aesthetic which ultimately overrides any categorisation of style and imagery according to such polarities. The transition from bark to Arches paper or canvas results in a loss of the third dimension, confining the painting to a neat hard-edged rectangle where it lies trapped, unable to extend beyond the frame.

Paddy Compass Namatbara
Two fighting mimih couples, 1963
56.0 x 52.0 cm
(see also page 209)

Nangunyari-Namiridali
A mimih dance: hunting the freshwater crocodile, 1960
53.0 x 73.5 cm
(see also page 213)

Jimmy Midjawmidjaw
Inalats Corroboree, 1960
54.0 x 73.0 cm
(see also page 220)

Perceptible boundaries: aesthetic experience and cross-cultural understanding with a view to John Mawurndjul

Claus Volkenandt

The following thoughts and ideas are an exploration into what would be an appropriate approach to understanding non-European art, with special emphasis on the works of John Mawurndjul. Asking questions in this manner has several implications: enquiry into the understanding evokes the problem of defining a concept of understanding whilst the question of appropriateness calls for a norm by which this kind of appropriateness can be specified; talking about art as such suggests a European concept with global ramifications, while introducing the notion of the non-European immediately connotes a Here and There. It evokes a conception of Otherness with what appear to be clear boundaries.[1] All these questions and assumptions come to a head when one is directly confronted with John Mawurndjul's works in the Museum Tinguely. The exhibition shows bark paintings that are unfamiliar to Europe; each work has a specific sensory presence of its own that is determined by, and results from, its presentation in a museum of art. In the tradition of European art exhibitions, presenting in this case means displaying a, for us, unfamiliar medium of painting on the white walls of a museum, to be perceived visually, i.e. above all to be experienced and appreciated aesthetically.[2] An encounter with the works of John Mawurndjul in a European museum thus consists of three moments: the tension created by, and existing between, the works themselves, the location where they are displayed and the challenge the works pose to one's visual perception. These three aspects form the constellation within which I develop my ideas and concepts. In terms of academic disciplines I am operating in a field between art history and anthropology, in regard to the works' provenance I raise questions about cross-cultural understanding, or, more precisely, about the potentials and the boundaries of such an understanding.

In the Australian context, which I will briefly go into here, these issues were discussed for quite a length of time in terms of the difference between the anthropological and the aesthetic approach to Aboriginal art. In the meantime, the gap between anthropology and aesthetics seems to have been at least partly bridged, especially on the merit of Howard Morphy's concept of an anthropologically informed art history.[3] Morphy rejects the brand of anthropology that looks upon the label 'art' as an exclusively European unit of categorization, thus making it an inappropriate reference system for Aboriginal art. At the same time, Morphy criticises the tradition of art history that draws on aesthetic universals without, as a rule, paying reference to, and reflecting on, their Occidental-European origins. As an alternative, Morphy calls for a cross-cultural definition of art that disengages itself from the otherwise strongly Western connoted concept of art. For Morphy this means opening up and expanding the term 'art' in order to overcome the distinction between 'art' and 'artifact' – the opposition between a work of art and an object of use.[4] He regards an aesthetic approach to Aboriginal art from a European perspective as a viable option but not without pointing to the danger of the cultural imprinting of aesthetic values. According to Morphy, people who wish to approach Aboriginal art from an aesthetic viewpoint should not fall prey to the illusion that they are experiencing a work in the same manner and at the same level as a member of the producing culture.[5]

In his criticism of the universalistic aesthetic option, Morphy's guiding idea, which he uses to counter any form of European aesthetics, becomes apparent. His frame of reference is a form of work appreciation that takes its bearings from the producing culture, that is the culture in which the art works originate. Howard Morphy's concept of an anthropologically informed art history appreciates Aboriginal artistic production as art whilst accounting for the mode and conditions of its production in order to resist any form of aesthetic isolation. According to Morphy, such an orientation towards the modes and conditions of production, i.e. by taking into consideration the contexts and the historical, social, cultural, economic and art-historical circumstances under which the works are generated, provides an appropriate key for appreciating Aboriginal art. Without this knowledge, says Morphy, any aesthetic interpretation becomes impoverished.[6]

Morphy's bridging the divide between anthropology and aesthetics from the bridgehead of anthropology has not gone without criticism in the ongoing Australian debate. On the one hand critics refer to the concept of context in his production-oriented approach and, on the other, to the epistemological suppositions that Morphy's guiding principles engender.[7]

In terms of epistemology Morphy's approach has been criticised for not taking into account that later viewers do not have resort to the primary experience of witnessing the situation under which the works were produced. The Australian art historian Elizabeth Burns Coleman, for instance, points out that at least some Aboriginal art works are created in the context of ritual practices. These not only differ from one Aboriginal group to the other, they also – and this is the

8 See Burns Coleman, E., 2004, *op. cit.*, pp. 240–241.

9 As an exemplary case see Morphy, H., *Ancestral connections. Art and an Aboriginal system of knowledge*, Chicago, 1991.

10 See Burns Coleman, E., 2004, *op. cit.*, pp. 241–244, esp. p. 242: "Yet, there seems to be a significant difference between religious appreciation of something and knowing that an object under appreciation has religious significance."

11 See Burns Coleman, E., 2004, *op. cit.*, pp. 239–244.

12 On this point see Gadamer, H.-G., *Wahrheit und Methode. Grundzüge einer philosophischen Hermeneutik*, 6th edition, Tübingen, 1990, pp. 169–174: Rekonstruktion und Integration als hermeneutische Aufgaben (Reconstruction and Integration as hermeneutic issues).

13 See Scholtz, G., *Was ist und seit wann gibt es "hermeneutische Philosophie"*, Dilthey-Jahrbuch 8, 1992–93, pp. 93–119.

14 See Volkenandt, C., 'Hermeneutik' in Pfisterer, U. (ed.), *Metzler Lexikon Kunstwissenschaft. Ideen, Methoden, Begriffe*, Stuttgart/Weimar, 2003, pp. 136–139, and Volkenandt, C., 'Ästhetik der Differenz. Überlegungen zum kunsthistorischen Umgang mit dem Fremden' in Dobbe, M. and Gendolla, P. (eds.), *Winter-Bilder. Zwischen Motiv und Medium*, Festschrift für Gundolf Winter zum 60. Geburtstag, Siegen, 2003, pp. 304–317.

15 In the ideas and thoughts presented here I rudimentarily apply Max Imdahls iconic approach that distinguishes between a recognising or re-acknowledging (i.e. knowledge-related) and a seeing or visual (i.e. form-related) mode of perception in an attempt to advance a cross-cultural perspective in art history. Whilst Imdahl, based on the experience of Modernism, applied the seeing mode of perception in order to disclose art history in its historic horizon, it would appear that for a cross-cultural perspective in art history the relationship between the 'seeing' and the 're-acknowledging' approach to perception should be reversed. Insofar as the visual intake of a picture is based on the aesthetic presence of a work, we are dealing with the seeing mode of viewing, whilst the re-acknowledging mode of perception – for instance in regard to the pertinent symbolic order or the narrative system of reference – is dependent on cultural knowledge which first has to be made accessible. What Imdahl termed apprehensive perception (erkennendes Sehen), i.e. the alternating propagation of the seeing and re-acknowledging mode of perception, granting the image a visuality

decisive point – presuppose knowledge acquired at various levels of initiation, in other words: the works require the possession of structured religious knowledge.[8] Many features of religious knowledge have been documented and described by anthropologists, notably Howard Morphy himself has made many contributions in this respect.[9] But, in regard to understanding, just knowing about the context of production cannot compensate for the actual experience of creating, having actually been involved in the process. There is a difference, or better, a gap, between actually being a party to the production of a work of art and merely retracing its production through scientific description. And: the gap is unbridgeable, it is there to stay. Picking up Howard Morphy's criticism of the European-focused nature of aesthetics, it is also an illusion to believe that the gap can be bridged by anthropological enquiry and knowledge.[10]

Elizabeth Burns Coleman also critically reviews Howard Morphy's concept of context. She contends that not only the context and the modes of production, which Morphy takes as the yardstick for appreciation and understanding, are of significance, but also that the meanings assigned to an Aboriginal artwork are dependent on the circumstances under which it is created. Thus, the meaning of each image-element of a work can differ and change from one ritual context to the next;[11] it is contingent on knowledge, which, in other words, means it is lodged in individual persons. Meaning-defining ritual knowledge is neither readably accessible nor has it been compiled encyclopaedically. It is knowledge that people have been instructed in and that has been transmitted orally; at the same time it is malleable knowledge, adaptable to the reigning situation. It is also action-oriented knowledge – expertise acquired through past experience and applicable in forthcoming action. Thus it has performance character.

What conclusions can we draw from the Australian debate with respect to our own considerations? To understand Aboriginal works of art from the perspective of their creation and function it would not only mean meticulously specifying the situational context of their production, it would also entail accepting the basic premise that such an attempt would be undertaken under the condition of always being one pace behind: ensuring understanding out of the context of creation and function is, in a sense, principally only of second-rate significance. In terms of one European philosophical tradition we are facing the problem of choosing between (historical) reconstruction and (contemporary) integration, i.e. either going, or putting oneself, back in time (Friedrich Ernst Daniel Schleiermacher), or discussing the object under the conditions of its present contemporaneity (Georg Wilhelm Friedrich Hegel).[12] In regard to philology, European hermeneutics gave an answer to this by establishing rules for the purpose of ensuring (historical) understanding, and in philosophy by developing different forms of hermeneutics that enquire into the prerequisites and potentialities of imaginative understanding or *Verstehen*.[13] This configuration was carried over into European art history. However, at present we are not addressing the difference between form-oriented and content-orientated art history, the main issue concerns the basic predispositions that actually render understanding possible: either the original conditions of creation and function, or the genuine presence of the object, its contemporaneity with the particular present.[14] The basic predisposition defines the manner in which one approaches and deals with the objects in question.

In the following, I opt for the second path, i.e. viewing and seeing the object in its genuine presence as I experience it when immediately facing the work of John Mawurndjul in the museum.[15] In doing so I elect the option of a form of aesthetic experience that builds on one's own sensory capability and potentiality and renders a direct encounter with, and reaction to, the works possible. The contemplation, or viewing of a work – one of the main objectives in art history – not only serves conceptual apprehension, it has an apprehension-logic of its own. By this I do not mean a form of innocent, quasi naïve, mode of perception, but a viewing with a cognizant eye, resulting in a form of sensory apprehension. This mode of apprehension is constituted visually, i.e. insight is possible through the eye and only the eye. In other words: seeing and viewing constitute acts of apprehension.[16] This approach I will now try to apply to the works of John Mawurndjul and enter into a descriptive dialogue with them.

The first feature the viewer recognizes in John Mawurndjul's bark painting is the rectangular workformat, reminiscent of the panel paintings seen in European art up to the present day. What a bark has in common with a European panel painting is its two-dimensional plane, slightly vexed by the unevenness of its surface and the obliquity of its format, but retaining its expressive character all the same. These features, in turn, have consequences for the way the eye perceives and orders what it sees in the picture before it. This visual ordering occurs *simul et singulariter*, i.e. the viewer perceives the image as a whole whilst at the same time identifying its constituent elements. The picture's single elements are perceived against the horizon of the image as a whole, i.e. they are located on the image-plane that in turn becomes their frame of reference.[17]

In the following I should like to focus on one picture by John Mawurndjul titled *Yawkyawk*, 2005, and discuss the potentials of this approach that has developed out of European constellations and options.[18]

The picture is in portrait format, being approximately 1.5 m high and around 75 cm wide. The first glance reveals a visual event and, at the same time, the invocation of a figure. Whilst the visual vibrancy stems from the inner structure of the painting itself, the figure is invoked by the shape of a head, or a face, in the upper half of the bark and two white lines suggesting the shape of a body. Figure and structure are interlocked, emerging and receding in unison and opposition simultaneously whilst constantly accentuating each other. These accentuations are brought to the viewer's notice not only through the visual vitality of the image and the contrast between the painting's structure and the figure but also because his eye is locked in the portrait format of the painting. This is effectively underpinned by a thin, black line that runs around the bark, thus delineating the theme of the painting from its support. It demarcates a representational field of its own which attracts the viewer's attention and holds it there.

Stepping closer to the painting you clearly recognize the crosshatching, the so-called *rarrk*, that gives the picture its intense visuality. Thin lines consisting of natural earth pigments constitute the base elements and create a design that is regular and irregular at the same time. Red is the dominating colour. On the one hand the design is graphically structured by horizontally running tiers of colour. Out of the crosshatching these flows are compacted, becoming black, white or ochre-coloured bands. On the other hand, black, free-hand drawn lines traversing the bark from top to bottom create a contrasting vertical order. Together with a number of single black lines that meander across the picture we perceive a network of lines which, through the effect of the flow of colours, invokes a set of topographical and geological allusions: a map of the territory showing all its pathways, a land register, a geomorphologic survey chart, geological layers and so forth.

This set of allusions is sustained by the unevenness of the bark itself. The artist does not paint his *Yawkyawk* picture on an even artificial surface, through it's steady flow of ups and downs and its three-dimensionality, the bark takes on the semblance of a landscape relief. Probably it is no coincidence that the white almond shape in the picture is located not only near the centre of the image but also in one of the bark's troughs. It creates a visual focal point and forms a highlighted spot in the landscape at the same time. The shape's white colour and black contour lines correspond to three similarly configured vertical lines. One passes the almond shape to the left, the other to the right and the third connects it directly with the head-shaped form at the top of the image mentioned above. They are reminiscent of features in the landscape while strongly invoking the figurative element at the same time.

The invocation is based on rudimentary elements: a strongly stylised head in white that is given a rather ghostlike facial expression by a pair of prominent eyes, an adumbrated mouth and two lines outlining the head's shape. From the perspective of this figure invocation the almond shape looks like an internal organ, directly linked to the head by a white line. The intimation of a figure, however, in no way revokes the landscape quality of the image intonated by the rarrk structure, the almond shape, and the bark's uneven surface. In fact, the almond shape acts as an important go-between in the picture in the sense that it mediates between the 'outside' and the 'inside' of the figure itself on the one hand and between the figure and the landscape on the other. Put rather succinctly and hypothetically: the landscape stands for the outside of the figure which itself is present in the landscape it represents.

In an attempt to go more deeply into the matter concerning the outside and inside of the figure and its relationship to landscape– by the way: are we sure it's a figure, and if yes, who is it? And can we speak of landscape here and if yes, in what form? – we must acknowledge that we have reached the limits to our viewing, the boundary of what we can understand through mere contemplation. It becomes apparent that John Mawurndjul works in a different iconic translation mode from the one we are accustomed to in the West. By translation I mean here the way through which reality (in the widest sense of the term) finds its way into imagery. This qualifies translation as a metaphoric process: the iconification of reality.[19] In order to better understand this translation process in relation to John Mawurndjul and his *Yawkyawk* picture we are dependent on information from anthropologists, Australian art historians and from the artist himself. What we need to know more about are the cultural contexts that inform these works and what makes the works of John Mawurndjul appear so unfathomable to us, which in itself appears to be culturally determined.[20] At the same time I believe it is useful briefly to refer back to the debate between Howard Morphy and Elizabeth Burns Coleman, which tells us that when addressing contextualisation we are not dealing with only one context but a whole set of contexts and that, as the Australian debate goes to show, no single context can ultimately claim sole accountability for itself.[21]

of its own and thus proffering the opportunity of a genuine iconic experience, is one of the central issues of a cross-culturally informed art history. On the iconic approach, see Imdahl, M., *Giotto Arenafresken. Ikonographie, Ikonologie, Ikonik*, München, 1980. For the stimulating discussions and the useful suggestions on these ideas I thank Edgar Bierende, Antje Denner and Christian Kaufmann.

16 See Boehm, G., 'Bildsinn und Sinnesorgane', in *Neue Hefte für Philosophie 18/19: Anschauung als ästhetische Kategorie*, 1980: pp.118–132 and Böhm, G., 'Sehen. Hermeneutische Reflexionen' (1992), in Konersmann, R. (ed.), *Kritik des Sehens*, Leipzig, 1997, pp. 272–298.

17 See Imdahl, M., 'Überlegungen zur Identität des Bildes (1979)', in Böhm, G. (ed.), *Reflexion, Theorie, Methode: Gesammelte Schriften, Max Imdahl Vol. 3*, Frankfurt/Main, 1996, pp. 381–423, esp. pp. 394–404

18 John Mawurndjul, *Yawyawk*, 2005, natural pigments on bark, 148 x 72 cm, irregular shape, Basel, Museum der Kulturen.

19 See Boehm G., *Paul Cezanne: Montagne Sainte-Victoire: eine Kunst-Monographie*, Frankfurt/Main, 1988, pp. 54–66; for the cross-cultural perspective see Mersmann, B., 'Bildkulturwissenschaft als Kulturbildwissenschaft? Von der Notwendigkeit eines inter- und transkulturellen Iconic Turn', *Zeitschrift für Ästhetik und Allgemeine Kunstwissenschaft* 49 (1), 2004, pp. 91–109, esp. pp. 107–109.

20 This shows the way to anthropology as the academic discipline that traditionally deals with the cultural 'Other'.

21 see also Volkenandt, C., 2003, *op. cit.*, pp. 311–313.

John Mawurndjul
Yawkyawk, 2005
154.0 x 72.0 cm
(see also page 151)

22 see especially the contributions by Jon Altman (pp. 30–41) and Luke Taylor (pp. 42–63) in this volume.
23 On European art history and the relationship between art and history see Volkenandt, C., *Rembrandt: Anatomie eines Bildes*, München, 2004.

Dealing with these contexts means gathering information that could help us to understand how, in the case of the *Yawkyawk* painting, this translation process works, what it accomplishes and how reality is translated. The contexts we are talking about include, for example, the mode and the conditions under which the work was produced and also the narrative reference system the painting is based on, in other – European – words: we are talking about the *Yawkyawk* painting's iconographic properties. At the same time we have to consider the iconic traditions that take effect here and also John Mawurndjul's conception of self as an artist, out of which his works come into being and take shape. In the course of shedding light on these various contexts, as a number of contributors to the present catalogue do,[22] one acquires a stock of anthropological and art historical knowledge on the *Yawkyawk* picture which, in turn, connects with the painting's aesthetic presence.

In sensory terms John Mawurndjul's paintings are for us (Europeans) both familiar and unfamiliar. They express both: sensory closeness and dimensions of 'Otherness'. In this sense they contain aesthetic presence as well as cultural distance. An encounter with his works reveals paths of access to an understanding; at the same time it marks out perceptible boundaries.

One point I should like to make here is that the aesthetic presence of John Mawurndjul's paintings and the anthropological and art-historical knowledge on them are simply two sides of the same (work-) coin. I do not wish to play off aesthetic presence against cultural knowledge, or to subordinate one to the other. They form two sides, or better two moments of a work.[23] This duality is possible because the works are produced under certain conditions and serve specific purposes in various contexts but they are also capable of transcending these contexts without becoming completely absorbed by them and of stepping into, and facing, new actualities (in the same or different contexts). In this sense, both art-historical and anthropological knowledge are merely building blocks to an understanding of the works of John Mawurndjul. Knowledge – both anthropological and art-historical – must, however, be made accessible in perceptible terms, allow for visual perception, otherwise it does not go beyond reciting empty phrases. Images, just as language, are more than merely the sum of their components: meaning is generated in the space between the components through the act of speaking, or in our case, of viewing. Images and language are not merely symbolic orders that end with the identification of their constituent parts. Moreover, knowledge of these constituent parts, itself lodged in cultural knowledge, provides insight into the completely different mode through which John Mawurndjul translates reality into images. In this way, i.e. in experiencing works that have 'Other' origins, it should be possible to enlarge our European understanding of what an image actually is and what reference it bears to the world around it. Formulating this approach here has had primarily programmatic character while, at the same time, it was intended to delineate the contours of a cross-culturally oriented art history informed by European traditions and options.

The inevitable collision between politics and Indigenous art

Gary Foley

In the past thirty years we have seen a revolution in the history and politics of Australian Indigenous art. Since the late 1960s perceptions of Indigenous art have progressed from quaint disinterest to international excitement and the creation of a multi-million-dollar industry. From a tiny 1.7 percent of the Australian population, Aborigines make up at least 25 percent and probably around 50 percent of working visual artists as well as creating more than half the total value of Australian visual fine art and dominating the export market. Australia-wide the Aboriginal art industry is estimated to make in excess of $200 million a year and to be growing at 10 percent a year. Aboriginal artists in the Northern Territory are the largest producers in the industry. Their work has an estimated value of $110 million annually.[1]

Unfortunately, the practitioners and custodians of the artwork itself continue to be marginalized and exploited to such an extent that less than one percent of the millions generated by their work is returned to them or their communities. Further, the intense international interest created by Indigenous art rarely translates into an appreciation of the enormous historical injustices that continue to have a destructive effect on Indigenous peoples throughout Australia.

The whole world it seems is excited by Indigenous art of Australia. The same whole world simultaneously demonstrates total disinterest in the reality of the present day Indigenous social, political and economic condition. That such appreciation of art and in-difference to suffering can reside together is a contradiction that shall be examined in a small way in this essay. Through an examination of a few significant moments in the recent history of Indigenous Australia I shall illustrate the struggle by Indigenous artists to assert their self-determination, challenge exploitation at the same time as altering the cultural and political landscape of Australia.

The three significant moments I shall refer to are, the political assertion of control of the Aboriginal Arts Board of the Australia Council in the 1980s; the 1988 Bicentennial celebration, dubbed by Indigenous activists as the 'Great Masturbation of the Nation'; and the Australian High Court Decision in the Mabo case and the resultant *Native Title Act* in 1993. Each of these three events elucidate the contradictions of the intense cultural wars that are currently waging in Australia.

The lunatics take over asylum (Aboriginal Arts Board 1982–86)

In 1982 the newly elected Labor government of Bob Hawke appointed as chair of the Aboriginal Arts Board (AAB), Mr Charles (Chicka) Dixon, a former wharf labourer and long-term political activist. Dixon recruited myself as the director of the board and we set about with a clear political agenda to 'Aboriginalize' the board. By that Dixon meant that it was time for Indigenous artists to seize control of the Indigenous arts bureaucracy. From its creation a decade earlier, the AAB had been run by an exclusively non-Indigenous administration. Dixon and his board felt that non-Indigenous administrators had not done enough to protect or promote the interests of Aboriginal artists and performers and so set about implementing aggressively pro-Aboriginal policies.

Dixon also felt there had been an undue preference in previous funding that favoured so-called 'traditional' artists in northern Australia, so he introduced new policies to correct the imbalance. Among those who immediately benefited from these new policies were artists such as Tracy Moffatt, Lin Onus and Bronwyn Bancroft. The AAB under Dixon also effectively doubled funds available to assist Indigenous artists by introducing a rule that only Indigenous artists should be funded by the Aboriginal Arts Board. It might seem amazing today, but Dixon had found that in the 12 months prior to his becoming chair of the board, it had given more than fifty percent of its annual arts grants to *non-Indigenous people*! So as if to further emphasize his point about Aboriginal control, he told the 13 non-Indigenous staff of the board (there was only one Indigenous employee) that he intended to 'Aboriginalize' the AAB and that they should seek alternative employment.

Within three months the board had 14 staff (only one non-Indigenous staff member). The Dixon AAB also aggressively pressed other boards of the Australia Council to increase their funding of Indigenous projects, and many of today's significant Aboriginal and Islander theatre and dance companies were to benefit from such policies. Indeed, the veritable explosion in Indigenous creative arts that has occurred during the past twenty years can in part be attributed to the work of Chicka Dixon's Aboriginal Arts Board and that of Lin Onus' subsequent chairmanship.

Here was an example of the necessity of Indigenous people (in this case artists) regaining control of their own affairs and subverting the institutions that

[1] The author makes summary reference to the following publications, including on-line sources:
– Attwood, B. and Markus, A. (eds.), *The struggle for Aboriginal rights: a documentary history*, Allen and Unwin, Melbourne, 1999.
– Cowlishaw, G. and Morris, B. (eds.), *Race matters*, Aboriginal Studies Press, Canberra, 1997.
– Goodall, H., *Invasion to embassy: land in Aboriginal politics in NSW, 1770–1972*, Allen and Unwin, Sydney, 1996.
– *Mabo and Orr v Queensland* (1992), High Court of Australia, CLR.
– Morris, B., *Domesticating resistance: the Dhan-Gadi Aborigines and the Australian state*, Berg Publishers, Oxford, 1989.
– Rose, M., *For the record: 160 years of Aboriginal print journalism*, Allen and Unwin, Sydney, 1996.
– Smith, L. Tuhiwai, *Decolonizing methodologies: research and Indigenous peoples*, University of Otago Press, Dunedin, 1999.
– Bell, R., *Aboriginal art: it's a white thing* ttp://www.kooriweb.org/bell/theorum.html
– Morgan, T., *Who's dreaming now?* www.kooriweb.org/bell/article2.html
– Croft, B. L., *Cultural con/texts: apologists vs. apologies* www.kooriweb.org/bell/article9.html
– Langsam, D., *Aboriginal art – $100 m hidden industry* http://ourworld.compuserve.com/homepages/dingonet/aborigin.htm

affected them. As such it was a continuation of the ideas and philosophies that had exploded in Australia during the late 1960s and early 1970s, in the form of the so-called Black Power movement and the 1972 Aboriginal Embassy. It is important to note that Chicka Dixon was one of the key architects and planners of the Aboriginal Embassy, and it was the political principles he had espoused at the Embassy that he brought to the Aboriginal Arts Board in 1982.

The ideas of the Embassy in turn had derived and evolved from the famous 1938 'Day Of Mourning' protest which was the significant challenge to white sovereignty and hegemony of its era. Thus the radical actions of Dixon in 1982–6 could be regarded as very much part of a long-established political resistance, and thereby it cannot be said that the situation today in the world of Aboriginal art is disconnected from the political struggle for justice.

This politicization of the primary administrative and support structures in the 1980s in part produced a parallel overt political artistic outcome in the emergence of artists like Lin Onus, Gordon Hookey, Richard Bell and Gordon Bennett. The work of these artists and others who were encouraged and nurtured by the Dixon AAB changes, make a more direct challenge to the status quo. As Brenda Croft has pointed out, "socio-political circumstances always impact upon, and are reflected in Indigenous cultural expression".

One of the most important exhibitions to germinate during the Dixon led AAB was the Aratjara exhibition that toured Germany, England and Denmark during 1993 and 1994. Aratjara was born when a Swiss artist called Bernhard Lüthi approached the AAB in 1984 and expressed the view that Australian Indigenous art should be exhibited in the modern art galleries of Europe rather than the ethnographic museums where at that time it languished. This idea was enthusiastically embraced by the AAB and they provided funding to enable Lüthi to develop the idea. This ultimately resulted in a major exhibition, comprising both so-called 'traditional' and 'urban' artworks that in 1993 and 1994 were shown in modern art museums in Dusseldorf, London and Copenhagen. The Aratjara exhibition was to this day the most successful (in terms of people through the door) Australian art exhibition to ever leave Australia's shores. It also made a major contribution to the expanding international interest in Indigenous art from Australia.

1988 – 'The Great Masturbation of a Nation' Bicentennial

The period of Chicka Dixon's chairmanship of the Aboriginal Arts Board coincided with the lead up to the 1988 Bicentennial activities during which Australians were asked to celebrate 200 years of white occupation of Aboriginal lands. There was always going to be tension between those who wished to celebrate and those who regarded the event as a 'Day of Mourning', but the situation was exacerbated by the actions of the Hawke Federal Labor government since coming to office in 1983. When Hawke had been first elected Prime Minister, he had unequivocally declared that his government would deliver justice to Indigenous Australia through 'national uniform land rights legislation'. This legislation would enable Aborigines to claim land in freehold title and begin the process of re-establishing self-determination by way of economic enterprise leading to full economic independence.

Unfortunately, Hawke was attacked by representatives of the powerful pastoralist and mining industries who saw Aboriginal land justice as a threat to their vested interests. Under intense pressure, Hawke wilted and land rights for Aborigines was off the agenda. In the face of such political cowardice, the Aboriginal political movement staged major demonstrations at the Brisbane Commonwealth Games and threatened to disrupt the 1988 Bicentennial celebrations. Tension mounted and soon Hawke's Minister for Aboriginal Affairs began to interfere in the administrative operations of the Aboriginal Arts Board. This interference became intolerable for myself as director of the board and on 1 May 1987 I tendered my resignation.

As the Bicentennial approached the tension between the Hawke government and Indigenous Australians became more intense. Prominent among those critical of the government were Indigenous artists and performers who developed a strategy of challenging the powerful cultural mythology of what the Bicentennial represented. Part of that strategy involved the creation of a music and art project called 'Building Bridges', which was designed to communicate to white Australia an alternative understanding and vision for the future.

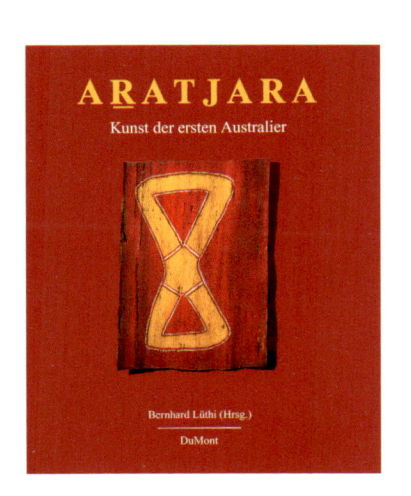

Catalogue
Aratjara – Art of the First Australians
Traditional and Contemporary
Works by Aboriginal and Torres
Strait Islander Artist
Kunstsammlung Nordrhein-Westfalen
Düsseldorf 1993

On 26 January 1988 the Australian Bicentennial celebrations went ahead in a white orgy of fireworks and alcohol. In contrast, with a remarkable expression of restraint and dignity, the biggest assembly of Indigenous Australians in 60,000 years marched and rallied in the heart of the city of Sydney. This moment clearly showed that Black Australians were able to culturally subvert the underlying themes of the Bicentennial. Simply by still surviving and resisting both the original invasion and 200 years of attempts to eliminate them through programmes of 'assimilation'.

The Mabo decision – 'Native Title is NOT Land Rights!'

By the end of the 13-year term of the Hawke/Keating Labor government, Aboriginal Australia not only did not have the Hawke-promised 'national uniform land rights legislation', but in fact were further dispossessed through a legal sleight of hand called *Native Title*. In 1993 the High Court of Australia, in the Mabo case, finally dispensed with the fallacy of 'terra nullius', which had been the legal justification for the acquisition of sovereignty of Australia by the British for more than 200 years. Instead, the High Court declared, Indigenous Australians apparently had what British Law deemed 'Native Title' in 1788.

The 'catch-22' was that Native Title (being the most inferior form of land tenure under British Law) was 'extinguished' by Freehold Title. In other words, all the settled areas of Australia (i.e. the best land) were lands that could not be claimed under the new *Native Title Act*. Thus the Mabo decision of the High Court and the resultant *Native Title Act* drawn up by Labor Prime Minister Paul Keating, represented the greatest single dispossession of Aboriginal people (without compensation) since the arrival of Captain Cook in 1770.

The advent of the Liberal government of John Howard has further exacerbated the sense of alienation felt by Indigenous communities throughout Australia. Today we are in the midst of major 'culture wars' in which Prime Minister Howard has taken a clear public stance by declaring his support for historian Keith Windshuttle who claims he is fighting against 'black armband" histories. Those who Windshuttle has deemed the 'black armband brigade' of historians include the few Australian historians of the past thirty years who have begun to explore the history of this land from an Indigenous perspective.

This exploration of the unspoken aspects of Australian history is perceived as a threat by a Prime Minister who some might say has embraced a racist position on history in order to win over the significant minority of Australians who voted for the racialized policies of Pauline Hanson. Hanson was an Australian version of populist racist political groups that have emerged throughout Europe in the past 20 years. Given that the voice of Indigenous historians has effectively been silenced in the great debates of today's culture wars, it has been Indigenous artists and performers who have become the most effective resistance fighters.

The win by Richard Bell in the 2004 Telstra National Aboriginal Art Award signifies the central importance of contemporary artists such as him, Gordon Bennett, Vernon Ahkit and others as the Indigenous voice in the debates that form the culture wars. Their subversive work has a subtle undermining effect on nationalist assertions that attempt to normalize British notions of Australian 'history'. In doing so they place themselves (wittingly or unwittingly) at the centre of the political-cultural argument that will define Australian identity for the next few decades.

An integral part of the strategy is the use of humour in their work. As Richard Bell states, "I like to use satire and other tools of humour to soften the blow, so to speak, because ultimately, it's about communication." Whether the art utilizes humour or other means, the important point remains that the cultural-political integrity of Indigenous Australia is as much under threat as it ever was.

Bell's win of the National Aboriginal Art Award is one of the most powerful recent statements by an Indigenous person who rightfully insists on being regarded as a 'contemporary Australian artist'. His winning entry, *Scienta E Metaphysica (Bell's Theorem)* 2003, was accompanied by a 4600 word essay titled *Aboriginal Art: It's a White Thing* in which he challenged not only the Aboriginal art industry, but also the ongoing denial of justice for Indigenous people. The fact that such an overtly political piece of work would win the most prestigious Indigenous art award in Australia clearly placed politics at the centre of the Indigenous art mainstream.

The fact that John Mawurndjul won the respected Clemenger Award for Contemporary Art in 2003 shows that Indigenous people in northern Australia may count yet another extraordinary personality amongst their members, an artist who proves to attract attention just by showing his works. This is also a valid way of sharpening the profile of Indigenous cultures as forming a lively part of Australia. I remember with respect the personal initiative by the late Lin Onus, chairman of the Aboriginal and Torres Strait Islander Arts Board of the Australia Council, to establish personal relationships between artists from the South and artists from the North.

Today's most important Indigenous artists are 'wise to and savvy about the economic and political context in which they work.' As Indigenous people first, before they are Indigenous artists, they are as conscious as any person in the Indigenous community of the new hostile political landscape that confronts us under the vision of John Howard. The irony of this is that in the world of John Howard's most ardent supporters, namely the boardrooms of corporate Australia, one would be hard pressed to find a boardroom or corporate headquarters that does not have at least one mandatory work of Indigenous art gracing their walls. This point returns us to the beginning of this essay, emphasizing again the contradiction between the vast amounts spent on Indigenous art by some of the wealthiest people in the world, yet the people who produce this work are among the poorest and most oppressed in the Western world.

Hopefully in exhibitions such as this people might remember that there is another dimension to the wonderful art work before you, and sometimes realize that these Indigenous people and their present political and economic situation should be a consideration in your appreciation of their art.

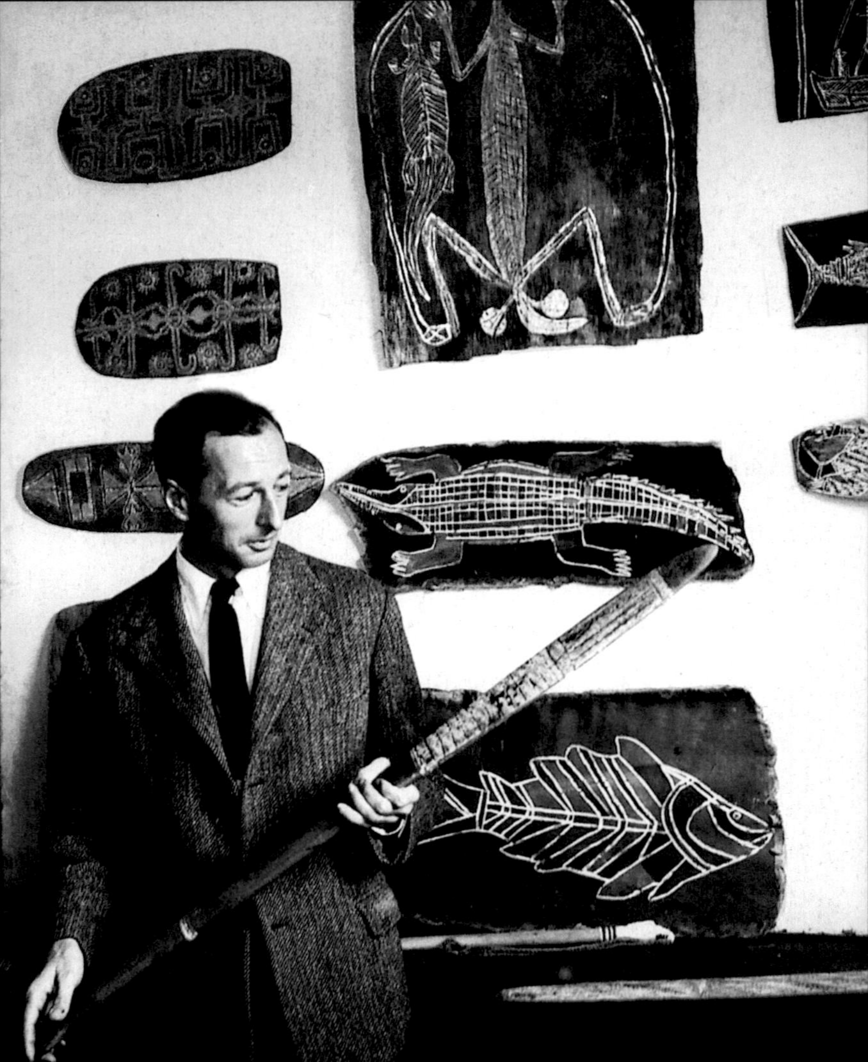

THE KAREL KUPKA COLLECTION

Bark painting from West Arnhem Land

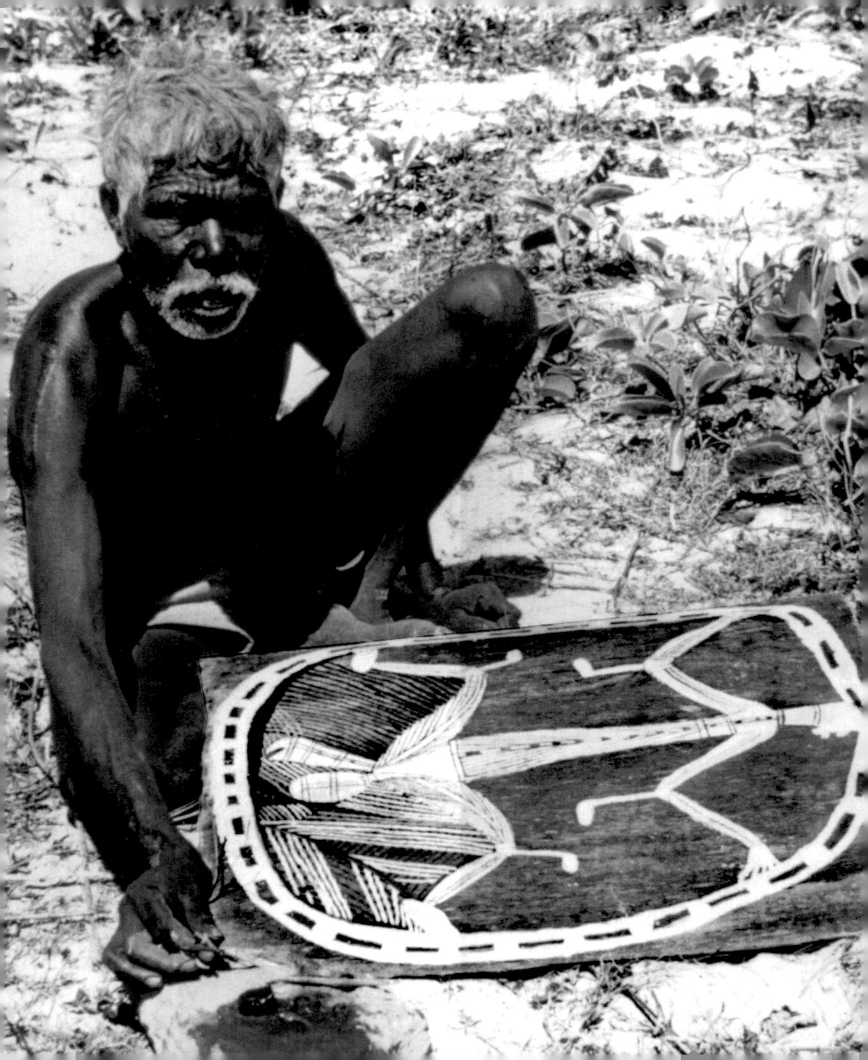

Karel Kupka in Australia: artist, collector, writer, anthropologist

Richard McMillan

Czech-born Karel Kupka (1918–1993) extended the awareness of Aboriginal bark painting in Europe by bringing large collections from Arnhem Land to museums in Basel and Paris. These collections, made between 1956 and 1964, are documented in photographs and notebooks befitting the scientist he eventually became, and were the fruits of commissions he had devised himself after university training in law and art, first in Prague then in Paris. He wanted to go to Arnhem Land because there, he believed, artists and their families were living as the first people had, "the sole survivors of the paleolithic age."[1] In Kupka's own words: "To satisfy my curiosity [about Aboriginal art] I studied all available information abroad and made a trip to Australia in 1951 ..."[2] The 1951 study-visit to Australian cities enabled him to assemble relevant information at a time when more was becoming available thanks in part to the consolidating efforts of Professor A.P. Elkin, head of the department of anthropology at the University of Sydney and, after two decades of fieldwork, to Elkin's foremost authority on the lives and art of Indigenous Australians. Kupka's long and filial relationship with Elkin, who had contributed two chapters to *Art in Arnhem Land* the year before, may have begun in 1951.[3] He also formed enduring friendships in Sydney, with the artist Carl Plate and his family for one. Following his return to Paris, Kupka secured a mission from Professor Alfred Bühler, director of the Basel Museum of Ethnology, to collect in Arnhem Land in 1956. The success of this mission ensured another from Basel in 1960–61. In 1963 Kupka collected for the National Museum of African and Oceanic Arts (MNAAO) in Paris, which had been established in 1960 by André Malraux, French Minister for Culture.[4]

First impact

Kupka, after his first period of collecting, did much to raise awareness of Aboriginal art in Sydney. He initiated two exhibitions of material he had collected: at Sydney's main art school, East Sydney Technical College, in November 1956, and at the Bissietta Gallery the following month. Both were noted in the afternoon newspapers and visited by an audience, primarily, of artists and their supporters.[5] Elkin spoke at the Bissietta Gallery opening. Editor of the scholarly journal Oceania, Elkin invited Kupka to contribute a summary of his fieldwork to the publication. When the article "Australian Aboriginal Bark Paintings" appeared the next year, Kupka was introduced by the editor as one who had studied Aboriginal art, not only in museums, but also in Arnhem Land where he had "spent several months amongst the local artists, observing them." Kupka concluded his text thus: "This most popular and widely known form of Aboriginal artistic expression [bark painting] is nowadays flourishing more than ever ... More painters, and competent collectors should be interested in Aboriginal work, and, by good choice, encourage this true art. Public art galleries should follow the example of the Queensland Art Gallery in Brisbane, where three bark paintings, well exposed, add happily to its fresh and youthful collection."[6]

Commissioned again by Bühler to collect in Australia in 1960, Kupka secured a letter of introduction from Professor Elkin to support his visit to northern Queensland: it begins by describing Kupka as "an artist of distinction from Europe whom I have known for several years," cites his study in Arnhem Land, his article on Oceania, and expresses gratitude for "the help and facilities which you can afford him."[7] No further documents of Kupka's visit to Queensland have yet been found in Sydney, though Kupka reports in some detail on the delicate transfer of the bones of a deceased painter to the university museum in St.Lucia; this happened at the request of the family.[8]

---

1 Ruhe, E. L., 'Poetry in the Older Australian Landscape, in Eaden, P.R. and Mares, F.H. (eds.), *Mapped but not known: the Australian landscape of the imagination; essays & poems presented to Brian Elliott*, Wakefield Press, Adelaide, 1986, p. 45, quoting M. Mauss 1923 in Bulletin de la société française de philosophie, Paris, that Australian Aboriginies were "the sole survivors of the paleolithic age."
2 Kupka, K., 'Artists and workers in Arnhem Land', *The Missionary Review*, (Sydney), 65 (9), March 1957, pp. 8–9.
3 Elkin, A.P., Berndt, C. and Berndt, R., *Art in Arnhem Land*, F.W. Cheshire, Melbourne and London, 1950.
4 Viatte, G., 'Malraux et les arts sauvages', in *André Malraux et la modernité*, (exhibition catalogue), 20 November 2001–24 March 2002, Musée de la Vie Romantique, Paris, (http://www.quaybranly.fr/article).
5 Cook, J., 'Loan exhibition of paintings', Daily Telegraph (Sydney), 16 November 1956, p. 13; by same author: 'An exhibition of Aboriginal arts and crafts', Daily Telegraph (Sydney), 4 December 1956, p 26. ["Some pastel portraits made by Mr. Kupka during his trip to Arnhem Land and surrounding areas are the only works on sale."]
6 Kupka, K., 'Australian Aboriginal bark paintings', Oceania 27, 1957, pp. 266–267, [Summary of fieldwork undertaken in 1956; Kupka describes figurative painting of the interior of Arnhem Land and Groote Eylandt, ceremonial art of the coast, Port Keats 'retranscriptions' and Tiwi painted baskets].
7 Elkin, A. P., Personal archives of Professor A. P. Elkin [henceforth referred to as *Elkin Papers*], P130, Archives and Records Management Services, University of Sydney: Series 29, "Australian Institute of Aboriginal Studies," Series 44 "Personal correspondence general 1956–1979": 22, June 1960 [Guide available at http://www.usyd.edu.au/arms/archives, under Personal Archives E-G.].
8 Kupka, K., Peintres aborigènes d'Australie, Publications de la Société des Océanistes no. 24, Musée de l'Homme, Paris, 1972, p. 81, note 166. A Queensland shield was also illustrated in Kupka, *op. cit.*, 1962, p. 184 as well as in *op. cit.*, 1965, p. 164.

9 Kupka, K., 'Centre for Aboriginal art', *Sydney Morning Herald*, 11 June 1960 [includes three photographs by Kupka; text written in 1959, possibly as part of an application to the Bollingen Foundation in New York; see Elkin, A. P., *Elkin Papers*, P130, Archives and Records Management Services, University of Sydney: Series 29, 'Australian Institute of Aboriginal Studies', item 9: correspondence and papers concerning Karel Kupka.

10 Kupka, K., 'Why not a centre for Aboriginal art', *West Australian* (Perth), 2 July 1960, [includes two photographs by Kupka. Word for word as item quoted in note 9].

11 Caruana, W. and Lendon, N., *The painters of the Wagilag Sisters' story 1937–1997*, (exhibition catalogue), National Gallery of Australia, Canberra, 1997, pp. 13, 28, 32 – see also catalogue checklist nos. 3, 10, 13, 49, 52, 79 for works collected by Kupka for Basel, Canberra and Paris.

12 Kupka, K., ,Artists and workers in Arnhem Land', *The Missionary Review*, 65 (9), March 1957, p. 9.

13 Report on Karel Kupka, McCarthy, F. D., 15 October 1963, AIAS document #63/68; copy with *Elkin Papers* 29:9 as per note 9.

14 *Elkin Papers* P 130, Series 29:9, as per note 9.

15 Letter to Karel Kupka of 2 July 1964, in *Elkin Papers* 29:9, as per note 9.

16 Reviews by Berndt, R. M., *Art and Australia* 4 (2), 1966, p. 111, as well as by Stanner, W. E. H., *Mankind* 6 (10), December 1967, p. 257-258 . Later Berndt, in as harsh a comment as he might make in a letter to his former teacher and long-standing mentor, complained that Kupka "did not treat the AIAS well and left a trail of promises behind him in Arnhem Land." [Letter, 4 June 1970, in *Elkin Papers*, Series 44, box 223, as per note 7].

While in Sydney, Kupka published an illustrated article in the city's main daily newspaper.[9] This accomplishment was repeated the following month in Perth, capital of Western Australia.[10] In both articles Kupka argued for the creation of "an organisation to help systematic research" into Aboriginal art and culture in Australia. He chastised art lovers for not visiting the two rooms of Aboriginal art at the Art Gallery of New South Wales (AGNSW) in Sydney.

Writer

Kupka's visits to Arnhem Land also resulted in an expertly designed, illustrated and produced book. *Un art à l'état brut* (1962) was later published in the author's own translation as *Dawn of art* (1965), first for distribution in Australia, later for the United States and Canada. The book included a 'text' by André Breton which was accorded the privilege of poetry in the English edition, being printed in the original French with an English translation. Breton establishes a dense context, beginning with "the untutored eye" for the "magnetic" subject, and quoting Claude Lévi-Strauss on totemic representation; he also compares designs on barks to ornaments on seashells. A foreword in each edition was contributed by important mentors of Kupka: in Switzerland by Alfred Bühler, who, as director of the Basel Museum of Ethnology, had commissioned Kupka's travel to Arnhem Land in 1956 and 1960. In the 1965 edition of *Dawn of art* Elkin anticipated the fruits of Kupka's work for the Australian Institute of Aboriginal Studies (AIAS), and distinguished him in 'approach', as Breton and Bühler do, from anthropologists. As well as Kupka's own "observations and insights, questions and evaluations" (Elkin's foreword) the book also contains an array of field photographs of artists in ceremony, and at work painting on barks as well as on sculptures. Selected photographs are presented in clear, large colour reproductions. In all, this created an attractive introduction to the art of a determined people. Kupka also used his collections and writing to support exhibitions in Basel (1958), Lausanne (1962–63), Geneva (1966), Paris (1969), Prague (1969) and, with the involvement of Qantas Airline, Paris and Rome (both 1964).

During his 1956 visit to Australia Kupka produced a brochure of six of his photographs with some paragraphs of general introduction to bark painting from northern Australia, published by the Legend Press in Sydney. A photo-portrait of the artist (Tjam) Yilkari Katani from Milingimbi painting a Wagilag story bark gave the enterprise special resonance, not least because of the renown created for the painter and the story by the National Gallery of Australia's 1997 exhibition *The Painters of the Wagilag Sisters' Story 1937–1997*, where nine early examples of Yilkari Katani's work were shown.[11] Kupka also contributed an account of his first visit to Arnhem Land to The Missionary Review, in acknowledgement of the support of the Methodists. Although unmentioned, the supervisor and supporter of artists Rev. Edgar Wells was at Milingimbi between 1949–59, as were many important artists. "During my trip in and around Arnhem Land I collected bark-paintings from practically every area where they are made. Those from Milingimbi are amongst some of the best."[12]

On his following visit to Australia in 1963 Kupka was one of the first, thanks to the support of Emeritus Professor Elkin, to benefit from the budget for 'urgent research' allocated by the Prime Minister shortly before the establishment of the Australian Institute for Aboriginal Studies (AIAS). This 1963 visit was again funded by MNAAO and by the artist himself.[13] At the end of this visit a dispute broke out between Kupka and AIAS. It is documented in a collection of letters and other papers assembled by Elkin.[14]

Eventually the conflict was resolved in the following way: AIAS representatives chose a collection of Arnhem Land material, now at the National Museum of Australia, from a larger collection shown to them by Kupka at the artist

Stanislaus Rapotec's apartment in Kings Cross, Sydney. Kupka left as scheduled in January 1964 with the rest of his collection, some of which the Institute had not seen. Elkin hoped that "there should be not be any further bother" following export clearance by Australian Customs.[15] But younger men would remember: critical reviews of *Dawn of art* by two of his adversaries appeared in prominent Australian journals, making veiled reference to his misdemeanours.[16]

While Karel Kupka continued to visit Australia, and Arnhem Land in the 1970s, his ability to generate publications and exhibitions in Australia had evaporated. The "false criticism" of Kupka that Elkin noted in a letter to Harry Geise in Darwin continued to undermine Australian recognition of his achievement until more recent acknowledgments.[17] In 1984 the National Gallery of Australia acquired an important collection of art works that Kupka would have assembled in view of eventually making them available to Australians.[18] Whether Kupka's open-hearted association with artists and art critics enlarged the distance between him and the circles of competitive anthropologists, remains an open issue.

Anthropologist

The interview with Kupka about the painter Daingannan published in Paris in 1964 was one of the earliest texts focusing on an individual Aboriginal artist, and also featured photographs taken by Kupka at Milingimbi.[19] A summary of his fieldwork in relation to an exhibition in Geneva was published in 1966, again with some of his photographs.

Kupka extended his involvement with individual artists in Arnhem Land – as a fellow-artist observing and admiring their painting and collecting their artwork, a combination of talents that won him Bühler's praise[20] – thus extending his commitment to anthropology. Kupka prepared a thesis, *Anonymat de l'artiste primitif*, which was submitted to a jury under the chairmanship of the distinguished prehistorian André Leroi-Gourhan.[21] He defended this thesis in 1969 at an exhibition of the barks in a special gallery of the National Museum of African and Oceanic Arts (MNAAO) in Paris before an invited audience. The jury awarded it 'maxima laude'.[22] The thesis, revised, was published by the Société des Océanistes in 1972, but regrettably sub-edited while the author was in Australia.[23] As a fellow in anthropology of the CNRS (Centre national de la recherche scientifique) Kupka returned to Australia several times in the 1970s to study aspects of kinship, and genealogies, particularly of artists whose work he had collected and friendship sustained.

A herald for Aboriginal art

Kupka's 1960 article in the Sydney Morning Herald was published only months before the opening (again by Elkin) of an important survey exhibition, *Australian Aboriginal Art*, 1960-1961, which later travelled to all capital cities of Australia. Karel Kupka's articles had helped to create an audience for this survey-exhibition. He knew the exhibition's organiser Tony Tuckson, AGNSW's deputy director, like himself an artist and traveller in Arnhem Land.[24] On November 15, 1960, Kupka gave a slide-talk in Sydney about his collection of Aboriginal art, with Tuckson and his wife Margaret attending.[25] As well as Tuckson, Kupka had other artist friends[26]: among them the poet Roland Robinson who in his autobiography, whilst referring primarily to the Aboriginal contacts he had given Kupka in 1956, also mentions Kupka's commission by the Roman Catholic Bishop of Darwin for painting an Aboriginal Madonna, now in the Darwin cathedral. Kupka visited the Ecole des Beaux-Arts in Paris between 1947 and 1948 and, at the same time, was there accepted to the studio of Jean Souverbie.[27]

As we have seen, Kupka, apart from collecting for museums in Europe, also established important collections for Australia. These are now held by the National Museum of Australia, and by the National Gallery of Australia,

17 AE to HG, 6 October 1970, in *Elkin Papers*, Series 44, box 223 as per note 7. – For a change of attitudes see Morphy, H., 'Seeing Aboriginal art in the gallery', *Humanities Research* 8 (1), Australian National University, Canberra, 2001, pp. 45, as well as Taylor, L., 'Fire in the water: inspiration from country', in Perkins, H. (ed.) *Crossing country: the alchemy of western Arnhem Land art*, (exhibition catalogue), The Art Gallery of New South Wales, Sydney, 2004, pp. 117–118, 121.
18 Caruana, W., 'National Gallery of Australia, Canberra', in Cochrane, Susan (ed.), *Aboriginal art collections: highlights from Australia's public museums and galleries*, Fine Art Publishing, Sydney, 2001, p. 13. [Brief account of purchase of 137 bark paintings and sculptures from Kupka in 1984. The works from Kupka's 1963 collection selected for the Australian Institute of Aboriginal Studies now in the National Museum of Australia are noted by David Kaus on p. 25].
19 Kupka, K., 'Daingannan, Artiste de la Terre d'Arnhem', *Journal de la Société des Océanistes* XX No. 20, 1964, pp. 45–55 [includes two Kupka photographs of artists and two of barks. Interview with Kupka conducted by Father Patrick O'Reilly, Secretary general of the Société des Océanistes].
20 Bühler in Kupka, K., *Un art à l'état brut: peintures et sculptures des aborigènes d'Australie*, La Guilde du Livre et Editions Clairefontaine, Lausanne, 1962, p. 14–15, with a text by André Breton and a preface by Alfred Bühler.
21 Souëf, M., 'Avant propos: Karel Kupka (1918–1993)', in Dussart, F., *La peinture des aborigènes d'Australie*, Édition Parenthèses, Marseille, 1993, p. 15.
22 Letter to Elkin, 15 December 1969, in *Elkin Papers* 44: 222 as per note 7.

23 Kupka, K., *Peintres aborigènes d'Australie*. Publications de la Société des Océanistes No. 24, Musée de l'Homme, Paris, 1972. – For the former title Anonymat de l'artiste primitif see Peltier, Ph., 'Karel Kupka, le témoin essentiel'/'Karel Kupka, the essential witness', in Ducreux, A.-C., Kohen, A. and Salmon, F. (eds.), *Au centre de la Terre d'Arnhem, entre mythes et réalité: art aborigène d'Australie/In the heart of Arnhem Land; myth and the making of contemporary Aboriginal art*, (exhibition catalogue), Musée du Hotel-Dieu, Mantes-la-Jolie, 2001, pp. 33–38.
24 Tuckson produced an exemplary catalogue for the survey, which Kupka was to laud in his PhD thesis: Tuckson, J.A., *Australian Aboriginal art. Bark paintings, carved figures, sacred and secular objects*. An exhibition arranged by the State Art Galleries of Australia, 1960–1961. Sydney 1960, see Kupka, thesis, *op.cit.*, p. 39. [. Particularly an exchange of letters from 1965-66 between Kupka and Hal Missingham, AGNSW director, Tuckson, AGNSW deputy director and William Boustead, AGNSW conservator; seeking information for Kupka].
25 Margaret Tuckson personal communication based on her agenda.
26 E.g. Carl Plate [Joslyn Plate interview 2004].
27 Robinson, R., *The shift of sands: an autobiography 1952–62*, Macmillan, South Melbourne, 1976, pp. 168, 173. For the Madonna see Kupka, K., *op. cit.* 1972, p. 52 and Flynn, F., 'Aboriginal Madonna and Native Art', in *Northern Gateway*, F.P. Leonard, Sydney, 1963, pp. 211–221. On Paris see Souëf, *op. cit.*, p. 10.
28 In a different view Arnhem Land residents were survivors, so to speak, not only of the paleolithic age, but also of visitations by the Macassans, the Japanese, the Anglo-Australians, etc., see Poignant, R., *Encounter at Nagalarramba*, National Library of

both in Canberra. Kupka insisted on the fact that Arnhem Land artists were contemporary fellow human beings, not people immobilised by their cultural past.[28] With the publication of his thesis in 1972, recognition for these meticulously documented collections was due. Had Karel Kupka not been reproached by Stanner and McCarthy, acting on behalf of his Australian sponsors, and informally discredited by the Berndts, fellow anthropologist-collectors, and their circle, he might have participated more fully in the renewed attention given to the art of Australia signalled in 1988 by *Dreamings*, the Asia Society's New York exhibition, tour and catalogue.[29]

Conclusion

Karel Kupka's publishing and collecting activities in the late 1950s and early 1960s changed the attitude of those collectors and professionals who knew about his commitment and assiduity. The Sydney Morning Herald's 1956 headline had warned of "A Parisian in Pursuit of our Aborigines' Art."[30] The collector Stuart Scougall suggested that "a mountain of material had already gone ...".[31] just as Kupka re-appeared in Australia to gather more for the enthusiastic museum in Basel. The example of a fit, mature and able enthusiast, devoted to art and keen to make a difference, was inspiring, in one way or another, to all who met Kupka. In retrospect his visits were salutary for Arnhem Land artists, their families and homelands. His contribution will stand as part of the history of the art of Arnhem Land, the "rising new industry" as he called it.[32] His care to document artists' names and stories was supplemented by his perceptive photography, and by his impact on individual artists, which will continue to augment biographies still being written.[33] As Breton rightly saw, referring to Kupka's collections for Basle, "Il éstime, à juste titre, que, de ce côté de la terre, un tel document vivant peut être encore – si tard qu'il soit – du plus grand prix, dans la mesure où, nous dénudant les racines de l'art plastique,

il ébauche en nous une certaine réconciliation de l'homme avec la nature et avec lui-même"[34] or, in the translation by John Ross "... a living document of this order can be of the highest value, for, by laying bare to us the roots of the plastic arts, it helps us to reconcile man with nature and himself."[35]

Australia, Canberra, 1996, p. 4. [Early history of Maningrida and district].
29 Jones, Ph., 'Perceptions of Aboriginal art: a history', in Sutton, P. (ed.), *Dreamings: The Art of Aboriginal Australia*, Braziller/Asia Society Galleries, New York, 1988, p 171.
30 A Staff Correspondent (Paul Haefliger?), 'A Parisian in pursuit of our Aborigines art', *The Sydney Morning Herald* 15 November 1956, p. 2 [one photograph; Kupka knew Haefliger, a German-born painter and art critic of the Herald from 1941 to 1957, personally and also quotes from his articles of 1941/42. See Haefliger, P., 'Australian Aboriginal bainting on bark from Arnhem Land', in *Art in Australia*, March-May 1941, pp. 33–36 and June-August 1942, pp. 67–70, see Kupka, *op. cit.*, 1972, p. 29, note 62.]
31 Scougall, S., 'Thoughts on Aboriginal art', *Art Gallery of New South Wales Quarterly* 1 (4), July 1960, p. 3
32 Kupka, K., *Dawn of art: painting and sculpture of Australian Aborigines*, Angus and Robertson, Sydney, Viking Press, New York, 1965, p. 90.
33 Mundine, D., 'The native born', in *The native born: objects and representations from Ramingining, Arnhem Land*, Museum of Contemporary Art, Sydney, n.d. (1997), pp. 65, 69–73. [Importance of Alan Fidock as agent crucial to Kupka, Tuckson, Scougall, Ruhe and Allen's collecting at Milingimbi. Gives a Poignant-Kupka link]; Taylor, L., Seeing the inside: bark painting in western Arnhem Land, Clarendon Press, Oxford, 1996, pp. 35, 44–45, 138, 224.
34 Kupka K., *op. cit.*, 1962, p. 11.
35 Breton, André, translation by John Ross in Kupka, K., *op. cit.*, 1965, p. 9.

Kunst der Uraustralier
Works from eastern Arnhem Land
Special exhibition
Museum für Völkerkunde
und Schweizerisches Museum
für Volkskunde Basel, 1958

Painter unknown
Head of a female buffalo
1960, Maningrida
Sculpture, wood, L. 36.5 cm

Painter unknown
Head of a male buffalo
1960, Maningrida
Sculpture, wood, L. 34.0 cm

«rarrk»

Painter unknown
Crocodile
1960, Maningrida
Sculpture, wood, L. 88.5 cm

Painter unknown
Crocodile (underside)
1960, Maningrida
Sculpture, wood, L. 86.0 cm

Painter unknown
Echidna
before 1931, East Arnhem Land
Sculpture, wood, L. 81.0 cm,
Collection T.T. Webb

Painter unknown
Macassan pipe
1960, Maningrida
Sculpture, wood, L. 66.0 cm

Painter unknown
Kangaroo
before 1931
120.0 x 50.0 cm
Collection E. Handschin

«rarrk»

Painter unknown
Goanna
before 1960, Oenpelli
73.0 x 35.0 cm

Painter unknown
Stingray
before 1959, Oenpelli
74.0 x 36.0 cm

«rarrk»

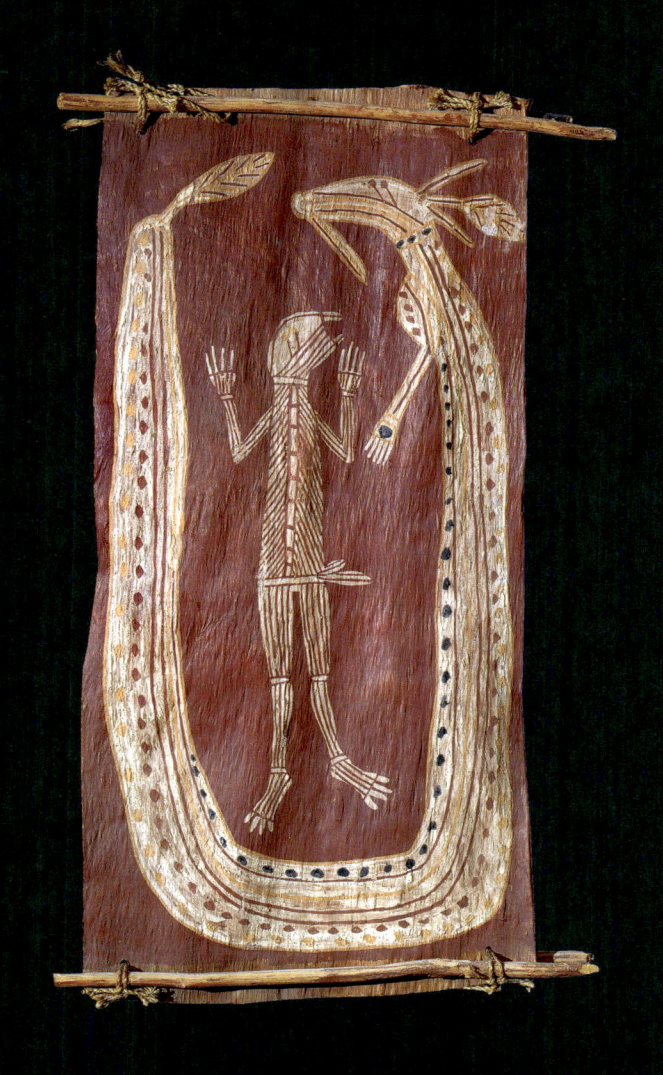

Peter Balmonidbal
Ngalyod, rainbow serpent,
with male figure
before 1975, East Alligator River
86.0 x 42.0 cm
Collection R. Sak

Djambalulu
Miliyara-corroboree,
dance of the white duck
1960, Croker Island
50.0 x 55.0 cm

Wumara
Copulating couple
1960, Oenpelli
68.0 x 34.0 cm

Wumara
Namarrkon, lightning spirit
1960, Oenpelli
61.5 x 44.0 cm

Marboa
Female figure
1960, Oenpelli
71.0 x 32.5 cm

Marboa
Freshwater turtle
1960, Oenpelli
54.0 x 46.0 cm

«rarrk»

Narlingmag
Crocodile
before 1960, Oenpelli
94.0 x 49.0 cm

Narlingmag (ascribed to)
Rayfish
before 1960, Oenpelli
54.0 x 44.0 cm

«rarrk»

Nagordo
Two female mimih spirits
1960, Oenpelli
56.0 x 61.0 cm

Nagordo
Mother kangaroo
1960, Oenpelli
37.0 x 42.0 cm

«rarrk»

Nagordo
Four kangaroos
1960, Oenpelli
64.0 x 45.0 cm

Paddy Compass Namatbara
Three mimih figures,
two female and one male
1963, Croker Island
92.0 x 53.0 cm

Paddy Compass Namatbara
Representation of yam
for ceremony
1963, Croker Island
Sculpture, wood
L. 47.0 cm, Dm. 5.5 cm

Paddy Compass Namatbara
Two fighting mimih couples
1963, Croker Island
56.0 x 52.0 cm

«rarrk»

Billy Yirawala MBE
Human figure with ceremonial
body painting
1963, Croker Island
Sculpture, wood, 40.5 x 9.0 cm (Dm.)

Billy Yirawala MBE
Two mimih figures dancing
1960, Croker Island
64.0 x 33.5 cm

Billy Yirawala MBE
Two female mimih
and a kangaroo
1960, Croker Island
56.0 x 28.0 cm

«rarrk»

Billy Yirawala MBE
Malicious spirit in its cave
1960, Croker Island
76.0 x 51.0 cm

Billy Yirawala MBE
Three mimih figures,
one male and two female
1963, Croker Island
117.0 x 56.0 cm

Nangunyari-Namiridali
A mimih dance: hunting
the freshwater crocodile
1960, Croker Island
53.0 x 73.5 cm

Nangunyari-Namiridali
Mimih and crocodile
1963, Croker Island
74.0 x 26.0 cm

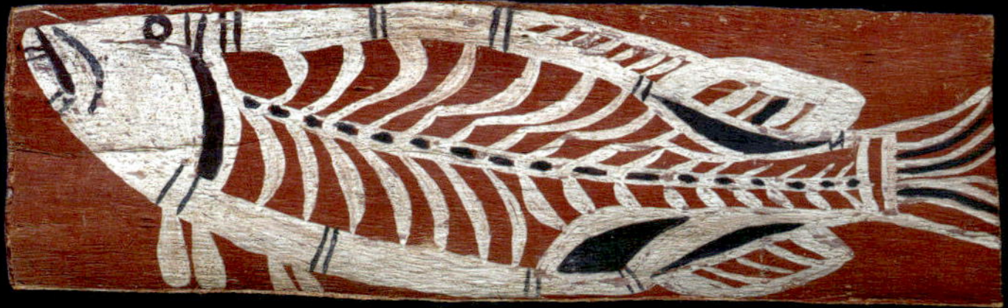

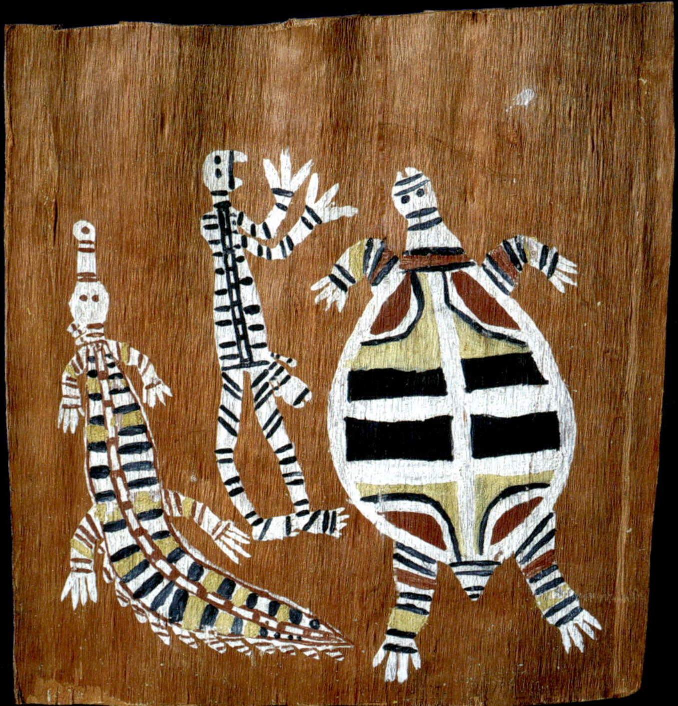

Nangunyari-Namiridali
Two couples of mimih figures
1960, Croker Island
53.0 x 73.0 cm

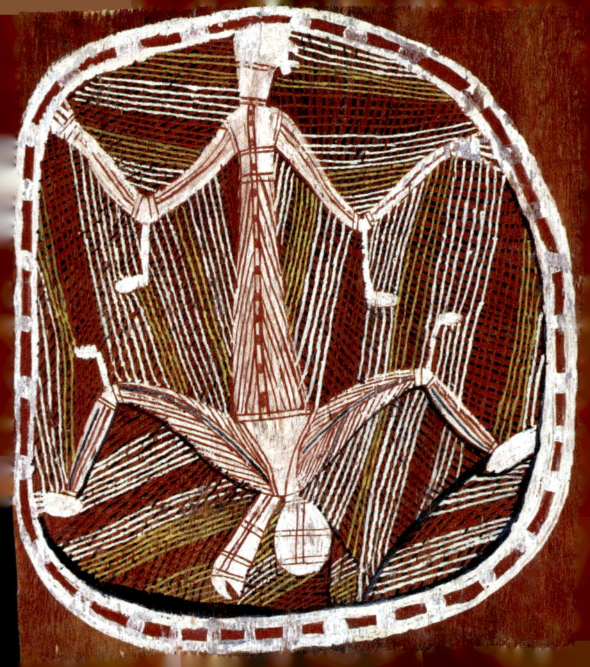

**Jimmy Midjawmidjaw
(ascribed to)**
Male thunder spirit
and crocodile
1963, Croker Island
70.0 x 60.0 cm

Jimmy Midjawmidjaw
Female namarrkon, lightning
spirit, and kangaroo
1960, Croker Island
62.0 x 92.0 cm

«rarrk»

Jimmy Midjawmidjaw
Female mam, evil spirit
1963, Croker Island
103.5 × 55.5 cm

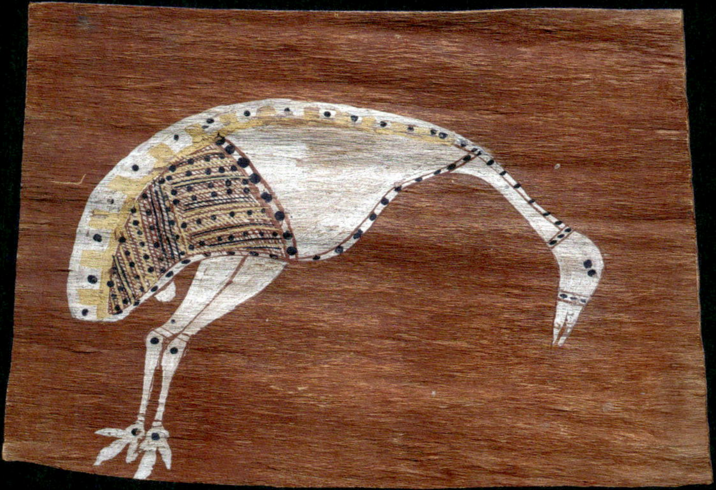

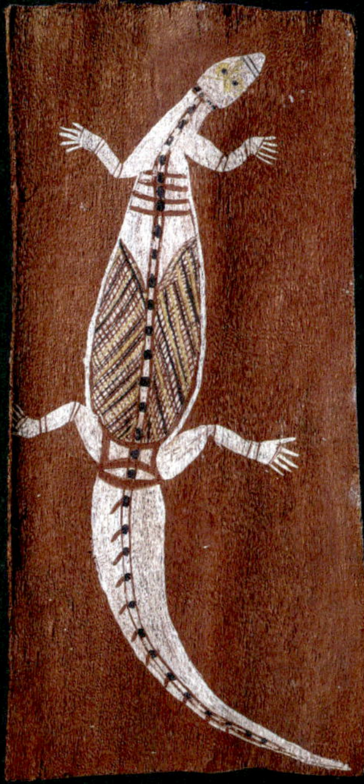

Jimmy Midjawmidjaw
Barramundi
1963, Croker Island
66.0 x 94.0 cm

Jimmy Midjawmidjaw
Inalats corroboree
1960, Croker Island
54.0 x 73.0 cm

Jimmy Midjawmidjaw
A schematic figure in the image of a
bone of Lumaluma, the mythical
creator of the Mardayin ceremony
1963, Croker Island
Sculpture, wood, 79.0 x 12.5 x 9.5 cm

«rarrk»

Aboriginal art from Arnhem Land – why in Basel?

Christian Kaufmann

How did it happen that the City of Basel with its magnificent public collection of paintings ranging from the old masters and including works by Konrad Witz and the Holbeins, to representatives of modern art came into possession of one the most significant collections of artworks from Arnhem Land? The story goes back to the early 1950s when Alfred Bühler, director of the Basel Museum für Völkerkunde (Museum of Ethnology) and professor of anthropology at the University of Basel commissioned the dedicated and talented Karel Kupka to assemble for the museum a collection of paintings and other objects of artistic interest in Arnhem Land. This must have been somewhere around 1955. But why Kupka and why precisely at this moment? One possible explanation is that Kupka impressed Bühler with his documentation on Aboriginal painting which he had compiled during his first visit to Australia. At that time the Basel museum had in stock only six bark paintings from northern Australia; four of them had been brought back from an expedition by the Basel entomologist Eduard Handschin in 1931 and one painting had been donated by the missionary T.T. Webb shortly afterwards. By adding objects and artifacts from new and different regions to the Basel Oceania collection Bühler hoped to expand the museum's rather limited horizon beyond the narrow confines of ethnology. The year before, Alfred Bühler, together with the Swiss ethnologist Paul Wirz, had put on an exhibition under the heading *Kunst vom Sepik* (Art from the Sepik) that proved a success and received a considerable amount of attention. With this exhibition Bühler succeeded in highlighting and placing a new emphasis on Oceanic art, the foundations of which had been laid by Felix Speiser, Bühler's predecessor at the museum and at the university, in the course of the 1930s and culminating in the trend-setting exhibition *Kunststile in der Südsee* (Art styles in the South Seas) back in 1941.¹

In 1950, Georg Schmidt, then director of the Basel Kunstmuseum (Museum of Art), joined the administrative committee of the Museum of Ethnology. Whilst he was still director of the Gewerbemuseum (Museum of Arts and Crafts), Georg Schmidt and Felix Speiser and his team had, in 1931 and 1933, put on the first monographic exhibitions on art traditions in New Guinea and the Solomon Islands. Both events made a lasting impression on the Basel public. Thus, Karel Kupka's commission to assemble a collection of artworks including anthropological documentation proves to be nothing less than the logical continuation of an earlier tradition. The fact that at the time of Kupka's first commission in the mid-fifties there was an especially lively interest in non-European art in the Basel scene – for instance on the part of the Group 33 and Group 48 artists – gave the venture an additional boost. The project was, for those days, an extremely costly affair – it exceeded the annual salary of the director of the museum – so it was helpful that the chairman of the museum's supervisory commission, that was responsible for the funding of the project, was the businessman J. R. Belmont who himself was an eminent collector of Indian art.²

Collecting art for presenting art

The commission Karel Kupka received from the Basel museum to collect works of art from Arnhem Land can be regarded as the foundation stone of the present exhibition project. Collecting art in this manner reflects two paths of development in terms of content and in relation to the era in which it occurred. The first trajectory refers to an expansion of the European concept of art through the inclusion of non-European forms of expression, mainly by presenting them in museums where they could be seen for the first time by a European public. The second path, at the other end of the scale so to speak, relates to the further step in the process of opening up the world of the Aboriginals to non-Aboriginals through collecting and learning more about their art. As the exhibition *Crossing Country* in the Art Gallery of New South Wales in Sydney in 2004 documented, a large majority of objects from western Arnhem Land that found their way to the museums from 1912 onwards was knowingly shown to, or purposely produced for, anthropologists and collectors who visited the region. The story runs along similar lines in the case of the anthropologists who came later such as A.P. Elkin, Ch. Mountford and Ronald and Catherine Berndt and the same can be said for the 'discovery' of Aboriginal art by the Australian museums and art galleries between 1956 and 1964.³

Kupka made several trips to Arnhem Land. The first visit in 1956 took him to eastern Arnhem Land with its centres in Yirrkala and on Elcho Island; later, in 1960/61 and 1963/64, he travelled to central Arnhem Land, the main station of which was located in Milingimbi on Milingimbi Island, and then on to the territory of the Gunwinngu (now Kunwinjku) to the west. The territory's main station at that time was based at the mission school on Croker Island which is even further out to the west, with a second station based inland in Oenpelli (Kunbarllanja). Maningrida had just been established as an outpost. His journeys took place at a time when the missionary societies in the area were trying to create income opportunities for the Aborigi-

---

1 Wirz, P., *Kunstwerke vom Sepik*, Sonderausstellung, Museum für Völkerkunde und Schweizerisches Museum für Volkskunde Basel 1954; Speiser, F., *Kunststile in der Südsee, dargestellt aus den Beständen des Museums für Völkerkunde*, Gewerbemuseum Basel, 1941.

2 The purchase of the collection was concluded under certain financial conditions in June 1957, while the contract itself was validated in March 1958, Sammlungsakten Museum der Kulturen zu Einlauf V 0292, 1957. The purchase of the 1961 collection was not finalised until 29 March 1965; Sammlungsakten Museum der Kulturen zu Einlauf V 0312, 1964. The correspondence between Kupka and Bühler, as far as it in the records, indicates a relationship of astonishing mutual trust.

3 Tuckson, A., 'Aboriginal Art and the Western World', in Berndt, R. (ed.), *Australian Aboriginal art*, London and New York, 1964, pp. 60–68; Morphy, H., 'Seeing Aboriginal art in the gallery', *Humanities Research* 8 (1), Canberra, 2001, pp. 37–50; Miller, S., 'Select chronology', in Perkins, H. (ed.), *Crossing Country*, Art Gallery of New South Wales, Sydney, 2004, pp. 211–215.

Unknown artist
Kangaroo, before 1931
120.0 x 50.0 cm

nals. While the collectors who had visited Arnhem Land immediately prior to Kupka were interested in the artworks mainly as objects of ethnographic record, Kupka was intent on discovering and learning something about the creative personality and individuality of the artists he met. In the course of his stays he not only found artists who were willing to assist him in his work, he also made friends with many of them. Not only was he able to get the names of most of the artists whose works he bought, he was often also given the story behind the themes of the paintings.[4] In some cases Kupka recorded the story on paper or at least he wrote down a brief summary. These were often clan-related narratives describing events during the age of creation, the so-called Dreamings [Abbildungen Kupka, Midjawmidjaw …]. Especially in Yirrkala and Milingimbi, Kupka accompanied the artists when they were busy preparing a new painting or he joined them during feasts and ceremonies. When he left in 1963, the artists on Croker Island organised a special, initiation-like ceremony for him.[5]

One trait that several collectors of Aboriginal art in the 1950s and early 1960s had in common was their closeness to individual artists or groups of artists in Paris, Sydney or Basel. Alfred Bühler, for instance, saw in the capacity of human beings to express themselves artistically a basic achievement available as a potential in mankind as such. He shared this conviction in Basel with Georg Schmidt. The two of them organised shows that were designed to differ markedly from ordinary ethnographic exhibitions. They did this as a token of their esteem for the creativity of the artists living and working in distant and foreign parts of the world, and in order to allow an artwork to speak for itself and to give its form-giving force the chance to express itself.

When there was not enough room in the Museum of Ethnology for their exhibitions they moved to other locations, for instance to the Museum of Arts and Crafts, to the Basel Kunsthalle (in 1962 for a comprehensive exhibition on art in New Guinea), or, on a later occasion, to the Basel Museum of Art itself.

Between 1954 and 1960 Bühler put on a whole sequence of innovative art exhibitions. Following *Heilige Bildwerke aus Nord-Neuguinea* (Sacred paintings from Northern New Guinea) in 1958 he staged an exhibition under the heading *Kunst der Uraustralier* (Art of the Earliest Australians) where the first part of the Kupka collection was exhibited. The series ended with *Kunststile vom Sepik* (Art styles of the Sepik) that included the findings of the latest research projects of the time.

Up to 1960, all the special shows and the new permanent exhibition were designed and installed by graphic designers who, in their main profession, worked as teachers in various subjects at the School of Arts and Crafts, now renamed University of Art and Design. The guiding principle for mounting the works on display was easy readability. This was effected by developing a clear-cut spatial order and an almost typographically strict grouping of object series, which, in turn, were supplemented by short commentaries in large lettering and visual media such as field photographs and maps.

The lighting – spotlights had not yet been introduced – was designed to be regular and neutral in order to avoid any form of distractive dramatisation. The filtered light of fluorescent lamps in daylight quality proved to be almost ideal. The walls of the exhibition hall were covered with so-called Kocher-canvas (i.e. unbleached canvas panels) similar to the fabric covering the walls of the rooms in the Basel Museum

Jimmy Midjawmidjaw
Frontispiece to *Un art à l'état brut*
Éditions Clairefontaine
Lausanne, 1962
(Photo Karel Kupka, 1960)

Jimmy Midjawmidjaw
Namarrkon, lightning spirit, 1960
70.0 × 60.0 cm
(see also p. 216)

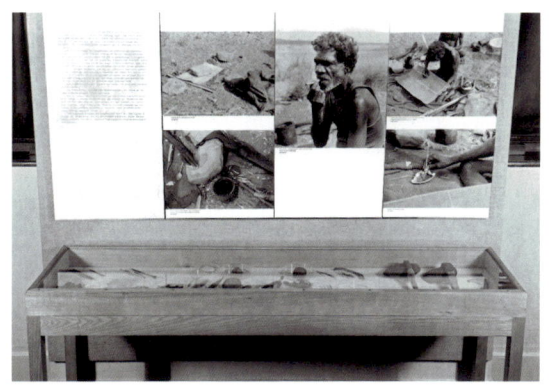

Kunst der Uraustralier
Special exhibition, Museum für Völkerkunde und Schweizerisches Museum für Volkskunde Basel
14 June to 31 August 1958

4 When working in an oral culture where terms and names are not held in writing, the spelling of names is often confusing for outsiders, even the spelling of one and the same name varies at times. We have tried to adapt Kupka's spelling to the current standard Australian form.
5 Kupka, K., *Peintres Aborigènes d'Australie*, Publications de la Société des Océanistes No. 24, Musée de l'Homme, Paris, 1972, p. 74, note.

6 This was Bühler's doctrine as he taught it in courses and seminars on museology at the University of Basel between 1960 and 1965.

7 The extension included, the exhibition was on from 14 June until 30 September 1958. The reviews by Maria Netter (m.n.) in the journal *Werk*, No. 8, 1958, by jpb. in the Basler *National-Zeitung*, No. 270 of 16 June 1958, by gb in the *Basler Nachrichten*, Vol. 114, No. 246 of 16 June 1958 as well as by H. Walter in *L'Alsace*, Vol. 14., No. 189 of 14 August 1958 all remark that the art aspect took centre stage in the exhibition. Only E. Briner (nr) in the *Neuen Zürcher Zeitung*, No. 1966 of 4 July 1958 noted a certain distance by emphasizing the ethnographic and craft aspects along with the artistic properties of the works on display.

8 Later renamed Musée National des Arts d'Afrique et d'Océanie (MNAAO). We are grateful to Philippe Peltier for the following information: On his fourth trip to Arnhem Land in 1963, Karel Kupka put together one last collection. When he got home, it was divided up between several cities: Canberra, Paris, and following an exchange, Basel. This dispersion is explained by the fact that Kupka had several sources of funding: in France, the Centre National de la Recherche Scientifique and support from the young Musée des arts africains et océaniens, whose Oceania department was headed by Professor Jean Guiart; in Australia, he enjoyed the support of the AIAS and Professor A.P. Elkin. The Paris collection – formerly held in the Musée des Arts d'Afrique et d'Océanie and recently transferred to the Musée du quai Branly – numbers 255 paintings and sculptures, to which must be added a donation of 55 paintings, made a short time later, from Kupka's 'personal collection'. While the Paris collection, in comparison with the one in Basel, is not the most important in terms of size, it is significant from the viewpoint of the history of its constitution. As the starting point of Kupka's thesis, which he defended in 1969, it was composed to substantiate an innovative approach to painters and their status and role in society. With the exception of a few works from Yirrkala (9 paintings) and Groote Eylandt (10 works), the main corpus of the collection comes from Croker Island, Milingimbi and Maningrida. Kupka focuses on these three production centres. While the names of forty-five artists are listed, the figure is deceptive. Some artists are represented by only one piece,

of Art. The showcases and glass display cabinets were designed to be as simple and uniform as possible so as not to distract the viewer and in order to give him an unrestricted view of the objects and the photographs showing the artists at work, thus allowing the viewer to retrace the actual encounter and the act of observing in the field.⁶

The exhibition of the first Kupka collection met these specifications almost perfectly. It was designed by Rudolf Hanhart who later became the director of the Kunstmuseum St. Gallen (Art Museum of St. Gallen) and head of the anthropological department there. The exhibition made it evident that there was too little room at the Museum of Ethnology for an exhibition of this kind and that the cramped spatial conditions greatly diminished the effect of the works on display. Nevertheless, the novelty of the event attracted a surprisingly large audience so that the exhibition had to be extended by four weeks.⁷ A short guide with a text by Karel Kupka, a preface by Alfred Bühler and six black-and-white photographs gave a good, though rather sober introduction to the forms and contexts of this art.

Unfortunately the Basel Kupka collection, which by 1964 had grown to include 398 objects, has never been shown in full up to this day. Until his premature death in 1993, Kupka dreamt of having a separate room at the museum where his collection could be shown in its full extent, in a similar way to the display at the Musée des arts africains et océaniens in Paris.⁸ Some of his pieces were shown in the exhibition on Oceanic art at the Basel Museum of Art in 1980 where they attracted considerable attention. A few pieces were incorporated in the permanent Oceania exhibition of the Museum of Ethnology where they were on display from 1985 to 2001, including the *Namarrkon* painting of 1960 by Jimmy Midjawmidjaw.

From the late 1970s on, the political aspects of Indigenous art in Australia moved to the foreground and the people's relationship to their land and its spiritual significance became ever more important, both for the individual Aboriginal and the communities as such.

This aspect comes out very clearly in the works collected by Kupka, so it came as no surprise that Ingrid Heermann asked for some of the pieces as loans for her exhibition *Gemaltes Land – Kunst der Aborigines* in Stuttgart; a number of other works from the Kupka collection were also shown at exhibitions in Canberra and Sydney.⁹

It is also worth mentioning that the objects in Kupka's collection have also posed a problem and a challenge in terms of physical conservation. A pioneer in this respect was Denis Guillemard in Paris who not only pointed out the technical aspects of conservation and developed appropriate methods but also raised basic questions concerning professional ethics in this context. These always sharply move into focus when one faces the task of conserving and restoring paintings that originally served to be mere glimpses of a representation.¹⁰

Outside the museums there were private collectors in and around Basel who collected Aboriginal works of art. The people at the museum got to know several of them in the course of time; some own valuable treasures as, for example, a painting from western Arnhem Land from the post-Kupka era showing a kangaroo.¹¹

Mediating art

*This point can never be overstressed: only through the gateway of emotion can one reach the royal road; otherwise the ways of learning can lead one nowhere.*¹²

In a first step André Breton repeats in his introduction to Karel Kupka's book a dogma of the surrealist movement. He goes on to cap it by observing that often the incidentals become the main issue.

Exhibition catalogue
Kunst der Uraustralier
Museum für Völkerkunde
Basel, 1958
(see pp. 190 and 217)

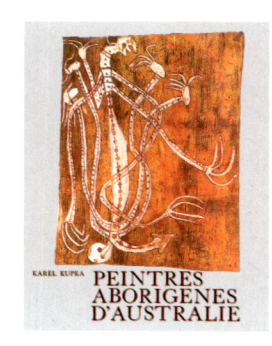

Publication by Karel Kupka
Peintres Aborigènes d'Australie
Musée de l'Homme
Paris, 1972

Dick Ngulungulei Murramurra (ascribed to)
Kangaroo, early 70s
122.5 x 49.5 cm

As discreet as the mimih spirits of Australian myth, who at the slightest alert breathe on a crack in the rock until it opens to let them pass, they play on the ephemeral and work by enchantment.[13]

In a reverse line of thought Breton then leaves magic behind and emphasizes quite a different aspect: *This is where Karel Kupka leads us, in showing the rise of works which he watches and studies for us from the very first moment of their conception. A searchlight, not a spotlight, has to be turned on the initial network of lines which, according to the decision of the artist and the artist alone, will serve to express, say, fire, the tangle of seaweed or a comb of wild honey. We are here at the source of conceptual representation; …*

And carries on:
… our epoch is slowly becoming aware that this is disdainfully independent of perceptual representation.[14]

In regard to the era that these lines were written, i.e. the early sixties, this statement is highly relevant: it bespeaks the rediscovery and the enhancement of the conceptual moment in art. Karel Kupka's expertly illustrated book successfully promoted the art of Arnhem Land beyond the narrow limits of anthropology. Bühler and Elkin, both anthropologists, were well aware of this as the prefaces to the French and English editions go to show. Bühler acknowledges Kupka's achievement of successfully integrating different perspectives to form a synthesis: on the one hand the view of the committed collector and observer, on the other, that of the artist who, by communicating closely with the painters who, he believed, were akin to him, is able to elicit more and different aspects than his academic counterpart.[15]

Following the success of the exhibition in 1958, Kupka's book *Un art à l'état brut* (1962) attained a broad readership thanks to the commitment and the support of the Guilde du livre and the Éditions Clairefontaine respectively. The first edition by the Guilde du livre amounted to 10,000 numbered copies, as well as a smaller book-sale edition. The book included illustrations of works from the two Basel collections (1956 and 1960). The enthusiasm the book generated amongst its readers was certainly partly due to Kupka's affinity to the exploration of rock art, which was attracting a lot of interest and attention in Europe at the time. When going through the book the reader was taken back in time, so to speak, and given the impression he was looking over the shoulder of a fellow contemporary and watching him paint, although the cultural roots of these 'contemporaries' – the true heirs of rock painting – go back far in time, to an age somewhere between the Mesolithic and the Palaeolithic. In terms of cultural history this linkage was quite a bold statement but it bothered only a few, not least because Kupka, now the true anthropologist, was able to show and explain the entire range of forms of artistic expression in northern Australia. In his descriptions Kupka conveyed the impression that painting as such was embodied in corporeal structures, not only where actual body painting was concerned but also when applying paint to sculptures. At the same time Kupka also referred to the circumstance that the barks which serve as painting surface never can be as flat and even as a primed canvas. Kupka also rightly pointed out that not only the painters' traditions and themes but also the act of painting itself was subject to an ongoing process of change. Through observations like this Kupka was able to phase down any form of anthropological speculation concerning the pre-figuration of eternally valid forms of cultural expression and values by depriving it of its empirical foundation. Such observations indicate Kupka's deeper insight into, and understanding of, the social contexts he was working in and which motivated him to carry on with his studies. He continued his research and later published a book titled *Les peintres aborigènes en Australie,* which, however, included only a few of his newer findings.

Unfortunately Kupka produced only an English translation of *Un art à l'état brut*;[16] his *Les peintres aborigènes en Australie* was never translated into English and neither book was ever published in German. Alfred Bühler's original introduction to the French edition was replaced by a preface by A. P. Elkin, Kupka's second important mentor – the reasons for this are discussed in Richard McMillan's contribution to the catalogue (see pp. 193–197). Elkin praised Kupka's book just as Bühler had done before. The gap between art history and anthropology only started to grow larger in the course of the decades that followed, when anthropology shifted its focus to more basic social-scientific issues and fieldwork became paramount as the foundation of anthropological knowledge and reflection.

New perspectives: change instead of fostering tradition

The present Mawurndjul exhibition, nearly fifty years after Kupka set out on his first collecting tour, is dedicated for the first time to the work of a single artist from western Arnhem Land and hence continues an old Basel tradition in a new form. Concentrating on the biography and work history of an individual artist replaces an earlier form of exhibiting where usually more attention was given to the general ethnographic background with the purpose of gaining a better understanding by providing an as detailed as possible insight into the cultural context. Bühler's method of displaying artistic forms of expression in all their diversity and existential complexity was useful and informative at others by large series. Furthermore, a single subject (figures or myths) may be treated by several painters. The attention paid to three sites, to a few creators and, finally, to certain subjects, is not without intent. Kupka wanted to show that, in those times of sweeping social change and artistic production, they were indeed artists in the Western sense of the term, that is to say painters capable of interpreting myths, of expressing their judgment on a subject, whatever the constraints imposed by law or ritual. As he maintained, "the Aboriginal painter constructs his own pictural architecture which is personal and totally subjective. It is not his intention to describe the way things look but to express his judgment, and that is why he transforms them so freely." This idea, which was novel at the time, was based on an acute sense of observation and many discussions with the painters. Recent developments in Australian painting show that it was well founded.

9 Heermann, I. and Menter, U., *Gemaltes Land: Kunst der Aborigines aus Arnhemland*, Linden-Museum Stuttgart, Dietrich Reimer Verlag, Berlin, 1994, Cat. Nos. 4–6, 21–25, 73–75, 94–95, 98; Lüthi, B. (ed.), *Aratjara – art of the First Australians*, Kunstmuseum des Landes Nordrhein-Westfalen, Düsseldorf, 1993; Caruana, W. and Lendon, N. (eds.), *The painters of the Wagilag Sisters story 1937–1997*, National Gallery of Australia, Canberra, 1997 (Wawilak Sisters), Cat. Nos. 3, 10, 52; Perkins, H. (ed.), *op.cit.*, 2004, pp. 24, 54, 227, 228, 331 figs.

10 Guillemard, D., *La conservation preventive: une alternative à la restauration des objets ethnographiques*, thèse de doctorat, Paris, 1995, Presses universitaires du Septentrion, Villeneuve d'Ascq, 2000.

11 In the ownership of Ulla Dreyfus. After comparing it with a painting from the Linden-Museum in Stuttgart and a number of paintings that were shown in the exhibition *Crossing Country* in 2004 the painting

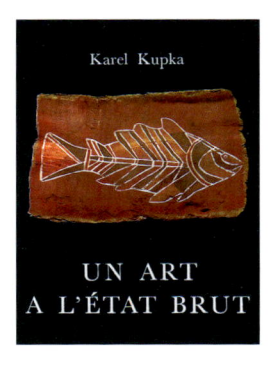

Un art à l'état brut
Karel Kupka
Éditions Clairefontaine
Lausanne, 1962

the time but today we need a more direct, face-to-face encounter with the artworks themselves and we need to know what our contemporaries – both in Europe and in Australia – read from these pictures and what they have to say to them. It is certainly useful to know something about the background of the artists and their families, where they come from, how they live, what troubles or pleases them and so forth. However, in my opinion it is more important to try and learn about the artist as a creative individual in, and through, the presence of his works and to explore the images he creates. Often, and rightly so, this poses a challenge to our inherited mode of viewing and seeing.

The anthropological practice of describing and explaining artistic forms of expression in association with the prevailing worldview of the respective culture was destined to raise suspicion among European art critics who tend to react to even the slightest hint of ideology by keeping their distance. This is especially the case in German-speaking countries. Taking into account their experience with totalitarian systems this is understandable but it is not really helpful in an intercultural approach to understanding art. For the anthropologist it is clear that art in any form, even if it wishes to be nothing but art, always contains a political reference, is always bound to the system of social orientation of the group in question. How this political moment takes stage varies from situation to situation. Gary Foley addresses several aspects of this issue in his review of Indigenous art in Australia during the last two decades (see pp. 185–188)

Faithful to the tradition of Kupka, the present catalogue includes a variety of views on, and approaches to, the art of John Mawurndjul and some of his predecessors. The various approaches, however, all share the same basic conviction that art unfolds a dynamics of its own through time. This is certainly also true for Arnhem Land where the development of art has gone through phases of acceleration alternating with times of retardation. At present we are witnessing a phase of rapid change. Paul Taçon discusses the dynamics of artistic formation in his article on the history of rock art through the ages and its various, at times overlapping, stages (see pp. 160–175).

Partly due to the lack of reliable and detailed information, the people in Europe up to the early 1980s looked upon the art of Arnhem Land as the continuation of an age-old, unchanging and unchangeable tradition – the art of the Primordial Australians. Today we know, at least in outline, more about the life histories of men such as John Mawurndjul, the members of his family and a number of earlier artists. Jon Altman and Luke Taylor contribute authentic descriptions of how, and under what conditions, John Mawurndjul grew up and how he became an acclaimed artist (see pp. 30–40 resp. 42–48). The artist is given a voice of his own in an interview with Apolline Kohen (see pp. 24–29). Taken all together the contributions present an exemplary commentary which, by explaining the past, highlights the path leading into the future. It makes you curious to know what lies in wait at the rock outcrop ahead or the next outstation.

The more we know about Arnhem Land and its peoples, the more the prejudiced views of the traditional way of life – the typical image of the hunter and gatherer shaped by his environment – become refuted, a different picture evolves showing Aboriginals successfully managing cultural contact situations and mediating between the Indigenous and the European worlds. Relationships of this kind go back as far as the year 1912 when, following a visit to western Arnhem Land by the Chief Protector of Aboriginals, Baldwin Spencer, Aboriginals around the cattle station of Oenpelli began producing bark paintings which they then sold and sent to Baldwin Spencer and the anthropological museum in Melbourne. This business-like relationship continued for several years.

The present exhibition in Basel attempts an approach which John Mawurndjul explicitly encouraged us to adopt: to contrast and compare selected earlier works from Kupka's western Arnhem Land by painters such as Jimmy Midjawmidjaw, Billy Yirawala and Paddy Compass Namatbara along with the paintings of John Mawurndjul himself. For this purpose, pieces from the Kupka collection are showcased in the rooms preceding the actual works of John Mawurndjul. For Mawurndjul himself this unique chance of comparing the two sets of works gives him the opportunity to reflect on the long road that has brought him here. By highlighting this development, his artistic accomplishment emerges with all the more lucidity. Mawurndjul's works are reviewed and discussed from different perspectives in the contributions by Judith Ryan (see pp. 64–68 resp. 176–180), Philippe Peltier (see pp. 155–158), Hans-Joachim Müller (see pp. 76–81) and Claus Volkenandt (pp. 181–184). After having learnt more about the paintings and different modes of seeing und appreciating them, we can return to the original paintings exhibited in their full corporeality. John Mawurndjul's paintings have outgrown the narrow confines of traditional lore, making way for new and surprising ways of looking at and seeing underlying relations and deeply-rooted linkages and giving the artist a distinctive profile of his own. Thus, under completely new and different circumstances, one of Karel Kupka's visions has come true at last, precisely in Basel: recognition of, and appreciation for, the entire work up to the present of an exceptional Arnhem Land artist in a European museum of art.

Appendix

List of exhibited works

© John Mawurndjul, courtesy Maningrida Arts & Culture

Bambil, echidna, and mimih, 1979
68.0 x 46.0 cm
Jon Altman
(Ill. p. 84)

Ngurrdu, emu, 1980
47.0 x 38.0 cm
Jon Altman
(Ill. p. 85)

Namarrkon, lightning spirit, 1979
96.0 x 57.7 cm
Museum and Art Gallery of the Northern Territory
Collection, Darwin, ABART 0751
(Ill. p. 86)

Ngalyod, rainbow serpent, at Dilebang, c. 1979
127.2 x 88.8 cm
National Gallery of Victoria, Melbourne, Australia
Gift of the Premier's Department, 1980, O.1-1980
(Ill. p. 87)

Lorrkkon, hollow log, 1980
93.5 x 24.5 cm
Peter Nahum at The Leicester Galleries, London
Courtesy Vivien Anderson Gallery, Melbourne, Australia
(Ill. p. 88)

Ngalyod, rainbow serpent, 1980
72.0 x 56.0 cm
Maningrida Arts & Culture, The Djómi Museum
(Ill. p. 89)

Namarrkon, female lightning spirit, 1981
c. 60.0 x 20.0 cm
Francesca Baas Becking
(Ill. p. 90)

Ngalyod, rainbow serpent, 1982
100.0 x 44.0 cm
Private collection
(Ill. p. 91)

Namarden, female lightning spirit, 1982
64.0 x 37.0 cm
Museum der Kulturen Basel,
Collection Marlies Staehelin, Va 1408
(Ill. p. 92)

Namarrkon ngal-daluk, female lightning spirit, 1983
136.9 x 40.4 cm
National Gallery of Victoria, Melbourne, Australia
Gift of Geoff and Janette Todd, 1992, O.37-1992
(Ill. p. 93)

Female lightning spirit, 1984
52.5 x 32.5 cm
Carrillo Gantner
(Ill. p. 94)

Ngalyod, rainbow serpent, devouring the yawkyawk girls, 1984
123.5 x 74.0 cm
National Gallery of Australia, Canberra, 84.1956
(Ill. p. 95)

Yawkyawk, young girl – water spirit, 1985
50.5 x 27.0 cm
Art Gallery of New South Wales, Sydney
Purchased 1985, 216.1985.1
(Ill. p. 96)

Yawkyawk, young girl – water spirit, 1985
115.0 x 60.0 cm
Art Gallery of New South Wales, Sydney
Purchased 1985, 216.1985.3
(Ill. p. 97)

Lorrkkon, hollow log, c. 1986
224.5 x 16.0 cm
Art Gallery of New South Wales, Sydney
Purchased 1986, 243.1986
(Ill. p. 98)

Ancestral spirit beings collecting honey, 1985–87
110.5 x 61.0 cm
Museum of Contemporary Art, Sydney and Maningrida Arts & Culture with financial assistance from the Aboriginal and Torres Strait Islander Board of the Australia Council, 1994.346
(Ill. p. 99)

Yawkyawk spirits: the site at Kudjarnngal, 1988
106.0 x 64.0 cm
National Gallery of Australia, Canberra, 88.1541
(Ill. p. 100)

Yawkyawk spirits: waterholes at Kudjarnngal, 1988
104.5 x 51.0 cm
National Gallery of Australia, Canberra, 88.1540
(Ill. p. 101)

Nawarramulmul, shooting star spirit, 1988
219.4 x 95.0 cm
Museum of Contemporary Art, Sydney
Purchased with funds donated by
Mr and Mrs Jim Bain, 1989, 1989.2
(Ill. p. 102)

Ngarrt, short-necked turtle, with its eggs, 1989
213.0 x 96.0 cm
Peter Nahum at The Leicester Galleries, London
Courtesy Vivien Anderson Gallery, Melbourne, Australia
(Ill. p. 103)

Mimih at Milmilngkan, 1989
249.0 x 95.0 cm
Art Gallery of New South Wales, Sydney
Purchased 2002, 98.2002
(Ill. p. 104)

Namorrorddo, shooting star spirit, at Mankorlod, 1990
241.0 x 116.3 cm
National Gallery of Victoria, Melbourne, Australia
Purchased from Admission Funds, 1990, O.154-1990
(Ill. p. 105)

Yawkyawk, young girl – water spirit,
late 80s
164.0 x 69.0 cm
Collection Annandale Galleries, Sydney, Australia
(Ill. p. 106)

Buluwana, female ancestor, 1989
261.0 x 77.6 cm
Prof. Roger Benjamin & Ms. Kate Sands
(Ill. p. 107)

Kakodbebuldi, 1990
179.3 x 91.8 cm
National Gallery of Victoria, Melbourne, Australia
Purchased from Admission Funds, 1990
O.133-1990
(Ill. p. 108)

Rainbow serpent's antilopine kangaroo, 1991
189.0 x 94.0 cm
National Gallery of Australia, Canberra, 91.874
(Ill. p. 109)

Creator spirit, 1994
c. 240.0 x 86.0 cm (Dm.)
Groninger Museum, Groningen, 1995.0257
(Ill. p. 110)

Lorrkkon, hollow log, 1994
249.0 x 16.0 cm
Groninger Museum, Groningen, 1995.0256
(Ill. p. 111)

River whale shark, 1989
233.0 x 19.5 x 23.0 cm
On loan from the Australian National Maritime Museum, Sydney
00005795
(Ill. p. 112)

Mimih spirit, 1992
250.0 x 11.0 x 11.0 cm
Art Gallery of South Australia, Adelaide
Gift of the Friends of the Art Gallery of South Australia, 1993, 933S5
(Ill. p. 113)

Billabong at Milmilngkan, 1993
175.0 x 49.0 cm
Aimé & Jacqueline Proost Collection
(Ill. p. 114)

Mardayin design, 1993
152.0 x 74.0 cm
Aimé & Jacqueline Proost Collection
(Ill. p. 115)

Djatti, frogs, 1993
175.0 x 49.0 cm
Aimé & Jacqueline Proost Collection
(Ill. p. 116)

Buluwana, female ancestor, at Dilebang, 1993
174.0 x 74.0 cm
Aimé & Jacqueline Proost Collection
(Ill. p. 117)

Kunmadj, dilly bag, 1996
112.5 × 59.5 cm
Private collection, Paris
(Ill. p. 118)

Mimih spirits as dreaming beings under a rock at Ngandarrayo, 1994
86.5 × 40.0 cm
Sprengel Museum Hannover
(Ill. p. 119)

Ngalyod and the creation of sites at Kakodbebuldi, 1994
191.0 × 68.0 cm
Sprengel Museum Hannover
(Ill. p. 120)

Nadulmi, the rainbow serpent's pet antilopine kangaroo, 1995
197.0 × 74.0 cm
Sprengel Museum Hannover
(Ill. p. 121)

Wayuk, waterlily, at Dilebang, c. 1990
69.7 × 44.0 cm
Private collection
(Ill. p. 122)

Ngaldadmurrng, saratoga, 1997
189.0 × 89.0 cm
Reg & Sheila Smith, Sydney, Australia
(Ill. p. 123)

Mardayin ceremony, Theme 1, 1997
134.5 × 73.5 cm
Collection Annandale Galleries, Sydney, Australia
(Ill. p. 124)

Crow from Kurrurldul, Mardayin ceremony, Theme 4, 1997
154.0 × 81.0 cm
Laverty Collection, Sydney, ID 891
(Ill. p. 125)

Yawkyawk at Dilebang, 1997
194.0 × 19.0 × 16.0 cm
National Gallery of Victoria, Melbourne, Australia
Purchased, 1998, 1998.346
(Ill. p. 126)

Yingarna, mother of the rainbow serpent, 1997
183.0 × 82.5 cm
National Gallery of Victoria, Melbourne, Australia
Purchased, 1997, 1997.401
(Ill. p. 127)

Ngalyod, rainbow serpent, 1999
156.0 × 81.0 cm
Robert McG. Lilley
(Ill. p. 128)

Ngalyod, rainbow serpent, 1999
153.0 × 90.0 cm
L. A. Moran Collection
(Ill. p. 129)

Dilly bag, 1996
57.0 × 30.0 cm
The Ian Munro Collection
(Ill. p. 130)

Barramundi and catfish, 1997
79.5 × 63.0 cm
The University of Sydney Union Art Collection, 97/8
(Ill. p. 131)

Mardayin at Mukkamukka, late 90s
168.0 × 95.0 cm
Museum and Art Gallery of the Northern Territory Collection, Darwin, ABART 1624
(Ill. p. 132)

Mardayin ceremony, 2000
170.0 × 78.0 cm
Art Gallery of New South Wales, Sydney
Don Mitchell Bequest Fund 2000, 538.2000
(Ill. p. 133)

Mardayin at Kakodbebuldi, 2000
157.0 × 66.0 cm
Laverty Collection, Sydney, ID 1281
(Ill. p. 134)

Mardayin ceremony, 1999
153.0 × 88.0 cm
Laverty Collection, Sydney, ID 1170
(Ill. p. 135)

Turtle, 2000
153.0 × 65.0/73.0 cm
Collection of Gillian & Roderick Deane
(Ill. p. 136)

Mardayin at Mumeka, 2001
168.0 × 63.0 cm
Private collection, Paris
(Ill. p. 137)

Namarrkon, lightning spirit, 2000
58.0 × 23.0 cm
Private collection, Maningrida
(Ill. p. 138)

Lorrkkon, hollow log, 2001
148.5 × 14.0 cm
Beat Knoblauch, Sydney
(Ill. p. 139)

Two fish, 2002
67.0 × 58.0 cm
Jon Altman
(Ill. p. 140)

Buluwana, female ancestor, 2001
200.0 × 59.0 cm
Laverty Collection, Sydney, ID 1865
(Ill. p. 141)

Billabong at Milmilngkan, 2002
108.5 × 36.5 cm
National Gallery of Victoria, Melbourne, Australia
Presented through the NGV Foundation in memory of Axel Poignant by an anonymous donor, 2003
2003.170
(Ill. p. 142)

Billabong at Milmilngkan, 2002
186.0 × 78.5 cm
Art Gallery of South Australia, Adelaide
Santos Fund for Aboriginal Art 2003, 20032P6
(Ill. p. 143)

Mardayin design at Kakodbebuldi, 2002
172.5 × 69.0 cm
Laverty Collection, Sydney, ID 1698
(Ill. p. 144)

Mardayin at Kudjarnngal, 2003
152.5 × 76.0 cm
National Gallery of Victoria, Melbourne, Australia
Presented through the NGV Foundation by Anita Castan, Governor, Nellie Castan, Governor, Judith and Leon Gorr, and Ricci Swart, 2003, 2003.663. The Clemenger Award for Contemporary Art, 2003
(Ill. p. 145)

Mardayin at Dilebang, 2003
131.6 × 63.0 cm
National Gallery of Victoria, Melbourne, Australia
Presented through the NGV Foundation by Greg Rosshandler, 2003, 2003.662
(Ill. p. 146)

Mardayin design at Dilebang, 2003
212.5 × 108.5
National Gallery of Victoria, Melbourne, Australia
Presented through the NGV Foundation by Anita Castan, Governor, Nellie Castan, Governor, Judith and Leon Gorr, and Ricci Swart, 2003; 2003.661
(Ill. p. 147)

Dirdbim, moon, 2003
72.0 × 41.0 cm
Laverty Collection, Sydney, ID 2047
(Ill. p. 148)

Billabong at Milmilngkan, 2004
219.0 × 60.0 cm
Courtesy of Annandale Galleries, Sydney, Australia
(Ill. p. 149)

Mardayin, 2004
106.5 × 36.5 cm
Museum der Kulturen, Basel, Va 1428
(Ill. p. 150)

Yawkyawk, young girl – water spirit, 2005
154.0 × 72.0 cm
Museum der Kulturen, Basel, Va 1429
(Ill. p. 151)

Mardayin design at Milmilngkan, 2004
Etching, 76.0 × 56.5 cm
Museum der Kulturen, Basel, Va 1430
(Ill. p. 152)

Mardayin at Mukkamukka, 2004
Etching, 37.5 × 29.9 cm
Jean Kohen
(Ill. p. 153)

Komrdawh, turtle, 2004
Etching, 50.0 × 33.0 cm
Jean Kohen
(Ill. p. 153)

Mardayin at Dilebang, 2004
Etching, 50.0 × 33.0 cm
Jean Kohen
(Ill. p. 153)

Mardayin design, 2004
Etching, 50.0 × 32.5 cm
Jean Kohen
(Ill. p. 153)

In addition, by
Anchor Kulunba
Barramundi fish trap, c, 1985
vine and bark fibre string, 277.0 × 60.0 cm
On loan from the Australian National Maritime Museum, Sydney
00000449
(Ill. p. 25)

Artist's biography

John Mawurndjul was born around 1952 in the Mumeka region near the Mann River in central Arnhem Land. He is the son of Anchor Kulunba (c. 1917–1996) and Mary Wurrdjedje. Anchor Kulunba was not an artist himself but a renowned 'clever' man or shaman and famous for his skills as a maker of conical fish traps. Mawurndjul is a member of the Balang subsection of the Duwa moiety of the Kurulk clan. His language is Kuninjku. He is the third of six children. His elder brother Jimmy Njiminjuma (1947–2004) was also a well-known artist, as is his younger brother James Iyuna (born 1959).

John Mawurndjul first grew up in Mumeka and Marrkolidjban. Because of an illness he and his family moved, when he was aged about twelve, to the newly established settlement Maningrida. It was there that he first really came into contact with the Balanda world. Mawurndjul attended the local Maningrida school, but haphazardly, on an occasional basis. After schooling, he joined a Kuninjku work gang for a short time, cleaning up the township.

In 1973, in the course of the outstation movement, Mawurndjul with his family and other Kuninjku returned to Mumeka and his clan land. He married Kay Lindjuwanga (born 1957), the daughter of the renowned bark painter Peter Marralwanga. Today Kay is an acclaimed artist herself, as is their daughter Anna Wurrkidj (born 1975).

John's artistic talents had been noted earlier in his youth when he had made a name for himself by decorating the bodies of initiates during ceremonies. He began painting under the guidance of his elder brother Jimmy Njiminjuma and Peter Marralwanga, commencing with small barks which soon began to sell. Together with Jimmy Njiminjuma he produced a number of larger paintings, but the two brothers worked so closely together that it is difficult to ascertain who actually contributed what to these works, but they are usually accredited to Jimmy Njiminjuma.

During the eighties Mawurndjul began to develop his own specific technique and style of painting, thus gradually gaining artistic autonomy. He began to paint more significant and complex themes on increasingly large surfaces. During this phase, one of his favourite themes was the rainbow serpent often shown together with its companion, the antilopine kangaroo. Other important subjects were the yawkyawk – young girls transformed into water spirits – male and female lightning spirits, or Buluwana, a female ancestor of the Duwa moiety.

Mawurndjul has been collaborating with Maningrida Arts and Culture since the start of his career. This community-based establishment promotes the cultural assets, both artistic and knowledge-based, of the Aboriginal people of the area, through the documentation and marketing of art. In the early nineties, John Mawurndjul and his family left Mumeka and settled in Milmilngkan, near an important billabong and other significant sites of his clan. Approximately at the same time, he launched into a new phase of his artistic career.

He moved on from figurative painting and began to concentrate on large-size, more abstract forms of representation, drawing on themes and designs from the Mardayin, a ceremonial complex connected with initiation and burial practices. In these works, Mawurndjul addresses in his own distinctive manner basic issues of human existence, ranging from conception to death, but above all he explores the linkages to the spiritual power of the ancestors and the time of creation. These connections become manifest in the landscape, especially in numerous distinct, named and thematically specified locations – sites where the living and sentient quality of the land becomes especially apparent and which serve as nodes between the ancestral and the human world. In his paintings, Mawurndjul consciously makes explicit what used to be enshrouded and encoded in ceremonial secrets, however, without ever disclosing any of these secrets. This period is often described as Mawurndjul's Mardayin phase.

In recent years, Mawurndjul shows a tendency to explore and thematise the actual structuring principles that underlie his works. Most recently, he has discovered the art of engraving, during which he has not only learnt the technique of etching, but also does the actual printing himself, the final and decisive step in the production of a graphic artwork. Employing this new form of linework and thus forfeiting the use of polychrome colours, brings to light the importance John Mawurndjul places in structuring and ordering principles for expressing his ideas and for producing visual play. Tones of grey and black have replaced the earlier colour contrasts.

In the course of his career, John Mawurndjul has won a number of awards and prizes and his works have been shown at innumerable exhibitions, among them, for example, the seminal exhibition *Magiciens de la Terre*, 1989 in the Centre Pompidou/Grande Halle de la Villette in Paris where the works of fifty Western artists were contrasted with those of fifty non-Western artists. Mawurndjul made his first trip to Europe in 1993 for the opening of the exhibition *Aratjara – Art of the First Australians* in the Kunstsammlung Nordrhein-Westfalen in Düsseldorf. Also worth mentioning is the invitation to the *XXXIII Bienal Internacional* in Sao Paulo in 1996.

John Mawurndjul is one of Australia's internationally most renowned artists, with works on show in numerous museums and galleries across Australia and Europe. In spite of his fame, John Mawurndjul has remained a modest man. At home he is not only respected for his artistic achievement, he is also an excellent hunter and dedicated to the preservation of the natural environment. On the basis of his religious and ritual knowledge and experience, his age and his personality, John Mawurndjul ranks as one of the most esteemed leaders of the Kuninjku community.

John Mawurndjul lives with his family in Milmilngkan and Maningrida.

Sources: Maningrida Arts and Culture (www.maningrida.com); Luke Taylor (*Seeing the inside: bark painting in western Arnhem Land*, 1996 and article in this volume); Jon Altman (article in this volume); *Oxford Companion to Aboriginal Art and Culture*, Oxford University Press, Oxford and Melbourne, 1998.

Solo exhibitions

2004 *John Mawurndjul*, Annandale Galleries, Sydney, Australia
2002 *Kabarlekidyo to Milmilngkan, John Mawurndjul's country*, Gallery Gabrielle Pizzi, Melbourne, Australia
1999 *John Mawurndjul*, Annandale Galleries, Sydney, Australia
1998 *John Mawurndjul: recent works from Milmilngkan*, Gallery Gabrielle Pizzi, Melbourne, Australia
1995 Gallery Gabrielle Pizzi, Melbourne, Australia
1994 Savode Gallery, Brisbane, Australia
1993 Gallery Gabrielle Pizzi, Melbourne, Australia

Select group exhibitions

2004 *Crossing Country, The alchemy of Western Arnhem Land*, Art Gallery of New South Wales, Sydney, Australia
2003 *Moon, one icon, many stories*, Arthouse Gallery, Sydney
Maningrida threads, Museum of Contemporary Art, Sydney
Mythological beings from Maningrida, Hogarth Galleries, Sydney
2002 Kuninjku show, Rebecca Hossack Gallery, London, Great Britain
NATSIA, 19th Telstra National Aboriginal and Torres Strait Islander Art Award Exhibition, Museum and Art Gallery of the Northern Territory, Darwin, Australia
East + West, Annandale Galleries, Sydney
Dreamtime, Sammlung Essl, Klosterneuburg/Wien, Austria,
Fieldwork: Australian Art 1968–2002, National Gallery of Victoria, Melbourne
2001 *NATSIA, 18th Telstra National Aboriginal and Torres Strait Islander Art Award Exhibition*, Museum and Art Gallery of the Northern Territory, Darwin
Arnhem Land Carvings and Bark Paintings, Hogarth Galleries, Sydney
Outside – In: Research Engagements with Arnhem Land Art, Drill Hall Gallery, Australian National University, Canberra
Nhurra Kutu: 'Going Home' – a tribute to Turkey Tolson, Yiribana Gallery, Art Gallery of New South Wales, Sydney
In the Heart of Arnhem Land. Myth and the making of Contemporary Aboriginal Art, Musée de l'Hôtel-Dieu, Mantes-la-Jolie, France
'*A Century of Collecting 1901–2001'*, Ivan Dougherty Gallery, Sydney
MAC Unpacked, Museum of Contemporary Art, Sydney
2000 *Transitions: 17 years of the National Aboriginal and Torres Strait Islander Art Award*, Museum and Art Gallery of the Northern Territory, Darwin: on tour in Australia: Tandanya, Adelaide; Drill Hall Gallery, Canberra
Aboriginal bark paintings, sculptures & hollow logs, Annandale Galleries, Sydney
Biennale of Sydney 2000, various venues at various locations
Maningrida, Framed Gallery, Darwin
1999 *Fighting for Culture*, Indigenart, Perth
Aboriginal Art in Modern Worlds/World of Dreamings, National Gallery of Australia, Canberra, as well as in the State Ermitage Museum, St. Petersburg, Russia

My Country: Australische Aboriginal Kunst, Brandweer Kazerne, Utrecht, Netherlands
16th National Aboriginal and Torres Strait Islander Art Award Exhibition, Museum and Art Gallery of the Northern Territory, Darwin
The Memorial: a masterpiece of Aboriginal art, Musée Olympique, Lausanne, Switzerland and Sprengel Museum Hannover, Germany
Spinifex Runner: a collection of contemporary Aboriginal and Torres Strait Islander fibre art, Campbelltown City Bicentennial Art Gallery, Campbelltown; tour in Australia
1998 Sixth Australian Contemporary Art Fair, Royal Exhibition Building, Melbourne (Annandale Galleries)
1998–99 *A material thing: objects from the collection*, Art Gallery of New South Wales, Sydney
1997 *In Place (Out of Time): Contemporary Art in Australia* in the Museum of Modern Art, Oxford, Great Britain *Mawurndjul & Bulunbulun*, Annandale Galleries, Sydney
1996 *XXXIII Bienal Internacional de São Paulo*, São Paulo, Brazil
The Eye of the Storm: Eight contemporary Indigenous Australian Artists, National Gallery of Modern Art, New Delhi, India; National Gallery of Australia, Canberra
1995 *12th National Aboriginal and Torres Strait Islander Art Award Exhibition*, Museum and Art Gallery of the Northern Territory, Darwin
Stories my Parents Sang, National Maritime Museum, Sydney
1994 *Power of the Land: Masterpieces of Aboriginal Art*, National Gallery of Victoria, Melbourne
Art of the Rainbow Snake, National Gallery of Victoria, Melbourne
Gemaltes Land: Kunst der Aborigines aus Arnhem Land, Australien, Linden-Museum, Stuttgart und Hamburgisches Museum für Völkerkunde, Hamburg, Germany
1993–94 *Aṟatjara: Art of the First Australians*, Kunstsammlung Nordrhein-Westfalen, Düsseldorf, Germany; on tour in the Hayward Gallery, South Bank Centre, London, Great Britain; Louisiana Museum, Humlebaek, Denmark
1993 *The Tenth National Aboriginal Art Award Exhibition*, Museum and Art Gallery of the Northern Territory, Darwin
Aboriginal and Torres Strait Islander Art, Parliament House Art Collection, Canberra
1992 *Crossroads – Towards a New Reality: Aboriginal Art from Australia*, National Museum of Modern Art, Kyoto; National Museum of Modern Art, Tokyo, Japan
The Ninth National Aboriginal Art Award Exhibition, Museum and Art Gallery of the Northern Territory, Darwin
1991–92 *Flash Pictures*, National Gallery of Australia, Canberra
1991 *The Speaking Land and Sea*, Australian National Maritime Museum, Sydney
Canvas and Bark, South Australian Museum, Adelaide
1990 *Keepers of the Secret: Aboriginal Art from Arnhem Land*, Art Gallery of Western Australia, Perth
L'été australien, Montpellier Musée Fabre Galerie, Montpellier, France
Spirit in Land: Bark Paintings from Arnhem Land, National Gallery of Victoria, Melbourne
1990–91 *Contemporary Aboriginal Art 1990 from Australia*, tour in Third Eye Centre, Glasgow, Scotland; then Swansea, Wales and Manchester, England
1989 *Aboriginal Art: The Continuing Tradition*, National Gallery of Australia, Canberra
Kunwinjku, Deutscher Gertrude Street, Melbourne
Magiciens de la Terre, Centre Georges Pompidou/La Grande Halle de la Villette, Paris, France
1989–88 *Recent Work from Maningrida and Ramingining*, Roslyn Oxley9 Gallery, Sydney
1988 *Dreamings: the art of Aboriginal Australia*, The Asia Society Galleries, New York, USA
Gunwinggu Artists, Beaufort Convention Centre, Darwin
1986 *The Art of the First Australians*, Kobe City Museum, Kobe, Japan
1982 *Aboriginal Art at the Top*, Museum and Art Gallery of the Northern Territory, Darwin

Awards and grants

2003 First Prize, Clemenger Contemporary Art Award, Melbourne
2002 Telstra Bark Painting Award, 19th Telstra National and Torres Strait Islander Art Award, Museum and Art Gallery of the Northern Territory, Darwin
1999 Telstra Bark Painting Award, National Aboriginal and Torres Strait Islander Art Award, Museum and Art Gallery of the Northern Territory, Darwin
1991 Professional Development Grant, Australia Council for the Arts, Aboriginal Arts Unit, Sydney
1988 First Prize, Barunga Festival Art Exhibition, Barunga
Rothmans Foundation Award (Best painting in a traditional medium), National Aboriginal Art Award, Museum and Art Gallery of the Northern Territory, Darwin

Collections containing works by John Mawurndjul

Aboriginal Art Museum, Utrecht, Netherlands
Art Gallery of New South Wales, Sydney
Art Gallery of South Australia, Adelaide
Art Gallery of Western Australia, Perth
Artbank Sydney
Djómi Museum, Maningrida, Northern Territory
Groninger Museum, Groningen, Netherlands
The Holmes à Court Collection, Perth
Kluge Collection, Morven Estate, Charlottesville, Virginia, USA
Linden-Museum Stuttgart, Germany
Museum and Art Gallery of the Northern Territory, Darwin, Northern Territory
Museum of Contemporary Art, Maningrida Collection, Sydney
Museum der Kulturen, Basel, Switzerland
National Gallery of Australia, Canberra, Australian Capital Territory
National Gallery of Victoria, Melbourne
National Maritime Museum, Darling Harbour, Sydney
Parliament House Art Collection, Canberra, Australian Capital Territory
Queensland Art Gallery, Brisbane
Sammlung Essl, Klosterneuburg, Austria
South Australian Museum, Adelaide
Sprengel Museum Hannover, Germany

Works by John Mawurndjul are also held in a number of private collections in Great Britain, France, Germany and Australia.

Select works from the Kupka collection, shown only in Basel:

All works in the Museum der Kulturen, Basel; where not specified otherwise, in collection Karel Kupka.

Painter unknown
Head of a female buffalo, 1960, Maningrida
Sculpture, wood, L. 36.5 cm; Va 1236
(Ill. p. 199 left)

Painter unknown
Head of a male buffalo, 1960, Maningrida
Sculpture, wood, L. 34.0 cm; Va 1237
(Ill. p. 199 right)

Painter unknown
Crocodile, 1960, Maningrida
Sculpture, wood, L. 88.5 cm; Va 1235
(Ill. p. 200 left)

Painter unknown
Crocodile (underside), 1960, Maningrida
Sculpture, wood, L. 86.0 cm; Va 1302
(Ill. p. 200 centre)

Painter unknown
Echidna, before 1931, East Arnhem Land
Sculpture, wood, L. 81.0 cm; Va 598
(Ill. p. 200 right)
Sammlung T.T. Webb

Painter unknown
Macassan pipe, 1960, Maningrida
Sculpture, wood, L. 66.0 cm; Va 1296
(Ill. p. 200 below)

Painter unknown
Kangaroo, before 1931
120.0 x 50.0 cm; Va 356 (Ill. p. 201)
Collection E. Handschin

Painter unknown
Goanna, before 1960, Oenpelli
73.0 x 35.0 cm; Va 1183 (Ill. p. 202 left)

Painter unknown
Stingray, before 1959, Oenpelli
74.0 x 36.0 cm; Va 1185 (Ill. p. 202 right)

Peter Balmonidbal
Ngalyod, rainbow serpent, with male figure, before 1975, East Alligator River
86.0 x 42.0 cm; Va 1377 (Ill. p. 203 left)
Collection R. Sak

Djambalulu
Miliyara-corroboree, dance of the white duck, 1960, Croker Island
50.0 x 55.0 cm; Va 1189 (Ill. p. 203 right)

Wumara
Copulating couple, 1960, Oenpelli
68.0 x 34.0 cm; Va 1175 (Ill. p. 204 left)

Wumara
Namarrkon, lightning spirit, 1960, Oenpelli
61.5 x 44.0 cm; Va 1176 (Ill. p. 204 right)

Marboa
Female figure, 1960, Oenpelli
71.0 x 32.5 cm; Va 1173 (Ill. p. 205 left)

Marboa
Freshwater turtle, 1960, Oenpelli
54.0 x 46.0 cm; Va 1174 (Ill. p. 205 right)

Narlingmag
Crocodile, before 1960, Oenpelli
94.0 x 49.0 cm; Va 1177 (Ill. p. 206 left)

Narlingmag (ascribed to)
Rayfish, before 1960, Oenpelli
54.0 x 44.0 cm; Va 1178 (Ill. p. 206 right)

Nagordo
Two female mimih spirits, 1960, Oenpelli
56.0 x 61.0 cm; Va 1179 (Ill. p. 207 left)

Nagordo
Mother kangaroo, 1960, Oenpelli
37.0 x 42.0 cm; Va 1275 (Ill. p. 207 right)

Nagordo
Four kangaroos, 1960, Oenpelli
64.0 x 45.0 cm; Va 1180 (Ill. p. 208 left)

Paddy Compass Namatbara
Three mimih figures, two female and one male, 1963, Croker Island
92.0 x 53.0 cm; Va 1343 (Ill. p. 208 right)

Paddy Compass Namatbara
Representation of yam for ceremony, 1963, Croker Island
Sculpture, wood, L. 47.0 cm, Dm. 5.5 cm; Va 1306
(Ill. p. 209 left)

Paddy Compass Namatbara
Two fighting mimih couples, 1963, Croker Island
56.0 x 52.0 cm; Va 1344 (Ill. p. 209 right)

Billy Yirawala MBE
Human figure with ceremonial body painting, 1963, Croker Island
Sculpture, wood, 40.5 x 9.0 cm (Dm.); Va 1305
(Ill. p. 210)

Billy Yirawala MBE
Two mimih figures dancing, 1960, Croker Island
64.0 x 33.5 cm; Va 1190 (Ill. p. 211 left)

Billy Yirawala MBE
Two female mimih and a kangaroo, 1960, Croker Island
56.0 x 28.0 cm; Va 1191 (Ill. p. 211 right)

Billy Yirawala MBE
Malicious spirit in its cave, 1960, Croker Island
76.0 x 51.0 cm; Va 1192 (Ill. p. 212 left)

Billy Yirawala MBE
Three mimih figures, one male and two female, 1963, Croker Island
117.0 x 56.0 cm; Va 1335 (Ill. p. 212 right)

Nangunyari-Namiridali
A mimih dance: hunting the freshwater crocodile, 1960, Croker Island
53.0 x 73.5 cm; Va 1193 (Ill. p. 213 left)

Nangunyari-Namiridali
Mimih and crocodile, 1963, Croker Island
74.0 x 26.0 cm; Va 1336 (Ill. p. 213 right)

Nangunyari-Namiridali (ascribed to)
Fish, before 1959, Goulburn Island
54.0 x 17.0 cm; Va 1195 (Ill. p. 214 left)

Nangunyari-Namiridali
Mimih, turtle and crocodile, 1963, Croker Island
64.0 x 59.0 cm; Va 1337 (Ill. p. 214 right)

Nangunyari-Namiridali
Two couples of mimih figures, 1960, Croker Island
53.0 x 73.0 cm; Va 1194 (Ill. p. 215)

Jimmy Midjawmidjaw
Namarrkon, lightning spirit, 1960, Croker Island
70.0 x 60.0 cm; Va 1186 (Ill. p. 216)

Jimmy Midjawmidjaw (ascribed to)
Male thunder spirit and crocodile, 1963, Oenpelli
70.0 x 60.0 cm; Va 922 (Ill. p. 217 left)

Jimmy Midjawmidjaw
Female namarrkon, lightning spirit, and kangaroo 1960, Croker Island
62.0 x 92.0 cm; Va 1187 (Ill. p. 217 right)

Jimmy Midjawmidjaw
Mam, evil spirit, 1963, Croker Island
92.0 x 43.0 cm; Va 1339 (Ill. p. 218 left)

Jimmy Midjawmidjaw
Female mam, evil spirit, 1963, Croker Island
103.5 x 55.5 cm; Va 1341 (Ill. p. 218 right)

Jimmy Midjawmidjaw
Wild turkey, 1963, Croker Island
53.5 x 76.0 cm; Va 1338 (Ill. p. 219 left)

Jimmy Midjawmidjaw
Water goanna, 1963, Croker Island
80.0 x 35.0 cm; Va 1342 (Ill. p. 219 right)

Jimmy Midjawmidjaw
Barramundi, 1963, Croker Island
66.0 x 94.0 cm; Va 1340 (Ill. p. 220 left)

Jimmy Midjawmidjaw
Inalats corroboree, 1960, Croker Island
54.0 x 73.0 cm; Va 1188 (Ill. p. 220 right)

Jimmy Midjawmidjaw
A schematic figure in the image of a bone of Lumaluma, the mythical creator of the Mardayin ceremony, 1963, Croker Island
Sculpture, wood, 79.0 x 12.5 x 9.5 cm; Va 1307
(Ill. p. 221)

Contributors

Jon Altman is professor at and director of the Centre for Aboriginal Economic Policy Research at the Australian National University, Canberra. His work combines economic and anthropological approaches. He has been conducting research with the Kuninjku people since 1979. In 1989 he chaired a national review on the economic aspects of Aboriginal arts and in 2003 he assisted the Northern Territory government in the development of its Indigenous Arts Strategy. In 2004 he was involved in the preparations for the exhibition *Crossing Country* in the Art Gallery of New South Wales in Sydney.

Gary Foley is a lecturer at the University of Melbourne and presently working on his PhD thesis on the history of Aboriginal Movements. From 2001 to 2005 he was senior curator for South-East Australia at the Museum Victoria in Melbourne. Prior to that he participated in establishing a number of Aboriginal organisations. Among other things, he was director of the Aboriginal Arts Board of the Australia Council and head of the Aboriginal Medical Service Redfern. He was an adviser to the Royal Commission on Aboriginal Deaths in Custody and was a leading member of the National Coalition of Aboriginal Organisations.

Christian Kaufmann is a freelance anthropologist who has worked in Papua New Guinea and Vanuatu with artisans, horticulturalists and artists. He is a founding member of the Pacific Arts Association. From 1970 to 2005 he was curator of the Oceania Department of the Museum der Kulturen, Basel. Among many other projects, he conceptualised and organised an international exhibition on art in Vanuatu. Up to 2005 he gave courses in museology and art at the University of Basel.

Erika Koch is a freelance photographer und lives in Düsseldorf, Germany. Apart from her focus on industrial and architectural photography she has produced a number of cross-cultural work series, namely in Brazil and for the exhibition *Altäre der Welt* which was shown in 2001 in the museum kunst palast in Düsseldorf.

Apolline Kohen is arts director at the Manigrida Arts and Culture (MAC) where she organises exhibitions and runs the centre. After attaining her degree as curator at the École du Louvre in Paris she worked for the National Museum of Australia in Canberra. For MAC she has realised two international projects, first, the exhibition *In the Heart of Arnhem Land: myth and the making of Aboriginal art* in the Musée de l'Hôtel-Dieu, Mantes-la-Jolie in France (June to October 2001) and, secondly, the cultural exchange project *Crossings* which, in 2001 and 2003, brought together artists from Maningrida and France and which was shown in a media-mix presentation at the Darwin Festival 2003. In 2004 she participated in the realisation of the exhibition *Crossing Country: the Alchemy of western Arnhem Land Art.*

Jean Kohen is an artist trained at the École des Beaux-Arts in Paris. He has been producing graphic art for more than forty years. His works have been shown in numerous galleries across Europe and Australia. In 2004 he began working with artists from Maningrida in a local studio producing prints. Namely with John Mawurndjul he has produced an impressive series of works.

Bernhard Lüthi, curator and designer of the present exhibition, is a freelance artist involved in many cross-cultural projects. In 1989 he was chargé de mission for the exhibition *Magiciens de la Terre*, Centre Pompidou/Grande Halle de la Villette in Paris. At the same time he conceptualised and later realised the exhibition *Aratjara – Art of the First Australians* together with the Aboriginal and Torres Strait Islander Arts Board of the Australia Council and the former Power Gallery of the University of Sydney (now Museum of Contemporary Art). After a long-standing collaboration with the Kunstsammlung Nordrhein-Westfalen the exhibition opened in Düsseldorf in 1993, before being shown in the Hayward Gallery, London, and the Louisiana Museum in Humlebaek. From 1999 to 2001 he worked with the curators Jean-Hubert Martin, Aline Luque and Philippe Peltier in organising the exhibition *Altäre der Welt* which marked the opening of the new museum kunst palast in Düsseldorf in 2001.

Richard McMillan is a freelance art historian deeply involved in the world of art. He produced the catalogue on the artist Tony Tuckson (1921–1973), who only became known as an artist posthumously through his estate. On the basis of this work, in 1997 McMillan attained a Masters Degree at the College of Fine Arts at the University of New South Wales. Through his work on the biography of Tony Tuckson, who had been the deputy director of the Art Gallery of NSW and had been engaged in promoting Aboriginal art and artists throughout his life, McMillan discovered Karel Kupka and his work.

Hans-Joachim Müller is a freelance writer and lives in Freiburg and southern Italy. After attaining his degree in philosophy and art history at the University of Freiburg im Breisgau he joined the feuilleton staff of the weekly newspaper DIE ZEIT where he worked for many years; later he was on the higher editorial staff of the Basler Zeitung where he was head of the feuilleton department. He has published several books, among others, a book on the Basel Rudolf Staechelin collection.

Philippe Peltier is curator at the Musée du quai Branly and responsible for the Oceanic and South Asia collections. From 1993 to 2002 he worked for the Musée national des Arts d'Afrique et d'Océanie (MNAAO) where he realised an exhibition on David Malangi. He is an art historian and anthropologist (field research in Papua New Guinea) and is a lecturer in Oceanic art at the École du Louvre. Together with Michael Gunn from the St. Louis Art Museum he is preparing an exhibition on the art of New Ireland to be shown in Paris in 2007.

Judith Ryan is senior curator of Indigenous art with curatorial responsibility for Aboriginal and Torres Strait Islander art, Oceanic art and Pre-Columbian art at the National Gallery of Victoria, Melbourne's main museum of art. Judith Ryan studied fine arts and English literature (Honours) at the University of Melbourne, and education at Oxford University and began her art museum career in 1977 at the National Gallery of Victoria. Her special interest is Indigenous Australian art of the twentieth century - its diversity, dynamism and transformation in the face of social change. She has curated about thirty exhibitions of Aboriginal art and has published widely in the field. The topic of colour in Aboriginal Art is a recurrent theme in her work.

Paul S. C. Taçon is professor and research leader of the School of Arts, Gold Coast Campus, Griffith University, Queensland. From 1991 to 2005 he was based at the Australian Museum in Sydney, where, for the last seven years, he has headed the museum's research centre. In approximately sixty months of anthropological and archaeological research he has become a specialist in many fields, working on pre-historic art, rock art, landscape archaeology, material culture and contemporary Indigenous issues. One of his main interests is the relationship between art and identity.

Luke Taylor is deputy director of research at AIATSIS and adjunct professor at the Centre for Cross-Cultural Research of the Australian National University. He is an anthropologist who specialises in research with Aboriginal and Torres Strait Islander artists. Between 1990 and 2000 he was curator and then senior curator in the Gallery of Aboriginal Australia at the National Museum of Australia, Canberra. He has published several books and exhibition catalogues. Together with Jon Altman he co-edited *Marketing Aboriginal Art in the 1990s* (Aboriginal Studies Press, Canberra, 1990).

Claus Volkenandt is an art historian who studied art history, philosophy and new German literature in Bochum and Basel. He attained his doctorate in 1997 and is a lecturer in modern art history at the Department of Art History of the University of Basel and is working on his habilitation thesis. He has written several books and articles, among others, two contributions to the Metzler Lexicon on Art on abstraction and hermeneutics. He is the editor of *Kunstgeschichte und Weltgegenwartskunst. Konzepte – Methoden – Perspektiven*, Berlin, Reimer, 2004.

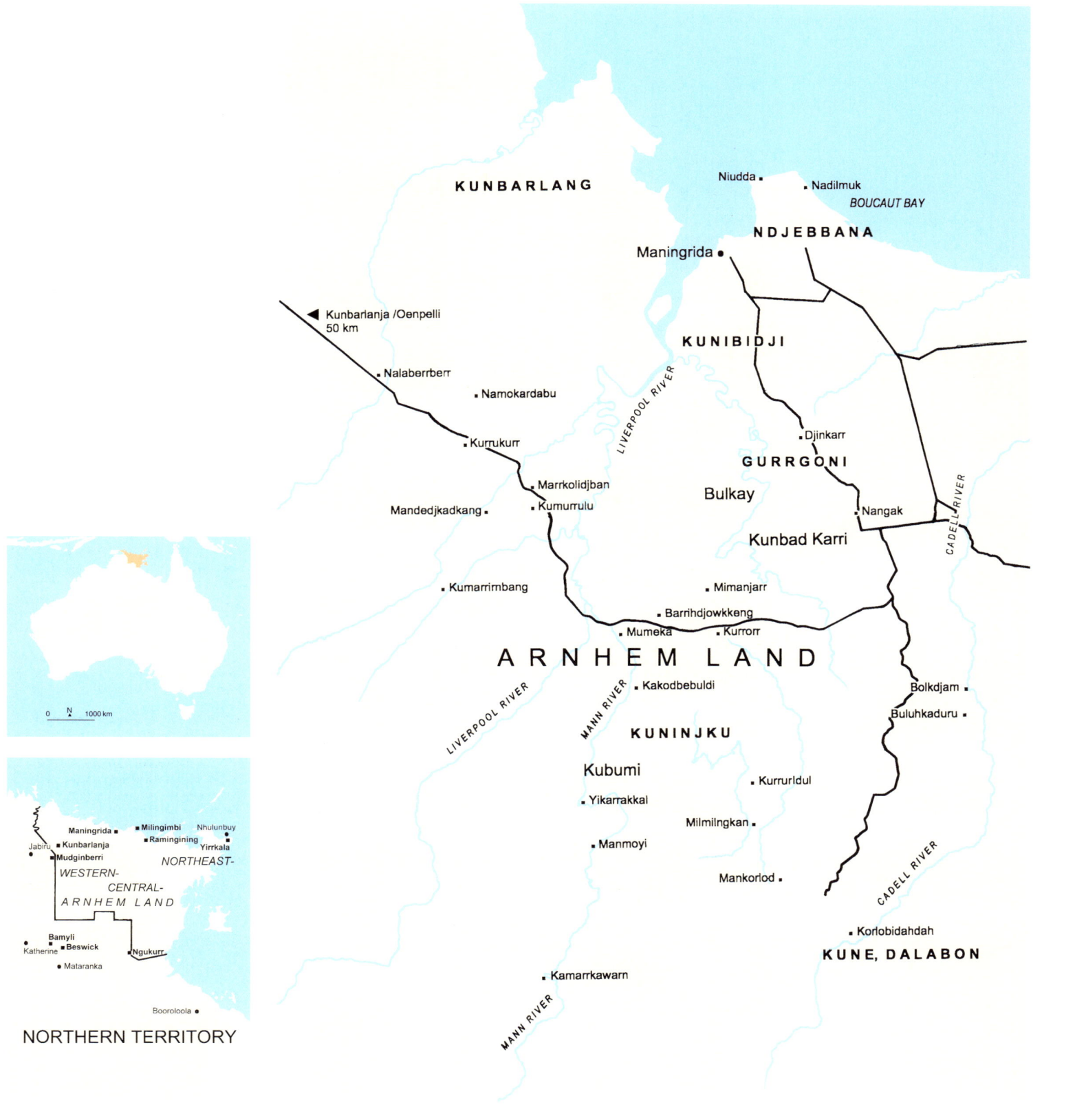

«rarrk»

Glossary

Aboriginal and Torres Strait Islander Arts Board of the Australia Council of the Arts assists Indigenous peoples to claim, control and enhance their cultural inheritance by promoting the continuation and recognition of cultural and especially artistic achievements.

Arnhem Land. The part of the Northern Territory of Australia between the Gulf of Carpentaria and the East Alligator River, named by Matthew Flinders after the ship *Arnhem* in which the Dutch expedition under J. Carstenszoon and W. van Coolsteerdt sailed westwards from Cape York.

Australian Institute of Aboriginal and Torres Strait Islander Studies (AIATSIS). Independent research institute funded by the Commonwealth of Australia, founded 1962.

Balanda. Common term for non-Aboriginal people. The name is borrowed from the original Macassan term *belanda*, meaning the Dutch (Hollander).

Bark painting. Painting executed on the bark of a eucalyptus tree. The bark is cut from the tree during the wet season when the tree is full of sap. It is then trimmed and heated over the fire in order to press it flat. Traditionally, brushes made from plant fibres or human hair served to apply the earth pigments, using orchid sap or – very rarely – blood as a fixative. According to early ethnographic accounts it can be assumed that bark paintings were used for illustrating stories and for instructing initiates whilst preparing ceremonial cycles. In eastern Arnhem Land the interrelationship between the motifs applied in ritual body painting and the designs used in bark painting appears to be closer than in western Arnhem Land.

Bark petition. In 1963, the Yolngu people of north-east Arnhem Land in the Northern Territory faced with their traditional lands being taken over by a huge bauxite mine, presented a petition to the Australian Parliament, in the form of a bark painting, calling for recognition of their land rights.

Bathurst Island. Island to the northwest of Arnhem Land. Its inhabitants, the Tiwi, attracted the attention of Australian museums and collectors through their painted sculptures used in mortuary ceremonies.

Billabong. A stretch of calm, stagnant water of varying size usually fed by a stream or a river. According to traditional Aboriginal belief, billabongs are a source of life and often the home of powerful spirit beings.

Bininj. Human being, people, common term referring to Aboriginal people as distinct from balanda.

Bininj Kunwok. The largest language group in western Arnhem Land; includes the dialect chain Kuninjku, Kune, Kunwinjku, Gundjeihmi/Mayali, Kundedjnjenghemi. Other languages in western and central Arnhem Land are, amongst others, Jawayn, Dalabon, Rembarrnga, Ndjébbana, Ganalbingu, Gurrgoni, Kunbarlang und Burarra.

Bir'yun. Yolngu term from eastern Arnhem Land designating the shiny and brilliant effect generated by the crosshatching (rarrk) on a painting that connotes a flash of ancestral or spiritual power and lends the work its desired quality.

Buluwana. Woman of the Wamuddjan subsection; one of the first ancestors to inhabit the Kurulk-Bordoh-Wamarrk clan estate.

Ceremonial cycle. Before the Mardayin ceremony was introduced to western Arnhem Land there was a regional ceremonial cycle called Ubarr and the secret Kunabibi ceremony that belongs to the Duwa moiety.

Clan. Land-owning descent group. In western Arnhem Land clans are patrilineal, i.e. clan membership is reckoned through the father's line of descent. Upon marriage, a woman moves to the land of her husband's clan but retains close relationships with her natal clan. Her children become members of her husband's clan but the mother-child bond remains strong throughout life.

Clemenger Contemporary Art Award. A triennal contemporary award granted by the National Gallery of Victoria, the leading art museum in Melbourne, named after Joan and Peter Clemenger who, in 1991, endowed the prize.

Daluk. Woman.

Delek. Kuninjku term designating white clay (calcium magnesium carbonate) used as pigment in painting; often described as Ngalyod's faeces.

Dilebang. Significant site of one of the Kuninjku clans, it features a prominent rock formation and a billabong.

Dird. Moon.

Djang. Sacred site, associated with events in the spirit world and the ancestral time of creation.

Djómi Museum. The regional museum in Maningrida is part of the Museum and Art Gallery of the Northern Territory and is run by MAC, see Maningrida.

Duwa. John Mawurndjul's moiety or ceremonial half. The complementary half is called Yirridjdja. As a knowledgeable leader, John Mawurndjul is responsible for the ceremonial and landed property of his clan; at the same time he is the manager, djungkay, of the Yirridjdja estate, his mother's moiety.

Escarpment. Western Arnhem Land is dominated by a massive quartz-sandstone plateau and fragmented outliers. The leading edge of the plateau includes an imposing escarpment and it is along this edge, on the steep-sided slopes below and on the plain's surrounding outliers and residuals that most of the rock shelters are found. In earlier times, these were inhabited especially during the wet season. This is evidenced by the many rock paintings found there. The most impressive rock formations are in the area around Oenpelli and in the Kakadu National Park.

Fish trap. The conical fish trap is made of a special vine found on the land of the Kurulk clan. John Mawurndjul's father, Anchor Kulunba, was a renowned specialist in the making of fish traps. The traps are used at the end of the wet season to catch fish in the estuaries of the local rivers.

Indigenous art. Common term today for what is also called Aboriginal art or, in the United States, Native art.

Kakadu National Park. National Park in northern Australia, established in 1979 in conjunction with the construction of the Ranger uranium mine and leased from its Aboriginal customary owners. With its centre in Jabiru it measures 19,800 square kilometres and has been on the UNESCO World Heritage list since 1981. Operations in the Ranger mine will go on until the uranium deposits have been exploited, probably by 2009. The originally planned Jabiluka mine is not going to be put into operation. The park's economic future lies in the development of a sustainable and controlled tourism industry.

Kunbarllanja (Kunbarlanja, Kunbarllanjnja). Indigenous name for Oenpelli.

Kunibídji, Aboriginal community with its own language. Maningrida lies on Kunibídji territory.

Kuninjku. Dialect of the Bininj Kunwok language group. The majority of the people in the Maningrida area speak Kuninjku. The superordinate language level is defined as Kunwinjku by the authors of this volume.

Kunwinjku. Previously called Gunwinggu; dialect group in western Arnhem Land with its centre in Oenpelli (Kunbarllanja). In the present volume the term Kunwinjku is used to designate the superordinate language level. See also Bininj Kunwok.

Land Title. According to British Law the claim to landed property that is not designated land belonging to the Crown (Crown land). A distinction is made between Freehold Title, meaning that the Crown (or government) has passed all interest in the land other than minerals onto the owner and so-called Native Title that is subject to certain restrictions. The colonisation of Australia was conducted under the false assumption that the land was unoccupied (terra nullius) since the Indigenous peoples appeared to be non-sedentary, seemed to lack any concept of landownership and had no developed form of social organisation. Land could therefore be claimed for the Crown and distributed to colonists by the government. This doctrine and policy was overturned when the Australian High Court passed the Mabo judgment in 1992 that granted the people of Murray Island in the Torres Straits legal ownership to their land. Since then numerous Aboriginal land claims have occupied the Australian Land Commissions. During the hearings, especially in Central Australia, images of landscape and the stories that go with them are often painted on canvas or tarpaulin in order to underpin the claim to traditional ownership. In Arnhem Land, which used to be an Aboriginal reserve, land rights were based on a different legal foundation which granted the Indigenous peoples better protection of their customary land (see also Native Title, Northern Land Council).

Lightning spirit. Called Namarrkon or Namarden in western Arnhem Land, it can either be a male or a female being. Lightning spirits are looked upon as the children of the rainbow serpent, Ngalyod. They inhabit the landscape; their presence is especially felt during the thunderstorm season (October to December) before the monsoon sets in. Lightning spirits are a common motif on rock paintings.

Lorrkkon. Hollow log, usually a tree trunk that has been hollowed out by termites. Hollow logs serve as surface for paintings that include designs similar to those seen on body decorations and on bark paintings. What makes them extraordinary is their three-dimensional quality. The form is derived from the hollow log coffins in which, during the final burial ceremony, the bones of the deceased were placed. For the Bicentennial celebrations in 1988, Aboriginal artists produced the *Aboriginal Memorial* consisting of two hundred painted hollow logs, each log representing one year of occupation. It now stands in the National Gallery of Art in Canberra.

Lumaluma. Ancestor being who created the Mardayin ceremony, associated with thunder, stormy weather and sacred fibre bags.

Macassans. Seafaring traders from eastern Indonesia, mainly from Sulawesi (formerly Celebes). The Macassans frequently visited the northern shores of Australia well before the arrival of the Europeans, and kept on doing so up to 1906, to collect and trade sea cucumbers or trepang. The goods were later sold to China as aphrodisiacs. The Macassans often stayed for months so that long-lasting exchange relations developed with the coastal population.

Mam. Free roaming spirits of the deceased. Mam are malignant, often causing harm to, or even killing, unwary hunters. They have claw-like hands for grabbing their victims and multiple limbs and genitalia. During the Mamurrng exchange ceremony the dance of the mam spirits is enacted.

Mangrove. Muddy swamp found on the coast and in estuaries, characterised by dense thickets of mangrove trees. These low trees are adapted to live in creeks of salt water; preferred habitat of crocodiles.

Maningrida. Township established in 1957. Today it has approximately 2600 inhabitants. It serves as the administrative centre of the area and offers educational and health services. It is also home to Maningrida Arts & Culture. MAC is a business enterprise of the Bawinanga Corporation. It promotes the cultural assets, both artistic and knowledge-based, of the Aboriginal people of the region through the documentation and marketing of art. MAC is supported by public funds and is managed by an arts director who usually stays there for several years. At present this is Apolline Kohen.

Mimih. The term mimih refers to a category of trickster spirit which is said to live in the rock country in western Arnhem Land. A mimih is imagined to be tall and thin so it can pass through cracks and enter into the rock. Mimih are not considered to have the same creation powers as Ancestral beings. They are regarded as precedent to human beings and are said to have taught them to hunt and instructed them in important cultural matters. Many bark painters begin their career painting mimih (see also Luke Taylor in this volume).

Missionary societies. Missions and Christian churches often suffer from the stigma of having been party to the colonial policy of driving Indigenous groups off their ancestral lands and relocating them in settlements. Through assimilation programmes they were to be transformed into 'normal' Australian citizens according to white, European standards. What is sometimes forgotten is that knowledge has been preserved because important aspects of traditional Indigenous culture were recorded and documented by missionaries.

Moieties. The land-owning clans and all their members belong to one of the two moieties called Duwa and Yirridjdja. The moieties regulate many aspects of social, political and ceremonial life and natural phenomena and features of the landscape are often assigned to either one of the moieties.

Namarden, see lightning spirit

Namarrkon, see lightning spirit

Namorrorddo. Shooting star spirit, at times malignant towards humans; they tend especially to steal the souls of people who have lost their way. The spirit's malignancy is indicated by the barb of a stingray.

Native Title. The entitlement of Indigenous communities and clans under common law to their customary lands and resources, based on the *Aboriginal Land Rights (Northern Territory) Act* of 1976 and the *Native Title Act* of 1993. Ever since the so-called bark petition of 1963 (a petition attached to a bark submitted by the Yolngu people claiming rights to their customary land and resources) Arnhem Land has been at the centre of the disputes concerning land rights, especially in connection with the enjoyment of usage rights of, and benefits from, mining projects. Over the last thirty years more than half of the land in the Northern Territory has been returned to its Aboriginal owners; in Arnhem Land the proportion is higher. Still contested are pastoral leases and sea rights.

Natural pigments. The most important pigments, red and yellow ochre, are extracted from ferrous lime- and sandstone and clay soil, and are prepared for use by crushing and rubbing. The white pigment, called delek, consists of white clay (huntite) which is found in deposits scattered in the soil. Charcoal is used for black. Indigenous pigments are an important trade item; they are supplemented by imported pigments such as Prussian blue and commercial products such as paints and fixatives made from polyvinyl.

Ngalkunburriyaymi. Mermaid, described as Yingarna's first daughter, and therefore sister to Ngalyod.

Ngalyod. Common term in western Arnhem Land for the rainbow serpent. Ngalyod is the creator and protector of all sacred sites. She is associated with, and responsible for, the cycles of natural and human regeneration. Ngalyod commands both creative and destructive powers and is mainly associated with rain, the monsoon season and rainbows.

Northern Land Council. Independent institution, founded in 1973, that strives for and coordinates the self-government of Aboriginal estates and issues the necessary permits to non-Aboriginals wishing to visit Arnhem Land.

Northern Territory (N.T.). The Northern Territory is a federal territory of Australia. The Northern Territory achieved political authority with the grant of self-government in 1978 but has not yet been granted full statehood. The Territory is exclusively subject to Federal Law.

Oenpelli. The settlement Oenpelli was founded by Australian pastoralists and Lutheran missionaries. Today it is the main hub for visitors arriving from the Kakadu National Park on their way to Arnhem Land to visit rock art sites. It is the main area of the Kunwinjku language and its local dialect. Its indigenous name is Kunbarllanja. In the 1950s and 1960s, Oenpelli had close ties to the mission station on Croker Island and the mainland opposite, respectively.

Outstation. A small Aboriginal settlement, home to a family with some of their relatives and usually located in geographically and culturally significant places. These settlements were established in the course of the Outstation Movement in the mid-seventies. Often they are only inhabited seasonally. Although quite self-subsistent, outstations are reliant on supplies and services from larger settlements and administrative centres such as Maningrida, Oenpelli, Ramingining or Yirrkala.

Rainbow serpent. The main ancestral creator in western Arnhem Land, usually known under its name Ngalyod (see Ngalyod), associated with rain and clouds. From a Western point of view, the serpent resembles the python Nawaran, the Oenpelli python (Morelia oenpelliensis).

Ramingining. Administrative centre approximately eighty kilometres southeast of Maningrida. Ramingining has its own local arts centre.

Rarrk. According to Luke Taylor (see this volume), the word rarrk is used throughout Arnhem Land to refer to designs that make use of crosshatching components. Crosshatching is a description of the way the designs are painted as a set of parallel lines which are overlaid by another set of parallel lines. A very thin brush consisting of a few very long fibres is used to make these lines. Colour changes in the respective sets of lines create a banding effect. The Mardayin ceremony for which these designs are produced was performed throughout the region although it is referred to generally as Ngarra in the east. In western Arnhem Land the term rarrk can also be used to refer to the design as a whole that is worn in the Mardayin ceremony. A full Mardayin ceremony has not been performed in western Arnhem Land for many years although senior men still look after the sacred objects for the ceremony and knowledge about Mardayin can be exchanged and incorporated in other important ceremonies.

Rock paintings. Important historical records in Arnhem Land; they document historical development phases that become evident through changes in the depicted themes (for example, from land-based animals to marine species such as the saltwater crocodile and a variety of fish indicating the proximity of the sea) and through layers of superimposed paintings and images. Many of the paintings were applied to the walls and roofs of rock shelters and are used by today's Aboriginals to illustrate and explain stories and traditional lore. Ceremonial paintings, some of which were frequently renewed up to the nineteen-sixties, are less common.

Social organisation. The social structure of Australian Aboriginals displays a number of specific features. Groups are divided into clans, moieties or sections, and subsections. Each individual belongs to one of either four or eight (as in Arnhem Land) subsections. Here, each moiety consists of four subsections. One of the main functions of these subsections is the regulation of marriage, in the sense that the men of one subsection always marry into the same subsection of the opposite moiety. This serves to uphold the rules of exogamy and to regulate the size and distribution of clans.

Spirits. According to the people of Arnhem Land, the spirit world co-exists with the world of humans. However, spirit beings populated the country long before the humans came into existence. One hallmark of spirits is their ability to change their shape. Spirits can appear to humans as corporeal beings (i.e. as human-like beings, animals, rocks, plants, even as rainbows and clouds) and, at the same time, act as invisible entities beyond the time-frame we are accustomed to; see also Ngalyod, lightning spirit, mimih, namorrorddo, yawyawk, Yingarna and mam.

Taille Douce. A special technique for producing prints. In contrast to other techniques such as mezzotint or drypoint where the engraving is applied directly to the copper plate, Taille douce, or etching, demands an intermediary step: the plate is first covered with a coat of wax or varnish about one millimetre thick and then worked using different etching needles to remove the varnish where desired and to create the image. The plate is then submerged in a series of acid baths each biting into the metal surface only where unprotected by the ground. The ground is removed, ink is forced into the etched depressions, the unetched surfaces wiped, and an impression is printed.

Yawkyawk. Literally: young woman. Sometimes used to designate composite beings of human-fishlike shape. They are said to be friendly towards humans. The yawkyawk girls were once devoured by the rainbow serpent and then spat out again to become water spirits and thus important mediators between the worlds. See also Ngalkunbur-riyaymi.

Yingarna. Mother of the rainbow serpent Ngalyod; also a frequent theme in paintings.

Yirrkala. Township and administrative centre in eastern Arnhem Land.

Yolngu. Indigenous name for the people in the eastern part of Arnhem Land.

Sources: Jon Altman (in this volume); Caruana, W., *Aboriginal art*, Thames and Hudson, London, 1993; Morphy, H., *Aboriginal art*, Phaidon, London, 1998; *The Oxford companion to Aboriginal art and culture*, Oxford University Press, Oxford and Melbourne, 1998; Perkins, H. (ed.), *Crossing country*, Sydney, 2004; Judith Ryan (in this volume), Taylor, L., *Seeing the inside: bark painting in western Arnhem Land*, Clarendon Press, Oxford, 1996; www.aiatsis.gov.au, www.maningrida.com, www.nlc.org.au

Photographic Credits[1]

Jon Altman, Canberra: pp. 30, 33 l., 33 m., 33 r., 34, 35

Annandale Galleries, Sydney: p. 118

Art Gallery of New South Wales, Sydney:
Jenny Carter: pp. 97, 98
Christopher Snee: p. 96
Brenton McGeachie: pp. 104, 133

Art Gallery of South Australia, Adelaide: pp. 113, 143

Mark Ashkanasy, Melbourne: S. 88, 94, 103

Australian National Maritime Museum, Sydney: pp. 25, 112

Christian Baur, Basel: p. 224

Michel Brouet, Sydney: pp. 84, 85, 90, 91, 106, 107, 131, 123, 124, 125, 135, 136, 139, 140, 141, 144, 148, 149

Peter Eve, Darwin: pp. 89, 130, 138

Tony Griffiths: pp. 36 l., 40/41

Groninger Museum, Groningen:
John Stoel: pp. 110, 111

Michael Herling/Aline Gwose: pp. 119, 120, 121, 122

Walter Klein, Düsseldorf: p. 37 r.

Erika Koch, Düsseldorf: cover, pp. 6/7, 8, 9, 10, 11, 12/13, 14, 15, 16, 17, 18/19, 20, 24, 26, 27, 42, 45 a., 49, 50/51, 52/53, 54/55, 56, 57, 58/59, 60/61, 62/63, 64 159, 160, 161 b., 162 l., 164 l., 166, 167, 168, 169, 170/171, 172/173, 174/175

Karel Kupka: pp. 192, 233

Bernhard Lüthi, Pieterlen: p. 161 a., 163 l.u., 165 l., 165 2.f.l.

André Morain, Paris: p. 137

Museum and Art Gallery of the Northern Territory, Darwin:
Gilbert Herrada: pp. 86, 93, 132

Museum der Kulturen, Basel:
Hans Weber: pp. 198, 223 a., 223 b.
Markus Gruber: pp. 92, 150, 151
Peter Horner: pp. 199–221

Museum of Contemporary Art, Sydney: pp. 99, 102

National Gallery of Australia, Canberra: pp. 95, 100, 101, 109

National Gallery of Victoria, Melbourne: pp. 87, 93, 105, 108, 126, 127, 134, 142, 145, 146, 147

Lin Onus, courtesy of Tiriki Onus, Upwey: pp. 36 r., 37 l.

Axel Poignant, courtesy of Roslyn Poignant, London: p. 43

Marc Raimondo, Sydney: pp. 70, 72, 73, 75
Sydney Morning Herald: p. 190 (after Françoise Dussart, La peinture des aborigines d'Australie, Marseille, Editions Parenthèses, 1993, p. 11)

Paul Taçon, Gold Coast: pp. 161 r., 162 r., 163 l.a., 163 r., 164 m.a., 164 m.b., 164 r.

Carl Warner, Brisbane: pp. 114, 115, 116, 117, 128

Maps

p. 71: © Crown copyright reserved
p. 233: The sketch-maps by Bernhard Lüthi are compiled from various sources.

[1] © All photographs remain the copyright of the photographers. Illustrations without reference to the author remain copyright of the lenders. For the small illustrations of works in the texts no photographers are mentioned by name.

This catalogue is published on the occasion of the exhibition

«rarrk» – John Mawurndjul: Journey through Time in Northern Australia

The (→ Museum der Kulturen. Basel.) Guest of the Museum Tinguely

Museum Tinguely, Basel
21 September 2005 to 29 January 2006

Sprengel Museum Hannover
19 February to 5 June 2006

Catalogue

Editors
Museum Tinguely, Basel
Christian Kaufmann

Publisher and Printer
Verlag und Druckerei Schwabe AG, Basel and Muttenz

Layout, Cover and Production
Bernhard Lüthi, Thomas Lutz and Michel A. Kilchherr

Translations
From the German: Nigel Stephenson
From the French: Nora Scott

Proof-reading
Norma Stephenson, Laurentia Leon

Production Assistant
Laurentia Leon

© 2005 Museum Tinguely, Basel and Schwabe AG, Verlag, Basel
© 2005 John Mawurndjul, courtesy Maningrida Arts & Culture, for the works by John Mawurndjul and Kay Lindjuwanga
© 2005 Estate of Anchor Kulunba, for the work by Anchor Kulunba
© 2005 for the work by Gawirrin Gumana, courtesy Buku-Larrnggay Mulka, Yirrkala
© 2005 for the photograph by Axel Poignant, courtesy Roslyn Poignant
© 2005 for the individual texts with the authors and translators

ISBN 3-7965-2201-7

www.schwabe.ch

Exhibition

Project Initiator and Guest Curator
Bernhard Lüthi

Co-Curators
Christian Kaufmann and Tiriki Onus

Exhibition coordination
Laurentia Leon

Film production
Insertfilm AG, Solothurn
Ivo Kummer, Daniel Leippert, Olivier JeanRichard, Pedro Haldemann, Nino Jacusso

Photo Essays
Erika Koch

Visitors' Brochure
Caroline Eichenberger

Shipping
Global Specialised Services Pty Ltd., Terry Fahey, Luke McColl
Möbel-Transport AG

Museum Tinguely	**Museum der Kulturen Basel**
Paul Sacher-Anlage 1	Augustinergasse 2
Postfach	Postfach
CH 4002 Basel	CH 4001 Basel
Tel. +41 (0)61 681 93 20	Tel. +41 (0)61 266 56 00
Fax +41 (0)61 681 93 21	Fax +41 (0)61 255 56 05

Director
Guido Magnaguagno / Clara B. Wilpert

Head of Exhibitions
Guido Magnaguagno

Conservation
Gloria Morales, Guest Conservator / Maria-Teresa Pol
Reinhard Bek / Christoph Zweifel

Public Relations
Laurentia Leon / Michael Schneider

Educational Services
Beat Klein, Lilian Schmidt / Gaby Fierz

Technical Services
Urs Biedert, Josef Imhof

Administration
Sylvia Grillon, Katrin Zurbrügg

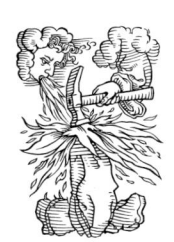

The mark of the printing and publishing house Schwabe, founded in 1488, dates back to the very beginnings of the art of printing and derives from the circle of artists around Hans Holbein. It is the printer's mark of the Petris, and illustrates Jeremiah 23:29: "Is not my word like as a fire? saith the LORD; and like a hammer that breaketh the rock in pieces?"